Nathan Strong

Sermons on Various Subjects, Doctrinal, Experimental and Practical

Vol. I.

Nathan Strong

Sermons on Various Subjects, Doctrinal, Experimental and Practical
Vol. I.

ISBN/EAN: 9783337161019

Printed in Europe, USA, Canada, Australia, Japan

Cover: Foto ©Lupo / pixelio.de

More available books at **www.hansebooks.com**

VARIOUS SUBJECTS,

DOCTRINAL, EXPERIMENTAL AND PRACTICAL.

By NATHAN STRONG,

Pastor of the North Presbyterian Church in Hartford, Connecticut.

VOL. I.

HARTFORD:
PRINTED BY
HUDSON & GOODWIN.
1798.

PUBLISHED AND SOLD BY
OLIVER D. & I. COOKE,
BOOK-SELLERS AND STATIONERS, HARTFORD;
ACCORDING TO ACT OF CONGRESS.

SERMON I.

On the goodness of God.   Page. 9

MATTHEW xix. 17.

There is none good but one, that is GOD.

SERMON II.

The evidence of divine goodness.   21

MATTHEW xix. 17.

There is none good but one, that is GOD.

SERMON III.

The justice of GOD.   41

REVELATIONS XV. 3.

—Just and true are thy ways thou king of saints.

CONTENTS.

SERMON IV.

The sovereignty of God.   Page 57

LUKE X. 21.

In that hour Jesus rejoiced in Spirit, and said, I thank thee, O Father, Lord of heaven and earth, that thou hast hid these things from the wise and prudent, and revealed them unto babes; even so Father; for so it seemed good in thy sight.

SERMON V.

On God's acting for his own glory.   73

ISAIAH xliii. 7.

—*For I have created him for my glory, I have formed him; yea, I have made him.*

SERMON VI.

Man's depravity.   95

ROMANS iii. 9, 10

—*For we have before proved both Jews and Gentiles, that they are all under sin; as it is written, there is none righteous, no not one.*

SERMON VII.

Man's depravity.   113

ROMANS iii. 9, 10.

Page.

—For we have before proved both Jews and Gentiles, that they are all under sin; as it is written, there is none righteous, no not one.

SERMON VIII.

Sinners under present condemnation.   129

JOHN iii. 18, 19.

But he that believeth not, is condemned already, because he hath not believed in the name of the only begotten Son of GOD.—And this is the condemnation, that light is come into the world, and men loved darkness rather than light, because their deeds are evil.

SERMON IX.

The connection between sin and misery.   141

ISAIAH lvii. 21.

There is no peace, saith my GOD, to the wicked.

SERMON X.

Regeneration.   157

JOHN i. 13.

Which were born, not of blood, nor of the will of the flesh, nor of the will of man, but of GOD.

CONTENTS.

SERMON XI.

Receiving CHRIST by faith.   *Page.* 179

JOHN i. 12.

But as many as received him, to them gave he power to become the Sons of GOD, even to them that believe on his name.

SERMON XII.

The life of faith.   197

HEBREW x. 38.

Now the just shall live by faith.

SERMON XIII.

Evangelical repentance.   213

EZEKIEL xxxvi. 31.

Then shall ye remember your own evil ways, and your doings that were not good, and shall loathe yourselves in your own sight, for your iniquities, and for your abominations.

SERMON XIV.

The objects of christian love.   225

1 JOHN iv. 16.

He that dwelleth in love, dwelleth in GOD.

CONTENTS.

SERMON XV.

Christian doctrines reasonable. — Page 243

ROMANS xii. 1.

—Which is your reasonable service.

SERMON XVI.

Christian duties reasonable. — 269

ROMANS xii. 1.

—Which is your reasonable service.

SERMON XVII.

Christian resignation. — 291

PSALM xlvi. 10.

Be still, and know that I am God.

SERMON XVIII.

On the evidence of forgiveness. — 311

JAMES ii. 18.

—I will shew thee my faith by my works.

SERMON XIX.

On working out our own salvation.   Page. 335

PHILIPPIANS ii. 12, 13.

—Work out your own salvation with fear and trembling. For it is GOD which worketh in you both to will and to do of his good pleasure.

SERMON XX.

Sanctification of the Sabbath.   353

EXODUS xx. 8.

Remember the Sabbath day to keep it holy.

SERMON XXI.

Benefits of the Sabbath.   375

EXODUS xx. 8.

Remember the Sabbath day to keep it holy.

SERMON I.

On the goodness of GOD.

MATTHEW xix. 17.

There is none good but one, that is God.

A TRUE conception of divine goodness, is necessary for a right understanding of God's infinite nature, and of his eternal government. The goodness or love of God, means his holiness, his whole rectitude, and all the moral perfections of his nature; which we describe by different names, from the various effects produced in the state of creatures, by the divine action. Every thing in the moral character of God, may be resolved into his goodness or holiness. Acts of justice, are also acts of goodness. God is as good in making a connection between sin and misery, and in punishing impenitent transgressors; as he is in giving life and immortality to the holy.

The idea, of there being some kind of opposition between the goodness and justice of God, arises entirely from the unholiness of men. If there had been no depravity in creatures, such an opinion would never have entered their minds, and they would have ascribed every event of the divine government, to unmixed and most glorious goodness.

It is very common for those, who live in sin, to please themselves with the attribute of goodness, and on this account think there is safety for them, while they are exceedingly afraid of justice; but if God's justice be a part of his goodness, these pleasing expectations are but a delusion. From the beginning, God hath and ever will, follow the dictates of goodness in his government. The divine love cannot, therefore, be admitted as any ground for security in sin; for ease in an unholy life; or for the neglect of experimental piety. Goodness when rightly understood, denounces terror to every sinner.

All will allow, that the love of God was displayed on the cross of Christ, to the highest degree; on the cross also we see his severity against sin. The cross of love, furnishes the most solemn warning to sinners, who delay and transgress; and the preacher of terror to ungodly men, will go to Calvary, for his most serious admonitions. It is from a very false idea of divine goodness, that any make it the ground of their security; for if God had not established a connection between sin and misery; if he did not punish sin, and keep up this connection in his government, it would be an easy thing to prove, in contradiction to our text, that he is not a good being; and if not a good being, not worthy of love, adoration and obedience.

It will be universally conceded, that the redemption of sinners, arose from the goodness of

GOD; and it ought also to be received, that the punishment of impenitents, arises from the same perfection. It is as much a part of infinite goodness, by no means to clear the guilty; as it is to be the LORD, the LORD GOD, gracious, merciful and long-suffering. Men in the practice of sin, are apt enough to hope from the goodness of GOD; but it would be much more for their advantage to fear a continuance in sin, from the same cause.

BUT why, it may be asked, shall we give this terrible appearance to the goodness of GOD? I answer, to whom is it terrible? To none but sinners who do not repent, and such have no right to any but terrible things. And why is it terrible to sinners, who do not repent? Because their whole temper is wrong; and wrong tempers and practices ought not to be soothed, and to do it is partaking in the sin. If it could be proved, that goodness when justly understood, doth not contain a warning to sinners, of great danger to themselves; by the same proof, it might be made evident GOD is not a good being. It is, certainly, a part of goodness in a Supreme Governor, to frown on every thing, either of temper or practice, which, in its nature, tends to destroy general peace and happiness. Whatever hath this tendency is sin. It is this tendency which makes it to be sin. The goodness of a Supreme Governor, requires him to frown on it by the most efficacious marks of his displeasure; and if he should not do it, our evidence of his goodness or moral rectitude, would be greatly diminished. After these general remarks on the subject, I propose the following method.

I. To describe the goodness of GOD, as it exists in his own infinite mind.

II. What evidence we have that God is good—to be followed by some inferences from the doctrine.

I. To describe the goodness of God, as it exists in his own infinite mind.

The goodness of God, consists in his love of the greatest sum of happiness, in the kingdom of which he is the head and supreme sovereign. His whole government, from first to last, conduces to this end. For this he created, rules, redeems, and will forever reign over angels and men.

The definition I have given of goodness, I think, is agreeable to holy scripture, to reason, and the common sense and feelings of men, in all cases, where they are not prejudiced to the contrary. We cannot call any being good, who prefers misery to happiness; nor infinitely good, if he prefers a lesser degree, to the greatest possible sum of happiness. Dispositions and actions, become morally good or holy, from their tendency in their own nature, to produce happiness or natural good; and if they have not this tendency, according to the construction of the intelligent universe, and its connection by social bonds and obligations, they cannot be called holy.

Happiness is valuable and a fit object of benevolent desire, according to its quantity, and not from its being enjoyed by this or another person. A similar degree of happiness, is as really valuable in one person, as in another; in one country, age or world, as in another; and the goodness of God disposes him, to make by his government the greatest sum of happiness in the whole.

It may be asked, how then can any intelligent creature contend with God's government? All intelligent creatures love and seek happiness, and if the nature, laws and government of GOD, seek the greatest sum of happiness, how can they rebel? If divine government seeks the greatest happiness, and creatures are seeking their own happiness in all they do, why is their temper forbidden and punished as a sin?

THE question, for its importance, deserves an answer; and it leads us to a direct sight of native depravity. The answer will equally illustrate the goodness of GOD, and the sin of creatures. Divine goodness desires the greatest sum of happiness in the universe. The sinful creature's desire of happiness is limited to himself, and that he may be the most happy possible whether he be deserving or not, and whatever effect his own exaltment may have, on the glory of GOD and the good of others. He seeks himself in all he does. To himself his desires are limited, and here all his motives center and terminate. By desire, he puts himself in the place of GOD, and his whole kingdom; and in this consists his idolatry—his unholiness and odiousness in the divine sight.

HERE arises the impossibility of a union between GOD, the head of his own kingdom, and sinners; until their hearts are changed by his sanctifying spirit, and made conformable to him in a love of the greatest happiness.

IT hence appears that pride, avarice, a love of sensual pleasure, and all the sin of mens hearts and lives, arise from a temper, that is directly contrary to the goodness of GOD and the interest and happiness of his kingdom.—They are not to be condemned for approving happiness, for this ought to be approved and desired. The sin is in loving themselves and their own happiness supremely—in undervaluing the real excellence and happiness of other beings—in making their own will and desire the measure of right and rule of action, in opposition to the nature of God, who is perfectly excellent, and to his will which seeks the greatest sum of happiness.

Plain as this truth is, to those who have felt in their own hearts, an affection conformable to the divine goodness; it is still very difficult, to give to those who never felt, a suitable idea of its nature or even of its reality. Having never felt such holy affection in themselves, nor seen its true glory in any other being, it is with difficulty they suppose it exists, or that there is any temper different from the selfishness, by which they have ever been governed. Even in their conceptions of the most holy God and his government, they are prone, from this reason, to suppose him a selfish being, and that when he punishes he acts in passion, in revenge, as selfish, self-willed sinners do. Whereas, in truth, the punishments and afflictions with which he visits creatures, are the fruit of goodness, and the effect of a scheme of counsel, which will produce the greatest sum of happiness, in the kingdom created by his power, and governed by his wisdom and goodness.

In the end, it will appear there is the most happiness possible, and that infinite power, wisdom and goodness have not labored in vain. God himself, whose boundless nature doth now and ever will contain, infinitely the greatest part of being, will be most happy and glorious; and in the created system there will be the greatest possible blessedness. A love of this, is the divine goodness; to accomplish this, is his desire, and the ultimate end of every event in his government. This is the love that composes his being; the goodness ascribed to him in his word; the tender mercy that is over all his works.

We find many instances recorded in the holy scriptures, in which acts of severity and punishment are ascribed to the goodness of God, as much as his bounties and the offers of forgiveness. God is often praised in his word for his righteous judgments on the wicked, and these judgments are considered as evidence that he is a good king.

God told Moses he would cause his goodness to pass before him; and in naming this goodness, he says, God *gracious, merciful, long-suffering, and that will by no means clear the guilty.* In the cxxxvi. Psalm, the smiting of the first born of Egypt—the destruction of Pharaoh—the ruin of great kings, and the slaying famous kings, are traced up to the glorious source that his mercy and goodness endureth forever. Tho' punishment implies pain to the person who endures it, it doth not imply any want of goodness in God, or that it is not his supreme delight to be good. On this ground we are commanded to rejoice always and evermore. There may be many cases, in which our own situation, if considered by itself, would be no reason for rejoicing; but there is no case in our own situation, considered in connection with the whole, which is not necessary for the general good; and thus there is always room to rejoice, that God is good—that he reigns—and by every existing event is promoting the sum of general happiness.

In this sense God always rejoices in his own government, tho' it be in many instances punitory; not because he delights in those punishments separately considered, for separately considered they are disagreeable; but in connection with the system of divine counsel, they are the most direct, and only possible means of the greatest happiness.

The remarks which have been made on the divine goodness, may be summed up in the following.

The goodness of God comprehends his whole moral perfection, and his infinite rectitude, in which he is glorious, and worthy of all love and adoration. It consists in a love of the greatest possible happiness in intelligent being, and to make this he created and governs nature. Every moral perfection of his nature, however named by us, is a part of his goodness. Every act of his government, thro' an eternity past and an eternity to come, will lead directly to his main design; and the incapacity of finite understanding to comprehend the ways of God, is not a sufficient reason to doubt of his love. Nothing less than the greatest sum of happiness can be the supreme object of a holy goodness. The pains endured by creatures, and the punishments inflicted by God, are as truly dictated by goodness, as the bestowment of particular favors, because they are designed by him for the general advantage; therefore God always rejoices in his own government, and the command to creatures, to rejoice evermore, is reasonable.

Several important inferences flow from this part of the subject.

1st. It teaches how worthy the Lord Jehovah is to be adored and served.

He is a God all goodness, and therefore all glorious. It is only to moral perfection or goodness, that excellency or glory are to be ascribed. Knowledge and power may be great and astonishing; but do not necessarily imply glory as goodness doth. A being who possesses power, which surprizes us, may be very inglorious and dreadful. Jehovah is both great and good. His goodness appears more wonderful, to those who see it justly, than his power doth. The amiableness of his character swells on our view, until it becomes glory inexpressible by the language of creatures, and inconceivable by finite minds.—The whole of his vast government is the work of goodness.—None will deny the blessings of creation, providence and redemption to be such; neither ought they to deny his punishments also to be such, for they are necessary in his kingdom to produce the greatest sum of happiness, as his bounties are. Thro' an eternity past, and an eternity to come, all has been, and will be, goodness in infinite action, to produce a most blessed kingdom, and the greatest good thro' an infinite duration.

IN thinking on this subject, our hearts ought to be warmed until we can say, *eye hath not seen, ear hath not heard, neither hath the heart of man conceived*, the cause we have to adore and love GOD. The motives of divine government being once justly understood, wherever we go, or whatever we see, administers reason to rejoice and adore the Lord. If called upon to produce the reasons of our rejoicing, we may appeal to all the bounties of providence, and all the blessings of redemption; yea more, to our very trials and groans, for tribulation worketh joy to those who receive it right, and even its effects on the obstinate will make the cause of GOD more glorious.

2dly. FROM the goodness of GOD, we learn the duty of cheerful submission to all the works of his government.

THE works of his government are always right, as they always tend to the supreme good. He hath infinite power and knowledge, to execute the purposes of infinite love; and can never be mistaken in the course to be pursued, or fail in choosing the best and most direct means of accomplishment. As this is the moral character, and these the natural powers of God, there can never be a reason to murmur, or think he doeth unwisely. Our incapacity, to see how all events are the consequence of infinite love, is no evidence against the fact. Every day gives new evidence of this truth, and it will be accumulating thro' eternity. Who by searching can find out God, or perfectly know the wisdom of his ways!—Every repining thought is impiety;—and every wish that the principles of his government should be changed, is opposition to his nature; for his law is an expression of his character, and his providence is his nature acted out, by external notices, to the knowledge of his creatures.

God suffers us to pray for deliverance from evil, and makes it our duty to use the means of preservation; but if our prayer be denied, and the means prove unsuccessful, we ought to acquiesce in his holy and wise ordering—to bless him under affliction—to say, *tho' he slay me I will trust in him*, I will adore the goodness which orders all events, without desiring his throne to be shaken, or his counsels altered in the smallest particular.

3dly. The goodness of God shows that sin is exceeding evil, and will forever be without excuse.

All sin is an opposition to God. If we opposed an unwise being—a being who is malevolent, and an enemy to the greatest good, there would be an excuse for the opposition, and our consciences would support us. But whom do we oppose? A good being—a friend of happiness—a God, who from the beginning, hath created and governed to produce the greatest sum of happiness—a Lord, whose requirements of us, have a natural tendency to make the most blessed kingdom, and to make us partakers in it, if we do not oppose him. What excuse can be made for this opposition? Shall we say it pleases us to oppose and disobey? The very excuse will condemn us, for the more we are pleased with opposing a sovereign, who is good in his nature, in his laws, and in his government, the more guilty we are. The transgressor's pleasure in sinning, is the proof of his guilt, and the only proof which will be needed in the day of trial. Shall we say, we loved our sins more than the spiritual duties of religion? This love is the sin, and pleading it, is in a sense pleading guilty. Who will stand on our side, when our sin appears to be a direct opposition to the infinite love of GOD? No creature, whose temper is right, will justify us. Our very companions in vice will condemn us, when they can no longer profit by our sins. Even our own consciences will condemn us. Self-condemnation is an awful ingredient in the punishment of sin, and it is one from which the guilty can never escape. If they could fly away from all other accusation, from this they can never fly. They must remain self-condemned so long as intelligence lasts. And the more evidently they see the good character of GOD, and the tendency of his whole work to produce the most happiness, the more miserable they will become by self-accusation.

4thly. THE nature of divine goodness is a proof, that selfish and unholy minds must be miserable, until there is a change of their temper.

THE good government of GOD is pursuing one end, and they another. GOD is seeking the greatest sum of happiness, a general good; and they are seeking their own happiness, a particular good, on the principles of exclusive advantage to themselves.—A consciousness that the power of God, who is opposed to them, will overcome, must be a source of constant inquietude.

In every respect, sin lays a foundation for sorrow and punishment.—Most of the sinful passions are painful in their very exercise—they cause an accusing conscience—they contend with God, who must overcome—the conviction of the sinner, that he is wholly under the power of God, whose purposes run counter to his own desires, must fill him with the utmost despair, after he hath sinned away the day of grace.

God is love—God is a consuming fire.—These two descriptions of the supreme nature, are perfectly consistent. That sight of infinite love, by which holy minds are purified and made happy; like fire will pain the selfish and unholy, and the goodness of God will seal their unhappiness.

How evil is the nature of sin, which renders creatures opposed to the general good, and wretched in themselves! How full of majesty is the Lord our God! Good in his own infinite mind, and building up around him a kingdom of holiness and everlasting glory. Amen.

SERMON II.

The evidence of divine goodness.

———

MATTHEW xix. 17.

There is none good but one, that is God.

IN a preceding discourse from these words, two things were proposed.

I. To describe the goodness of God, as it exists in his own infinite mind.

II. WHAT evidence we have that God is good.

To an inquiry for the evidence of divine goodness, or that God is a holy being, we will now attend. It has already been observed, that the goodness of God includes his whole moral perfection, all that rectitude, which makes him worthy of love, adoration and obedience.

THE evidence of divine goodness is derived from two sources. First, from the light of nature and reason; or in other words, it is known by the judgment, which a rational creature may form, from the evidence contained in creation, and the government of the world, and those moral agents who inhabit it.

The second source of evidence for divine goodness is in the revelation God hath made of himself, his will, and the ultimate design of his government. Each of these sources of evidence are sufficient to show, that God is good or holy. By the first, the heathen who have not a revelation, are rendered inexcusable for their sins; by the second, impenitent sinners under the light of revelation, which contains the greatest evidence of goodness, become the most guilty of mankind.

No one will deny, the evidence of God's goodness to be increased, in a very great degree, by his word; in which his character is drawn, his purposes and counsels made known, and his motives for appointing misery fully expressed. Some of the most plausible objections against the goodness of God are completely refuted in the scriptures, and the dark parts of his government explained to the understanding of men.

It is also allowed, that the light of revelation makes the natural evidence appear with more strength, than it could without a written word. Also that some of the instructing effects of a revelation, may have been found among most people, either by tradition or through some other means. Notwithstanding this, it is conceived, the works of creation and providence, do contain an evidence distinct from revelation, that the author and governor is good.

In men's inquiries on this subject, they are apt to mingle two questions, which ought to be kept distinct.

The first is, Whether there be natural evidence of God's moral character? The second, Whether men in general have seen this evidence, so as to be convinced of divine rectitude. There may be evidence, which is not sought after or received. If a man in christian lands, doth not read the books of revelation, or is so immersed in sensual pursuits and gratifications as to neglect the means of instruction, he will be ignorant of the revealed evidence of divine goodness. This is actually the case with the greater part of persons in christian lands. They neglect reading the holy scriptures.—Their thoughts are wholly on the amusements and interests of the world and the gratification of their own lusts.—Even in their attendance on public worship, their thoughts are in the ends of the earth. Such persons show an amazing ignorance of God's moral character, still this is no argument against plenary revealed evidence of his rectitude. So with respect to those, who are without revelation; though the books of nature and providence lie open, they have never read them. Perhaps not one in a million of such persons have attained to a knowledge of divine goodness, but this doth not prove the total want of natural evidence whether God be a good or evil being.

FURTHER, it is certain that the glory of truth is hidden from all unholy persons, though they have both the natural and revealed evidence; and a sight of the glory of truth is perhaps a source of higher conviction to the mind than any other.

THE following are some of the reasons for an opinion, that there is sufficient natural evidence of divine goodness.

1st. IF there be not evidence antecedent to revelation, both of the being and goodness of God, it is not seen how there can be a certain reliance on the truth of scripture.

IT is always required we give evidence from creation and providence, of the being of God, before we attempt to prove a revelation is from him. It also seems proper, to evince his goodness from the same source, before we call on mankind to receive his word as infallible truth; for if he be not a good being he may take delight in deceiving impotent creatures, and having great power, he might carry on the fraud through many ages, by miraculous operations, and by predicting and fulfilling his own predictions, to make a final disappointment the most distressing.—It appears, therefore, to be fit men should have prior evidence, both of the being and moral character of God, before they are called upon to receive his word as infallible truth.

2dly. The scriptures do in many places, either directly or impliedly, refer to creation and the governing providence of GOD, for evidence of his goodness and moral perfection. When GOD looked on creation he saw the whole to be good, both fitted to the use for which it was made, and to show the goodness of the creator. If the creation appeared fitted for a good design, this was evidence that the creator was a good being. The holy scriptures do continually appeal to the works of nature and providence, as evidence of GOD's moral perfection and our obligation to serve him. David, in calling on men to praise the LORD recapitulates the works of nature, and the events of divine government for evidence of the duty; but these must also be evidential of goodness, in order to show that we ought to praise GOD, for a being destitute of goodness cannot, in any case, have a right to our praise. Or, if any consider the works of nature, as evidence only of GOD's natural perfection, his knowledge and power; this is insufficient, for natural perfection of the highest degree without goodness, is not worthy of praise.

The apostle Paul, clearly decides this point, in the first and second chapters of the epistle to the Romans. He is expressly treating of the immoral character and guilt of the heathen, and considers the circumstance of their having no written law or revelation to teach them. (Chap. i. verse 19, 20.) *Because that which may be known of* GOD, *is manifest in them; for* GOD *hath shewed it unto them. For the invisible things of him from the creation of the world, are clearly seen, being understood by the things that are made, even his eternal power and* GODHEAD; *so that they are without excuse.*

THE clause, *so that they are without excuse*, fixes the apostle's meaning. The invisible things of GOD, and his eternal power and GODHEAD, which are said to be clearly seen by the things which are made, must include his moral as well as natural perfections; otherwise, they would not be without excuse. Men cannot be inexcusable for their sins without knowing a moral law, for where there is no law there is no transgression. They cannot know a moral law without a knowledge of the lawgiver. A knowledge of the law, and of the lawgiver's character, mutually imply each other. Knowing GOD's power only, never could have acquainted the heathen with a moral law, and being ignorant of this, they could not have been inexcusable.

THIS idea is confirmed by what the apostle says, (Chap. ii. verses 12, 14, 15,) *For as many as have sinned without law, shall also perish without law: and as many as have sinned in the law shall be judged by the law. For when the Gentiles which have not the law, do by nature the things contained in the law, these having not the law are a law unto themselves, which shew the works of the law written in their hearts, their conscience also bearing witness, and their thoughts the mean while accusing, or else excu-*

sing, one another. By having, or being without the written law, in this paſſage; is meant, having the law and inſtruction of revelation, or being deſtitute of it. He conſiders thoſe who have not the written law, ſtill as having the law, and a condemning or acquitting conſcience. How there can be a knowledge of the law, and a condemning conſcience to juſtify GOD in the day of judgment, which the apoſtle alſo mentions, is difficult to conceive, unleſs there be evidence of his moral character in creation and the works of providence.

IN the ſcriptures, the heathen are often deſcribed as ſinning againſt light and knowledge—as being wilful in their ſin—their idolatry in worſhipping ſtocks and ſtones, and the hoſt of Heaven, and in departing from the true GOD is charged as a great crime; but it is not ſeen how this idolatry could be ſo great a crime, if they had not evidence of GOD's moral perfections, and ſuch evidence as they would univerſally have ſeen if their hearts had been right. It is the moral perfections of GOD which entitle him to worſhip. It would be as unreaſonable to worſhip an infinitely evil being, as it is to bow before ſtocks and ſtones. In this manner, the ſcriptures bear teſtimony, that the goodneſs and rectitude of GOD are evidenced to human reaſon, even without a revelation.

3dly. THERE is a general tendency in the ſtructure of nature, and government of providence, to reward moral virtue with happineſs and to puniſh ſin with miſery; from which, we infer the divine goodneſs.

IF GOD be not a good being, why is the human body in all reſpects adapted to the convenience of the poſſeſſor. Why is the world ſtored with objects to ſatisfy our neceſſary wants. Why is material nature dreſſed in ſuch a profuſion of beauty? An evil GOD would certainly have ſpread it rouud with the curtains of deformity. Why is there a conſtant proviſion for the wants of man and beaſt. Why is there a preparation for all the ſocial relations, which with the aid of virtue, would make the human ſtate happy indeed. Why, in ſhort, is there a natural conſtitution to make the good happy and the ſinful miſerable, for this is the caſe in both.

THE wages or conſequences of ſin, are pain of body and mind, unhappineſs in the ſocial connections, and death. Intemperance is followed with diſeaſe and torment; diſhoneſty with loſs of reputation, and mens abhorrence; the gratification of ſinful luſts, with wars, fightings and infamy. Enmity and hatred are proper names to expreſs the inward torment of the ſinner, and a condemning conſcience, is certainly found in the ſinner's own breaſt, whether he hath a revelation or not. The moſt pleaſing ſinful enjoyments are followed with diſſatisfaction and a remaining ſenſe of want, which is not a ſmall degree of miſery. Take the moſt proſperous ſinner, one of whom the world will ſay he hath every thing to make him happy, he ſtill remains unhappy, thro' innumerable wants and deſires of an unſatisfied heart. Miſery is prepared both for immoral actions and an unholy heart; and ſuch a mind will forever remain unhappy.

ON the other hand, there is a tendency in nature and providence, to reward moral virtue with happineſs.

TEMPERANCE and induſtry promote health and mental vigor, and give us the neceſſary comforts of time. Truth and integrity obtain the confidence and love of mankind. A religious temper and practice produce peace of conſcience, and happiness in all the social relations; and where the objects of religious love are chosen, peace of mind follows. This general structure of nature and providence will appear to a person who considerately examines; and if there be found a tendency to reward virtue with happiness and to punish vice, it shows the creator to be pleased with goodness, and having found with what he is pleased, there is no difficulty in knowing what his moral character is.

Further, the existence of natural conscience in all men will not be denied. It is found in places where a revelation, in the common meaning of the word, never reached. Whence comes this judgment of natural conscience? It must either be founded on surrounding natural evidence addressed to the understanding, or be a constant revelation to the mind; and the latter is too absurd to suppose.

It is conceived, for these reasons and sundry others which might be mentioned, that the works of creation and providence contain evidence that God is a being of most glorious goodness.

The only reason mankind do not see this evidence, is the sinfulness of their own hearts. We know men have very different opinions of the divine character, and that vicious motives, and even the enormity of sin have been attributed to the Godhead. But is this confined to the places in which a revelation never shone? By no means. In christian lands, a multitude of people, with the Bible before them, form as false notions of God's moral perfections as the heathen do, and appear to be without true apprehensions of divine holiness,

WHERE was more grofs idolatry ever committed than in ancient Ifrael, who had the law and the prophets; or than in the modern antichriftian world, poffeffing the compleat cannon of fcripture? But we do not from this determine the holy fcriptures to be deficient in evidence of the divine holinefs, and his fole right to adoration, prayer and worfhip.

THE light fhineth in the darknefs, and the darknefs comprehendeth it not. This is the condemnation, that light has come into the world, and men love darknefs rather than light. One thing meant by light in thefe facred paffages, is evidence of truth. They were, perhaps, fpoken of revealed evidence of truth, but apply as well to natural evidence. The abfurd notions men have had of the divine character, are no ground to determine againft the fufficiency either of natural or revealed evidence, for the moral perfection of JEHOVAH.

SINFUL minds do not feek evidence; they are prejudiced againft it; they do not fee the glory of truth; they try to pervert it, that they may gratify their own hearts, and live with a quiet confcience, at eafe in fin. All this is no argument againft the fufficiency of light. In a thoufand inftances, it fhines in the darknefs of an unholy mind, and the darknefs comprehendeth it not.

SUPPOSE a creature of perfect holinefs were placed in the world, without a revelation; but with all the other means and opportunities to learn GOD's character, which men have. It is prefumed, that from creation and providence he would learn the holinefs of the Lord—that he is oppofed to fin and will punifh it—and would fay, nature is fo filled with evidence that GOD is good, and requires it in men, they will be inexcufable for all unholinefs, and cannot plead before the judgment feat, the impoſſibility of knowing the character of their judge.

But it may be objected, there is miſery in the world, and how do we know God doth not delight in miſery, rather than in happineſs? I anſwer, ſuch a holy mind as I have ſuppoſed, even from the miſeries of the world, as they are appointed and applied in the preſent divine government, would learn that the Lord is a good being. The pure and holy creature I have ſuppoſed, by means of his holineſs would ſee the infinite evil of ſin, the juſtice of God in condemning, and in appointing the greateſt degree of puniſhment for the guilty; and when he come to compare the demerit of ſin, with the miſery that actually happens, he would even from this determine God to be a good being. Seeing how much leſs miſery there is than ſin deſerves—how many mercies are mingled with human ſorrows and pains—how kind the Lord is to the evil and unthankful—how calculated his judgments are to warn, to reclaim, to prevent ſin; and attending to all the circumſtances under which pain and affliction exiſt, he would conclude the being who orders this, to be gracious and infinite in his goodneſs. The pains of another world will be retributive; but I think, that even without a revelation, there only needs a holy heart, to ſee that the pains and miſeries of this world, are ſo allotted and mingled with alleviations and mercies, as prove the preſent ſtate to be corrective and diſciplinary; and if God appears to act rather as a correcting than retributing judge, theſe very pains are evidence of his goodneſs.

It may be objected further; ſin exiſts, which God had power to prevent, and without a revelation, this would make it probable he delights in ſin rather than in goodneſs or holineſs. To answer this let us again suppose a mind of perfect holiness called in, to judge of God's character from the existing state of things in the world. And what would he see? He would see a world full of sinners, creatures made by God, who are evil instead of good. What beside this would he see? He would behold God treating them with great patience and long suffering—following their ingratitude with kindness—sending his rain and causing his sun to shine on the unjust—he would observe the general system of nature constructed to do them good, to reward every virtue with happiness and every vice with pain—he would see all things and events setting the most powerful motives before them to be holy and good. From the general prospect and viewing all its parts, notwithstanding the fact of there being sin, he would conclude the Supreme Creator to be good; and that if he were not good, he never could treat sinners as he doth, or fill nature and providence all around them with the most powerful motives to leave their sin; and though he might not be able to account for the event, would still determine it to be consistent with infinite goodness. It is conceived, our own sin and prejudice is the only thing that prevents our seeing a natural evidence of God's holiness.

I HAVE enlarged on this branch of evidence that God is good, because it is necessary for two points; to establish the holy scriptures, and also fully to expose human guiltiness, and set the criminal nature of sin in such a point of view, as it will appear at the day of trial and final judgment.

I KNOW, that some have endeavored to establish the sufficiency of a natural evidence of the moral character of God, hoping thereby to invalidate the need of revelation; but I am not in the least alarmed by the attempt. As a friend of revelation, I will thank all who oppose it, to assist me in collecting natural evidence of the goodness of God; for the more they collect, the more they will establish its truth, and not at all detract from the need of its being given. The more also, they will prove themselves to be very guilty sinners, and in need of such a salvation by sovereign and sanctifying grace as is taught only in the holy scriptures.

Whether God be infinitely good; and whether infinite goodness will ever save sinners, and if he will, how it must be done, are questions distinct in their nature, and ought not to be mingled. For the affirmative of the first we have both natural and revealed evidence, which shows the infinite evil of sin, and the transgressor's desert of eternal punishment. For the last, whether infinite goodness will ever pardon sin; and if he will, on what terms and by what expiation, we have only revealed evidence, the testimony of holy scripture.

Our second source of evidence for divine goodness, is in the revelation God hath made of himself and his will. Though there be a sufficient natural evidence, to render sinners inexcusable in the day of judgment; the revealed is more clear and explicit. The character of God is drawn in the best manner to assist us in conceiving of him. All holiness is attributed to him. The unity of his nature and counsels are asserted. The doctrine of the trinity, most important in the scheme of redemption, is revealed. The harmony of his perfections, which men conceive severally, is stated. The promotion of holiness and happiness, is told to be the great design of his government in all its dispensations. The immutability of his nature and councils, and perfect harmony of his design, in all he does, is illustrated. Many of the mysterious parts of his providence are opened to the understanding of creatures. The final rewards of his moral government, are placed before the hopes and fears of men, so as to act most powerfully upon them. And the inquiry, whether and how he will save sinners is determined beyond room for doubting.

By the character of GOD, which is drawn in revelation, we learn him to be all goodness and love.—Good in his mercies; in the afflictions which he appoints to men; in forgiving the penitent, and in finally punishing the impenitent.—All appearance of contradiction or partiality, in the exercise of mercy to some, and the execution of strict justice on others, is removed; and the good of the whole, which is the only object worthy of infinite love, is declared to be sought by GOD, in all his counsels and works.

Though there be natural evidence of divine goodness, infinite wisdom judged a revelation of his true character to be proper, for many reasons. Sundry have been hinted, and the two following ought to be particularly mentioned.

1. It gives great additional knowledge of the nature of GOD's holiness or goodness, and the spiritual purity of his law; whereby those who wish to serve him, are assisted in doctrine and practice, and wilful sinners are more apparently inexcusable. It is a dictate of goodness, that the nature, both of holiness and sin, should come into most plain view. The increase of evidence, increases knowledge. The increase of knowledge tends to promote more eminent holiness in the obedient, and

shows the exceeding sinfulness of sin in transgressors. By the union of natural and revealed light, God will become very glorious in the rewards he appoints. Especially, the guilt and just condemnation of sinners will be seen with convincing clearness, when it is known that they transgressed, both against great natural evidence, and the full blaze of revealed instruction.

2. But the most important purpose for which a revelation was given, is to determine the question; Whether infinite goodness will save sinners, and by what means redemption is effected. From a simple knowledge that God is good, though it be on the greatest evidence, we cannot determine sinners will be reclaimed, forgiven and made happy. The law which forbids sin and denounces eternal punishment, was ordained in goodness; and human reason, from natural evidence, never could be certain any transgressors would be released from this condemnation and punishment. Reason could not say, but sin and misery must be eternal, in every instance where they commence. No discovery could be made of any means, for glorifying God and advancing the happiness of his kingdom by the pardon of wicked creatures. For this knowledge we are wholly indebted to the scriptures, and therefore it is said, that by *Jesus Christ, life and immortality are brought to light*, that is, a holy and glorious life and immortality. God, in his word, has assured us some sinners shall be saved from their sins, and consequently from the miseries of the world to come. He hath taught us the method of redemption, by the life, obedience and death of his Son; by a satisfying atonement, and the sanctification of his Holy Spirit; by a gracious forgiveness, and title by free promise to the glorious blessedness of another world. The whole system

of gospel doctrine confirms this grace, and teaches us how the unworthy are taken from guilt and reigning sin and brought to glory. When we consider the manner of redemption; the connected doctrines in this wonderful scheme of grace; the character into which his people are formed by a divine influence; the evangelical affections and duties of real christians; the motives of divine wisdom in that mixed variety of events, which take place in this world; together with the descriptions of future glory to the saints, expressed by the highest images of present nature; the whole serves as an additional and the highest evidence of divine goodness. All moral perfections in the SUPREME NATURE, shine with new evidence and a great degree of manifestation, by revealed grace through a Saviour. The moral glory of JEHOVAH, is seen in the face of JESUS CHRIST, by men and angels, beyond what it could have been without a redemption of sinners. All this is conceded; but from this it by no means follows, there is not natural evidence of GOD's holiness. We have also reason to suppose, that evidence of GOD's true and glorious character, will be increasing through eternity. It is now, greater than it was under the Mosaic dispensation; will be greater when GOD's church shall fill the earth; greater still at the day of judgment, and continue growing through all the ages of endless duration.

FROM the subject we may infer,

1st. ALL, who deny a revelation, on the ground of sufficient natural evidence for the moral perfection of God; allow that, which proves their own guilt and misery, and leave themselves without a remedy.

SINNERS are individuals. The object of infinite goodness is the greatest sum of happiness in the whole, and this doth not certify us that all individual finners will be made the moft happy they can be. We could not have known, that one of them would ever have been forgiven, if a revelation had not contained the good news.

Persons who deny a revelation, do thereby deny a gofpel. From the goodnefs of God, they infer there is no danger for them, and thus live without fear of wrath to come; but they might as well infer, from the infinite goodnefs of God, there never had been any mifery; which being contrary to fact fhows the manner of reafoning to be falfe. Thofe who reject a revelation, in order to free themfelves from a fear of punifhment to come, and to avoid that holy life which the fcriptures command, becaufe they think there is a fufficiency of natural light concerning God's character and the duty of men, ought alfo to remember; that they have allowed enough to condemn themfelves and fhow the juftice of their eternal punifhment, and have left themfelves in a ftate of forlorn mifery and guilt, by denying God's word, which alone contains evidence of a redemption thro' the blood of Chrift. Is there natural evidence for the infinite goodnefs and holinefs of Jehovah? We allow there is. The fame evidence proves men to be finners, guilty beings, who deferve punifhment for rebelling againft infinite rectitude. Without the fcriptures they are proved to be guilty, and nothing appears but they muft be forever unpardoned. The more this argument is ufed againft revelation, the more certainly and juftly the perfons who ufe it appear to be condemned. It is ftrange, that any who believe a fufficiency of natural evidence, for the perfect holinefs and goodnefs of God, fhould wifh to banifh a revelation from the world. To help themfelves in one way, they fhut out help in another, and leave their own eternity under a moſt awful gloom. But perhaps ſuch perſons, by the goodneſs of God, do not mean his holineſs, juſtice, and high diſpleaſure with ſin. They may hope the goodneſs of God is a perfection diſtinct from his other moral attributes, and that its tendency is to make every creature happy whether he be holy or unholy, malicious or benevolent. If they have ſuch an idea, they are miſtaken in the nature of goodneſs. Goodneſs and holineſs are two general expreſſions, each of them denoting the whole infinite rectitude of Godhead. All ſuch as from inattention to the ſubject have thought differently are deſired to explain how an unjuſt being can be good. Is an unjuſt being good to the perſon to whom he is unjuſt? Or can we call an unjuſt being a good moral governor of the univerſe? Certainly not. In every caſe, what juſtice admits, goodneſs admits alſo, and God is good becauſe he is holy, juſt, true and righteous; and without theſe he could not be a good being. One way in which the goſpel declares God's goodneſs, is by evidencing his juſtice. He is juſt to himſelf, maintains his own right, aſſerts his prerogatives, claims the honor due to him, is juſt to his law, and to his rules of government in a univerſe of intelligent beings. If the goſpel ſaved ſinners, in any way that did not preſerve the rights of juſtice moſt entire, it would not prove God a good being. Juſtice is not only a part of goodneſs, but if one part be more eſſential than another, this is the baſis on which infinite goodneſs ſtands.

There is room to ſuſpect, that ſome who allow a natural evidence of God's goodneſs, do not mean to include in it the juſtice which condemns and puniſhes ſin; but to ſet ſuch perſons right, we ought to convince them that infinite goodnefs contains condemning juftice on impenitent finners; and not relinquifh the natural evidence of God's perfection to filence their unfounded cavils.

2dly. The fubject fhows the greatnefs of light which fhineth, and the weighty evidence there is of all moral and evangelical truth.

In the fame proportion as there is evidence of the divine character, there is alfo of moral truth. What could God have done more to inftruct us? Nature and all its parts are filled to teach us his holinefs. The laws of nature contain much information. Moral good and evil are taught us by caufes and effects in the natural fyftem. The fcheme of creation, as it comes to our underftanding, leads up to a God, holy and Almighty, who is pleafed with moral virtue, and difpleafed with fin. We cannot look either on the day or night; on the ftable earth, the animated fields, or glorious heavens; without beholding evidence of the creator's character, who is the pattern to be imitated. Doth not our confcious unlikenefs to him condemn us?

His providential government of nations and individuals teaches the fame truth. The hiftory of kingdoms and men contains a hiftory of God's counfels and rectitude. Divine revelation fhines with a brighter light, and teaches us how God the Son, came from heaven to earth to prove the holinefs or goodnefs of the Father. Natural and revealed evidence confirm each other, and in union contain the higheft fum of inftruction, which the prefent period of being admits. An increafe of evidence for any truth does not fhow, that there was not previoufly enough to convince an unprejudiced mind. It is often inquired why God gives increafing evidence of truth, and how this is equitable in his treatment of creatures. For doing thus he may have many reasons, and there is one that is necessary in the nature of things. The degree of present evidence often depends on past events. What God and men have been doing since the creation, directs our present judgment of his character, and thus there will be an eternal accumulation of evidence, for truth that hath always been witnessed sufficiently, to convince an unprejudiced mind. The ignorance of God's character, which there is in the world, comes from the depravity of mens hearts. Evidence will not instruct all individuals in a sinful world; for tho' it be sufficient the heart opposes, and this opposition is against both the light of nature and of revelation.

3dly. The subject teaches us that all who are finally impenitent will be inexcusable before God. When they are in the presence of the Holy Judge, as we all shall be after a few moments more; when their appetites are restrained by their situation, and there is no longer a possibility of possessing wordly objects of sin, they will be surprized at their own stupidity while mercy was offered. The greatness of light against which they sinned will prove their guilt. Through a consciousness of its being the greatest possible, their mouths will be stopped, and they will be self-condemned, as persons who have sinned against nature, providence and revelation. To a person in this situation how dreadful must a prospect of eternity be! How piercing the reflection, here I exist, and must exist forever, a miserable creature! My heart is at variance with my reason and conscience, and the conflict must be eternal! Here lies the gnawing worm in my own bosom! Outward afflictions for such an endless duration would be dreadful, but this inward pain who can bear! Every objection I offer against GOD or his government becomes evidence of my guilt and misery. I can neither flee, nor change, nor endure! I accuse myself, and still love the sin I accuse! If there might be an end—but eternity seals my despair!

If any in the pleasing security of sin should chance to read these lines, they will probably close the page, call the writer an enthusiast, and say; in these days we are not used to such a story, once it would have done, but now it is too late to affrighten men. But stay, my fellow mortal, I beg thee to consider. It is for thy own good this is requested. Hast thou examined the subject thoroughly? Art thou certain thy own hopes are well founded? Doth not thy own conscience sometimes upbraid thee, and say it is possible this may be true, and if it be, my condition is bad indeed: If thou wert on a death bed, would it be possible to put by these reflections? And is it not folly to postpone until the hour of dying, a preparation for eternity? This is of all times the most unfit, and there is little reason to expect, that GOD, who hath been long neglected, will then show mercy. Let the goodness of GOD, in which we all share, lead us to repentance. Our means of instruction are great. If the light be resisted it will be a favor of death unto death; but if faithfully improved, will guide us to mansions of glory in the kingdom of God. AMEN.

SERMON III.

The justice of GOD.

REVELATIONS XV. 3.

—Just and true are thy ways thou King of saints!

THE justice of GOD is a most amiable perfection.—Our text is part of the song of Moses and the Lamb.—Moses gave the law, and the Lamb of GOD gave the gospel of peace and reconciliation. The inhabitants of heaven sing an anthem, in which, law and gospel unite to praise GOD for his holiness and justice. *Great and marvellous are thy works, LORD GOD Almighty! Just and true are thy ways, thou King of saints! Who shall not fear thee, O Lord, and glorify thy name? For thou only art holy: For all nations shall come and worship before thee, for thy judgments are made manifest.*

THIS is sung by the holy inhabitants of heaven, introductory to the seven angels going forth with the seven last plagues, the vials of divine wrath, to be poured on a sinful world.—We are probably now in the midst of that period, the foresight of which caused the holy inhabitants of heaven to bless GOD.

THE song concludes with these words, *All nations shall worship before thee, for thy judgments are made manifest.* The punishing judgments of GOD upon the wicked, are here assigned as a proper cause for worship and praise.—Those who are perfectly holy, see a fitness that the judgments of GOD should be executed upon the wicked, and it is an amiable part of his character that he doth it. Every thing in GOD's character and government is rational and excellent, and there is as much propriety that sin be punished, as that virtue be rewarded with happiness.—In the Revelations made to St. John, we often find the holy saints of heaven, praising and blessing GOD, for his judgments on the wicked; and it is solely owing to the depravity of our hearts, that we have not the same view of his justice, in punishing sin.———I shall endeavor to illustrate the following doctrinal truth.

THE justice of GOD in punishing sin is an amiable perfection.

ALL are willing to allow that justice is amiable both in GOD and creatures, when it promotes their interests; and doth not carry with it either punishment or a denial of their desires. So far as this, we may find the most sinful and selfish, allowing the amiableness of justice. But in such cases, it is not the holy amiableness of justice which they approve; and even their acquiescence in this divine attribute is as sinful, as their own hearts be.—Indeed, it is not the real justice of GOD, as it exists in his infinite mind and is displayed in his government, which they approve.

I have limited the truth to be considered, to the justice of God in punishing sin; because the anthem of praise, from which our text is taken, appears to be predicated on his punitory judgments; and also, because, it is this part of the divine government, against which the corrupt heart most apparently rises, and judges to be unamiable.

Notwithstanding the frequency of such apprehensions, in this sinful world, we have the best reason to determine that none can be saved by the gospel of Christ, until they see the amiableness of divine justice, both in forbiding and punishing sin. Salvation by the grace of God in Jesus Christ, implies a state of the heart, which feels the justice of condemnation, and knows that God would be very glorious in punishing, if he saw it to be best. With no other views, can the creature sincerely pray, *God be merciful to me a sinner*, who have no right to plead, and whom thou mightest gloriously subject to the full penalties of the law.

Before I proceed to show the amiableness of divine justice in punishing sin, it is proper, I should make a remark or two to prevent misconception.

We must distinguish between the amiableness of divine justice, and the amiableness of the immediate effects produced by it. A punishment consisting in pain, either of body or mind, is the immediate effect produced; and this, in itself, can never be desirable. Pain or unhappiness, considered without regard to the consequences flowing from it, is alike undesirable both to good and bad minds, and to God himself.

It was undesirable to the holy Jesus, in his own case; still he prayed to the Father, *For this cause came I to this hour*, that I should suffer. *Father glorify thyself*, in causing me to suffer. His sufferings were undesirable; but he saw an infinite amiableness in the justice of GOD, which brought him to the hour of pain; and it was a most amiable temper in him, cheerfully to submit to his passion.

A MAN, in his own case, may very rationally prefer a natural evil, for the sake of a greater good to follow. The most holy governor of the universe, may appoint unhappiness to the sinner, which in itself is undesirable in his sight; for the sake of a greater good in his kingdom. This is nothing like delighting in misery; and those, who conceive the punishing justice of GOD to be of this kind, have never formed a true apprehension of this glorious attribute.

IT is, doubtless, a very common thing, for men to have this false notion of GOD's punitory justice; and from not inquiring into the true nature of the attribute, they find difficulty in reconciling it with goodness.—Goodness never delights in unhappiness for its own sake, neither doth punishing justice. In this respect, goodness and justice are agreed, as on examination, we shall find they be in all others. The reason men are so prone to form this false notion of justice, is their own sinfulness.—They have the depraved exercises of hatred and revenge, and it gratifies them to see the pain of their enemies. The holy and good GOD is never, in this way, delighted with the unhappiness of sinful creatures. It is not strange, that those who form an opinion of divine justice, on the model of their own bad passions, should find reason enough to fault it. While their own deformity is hidden from their sight thro' selfishness, they can in another being, see it to be unamiable, if opposed to their desires or interests.—We must go to very different sources, to discover the amiableness of justice; which I shall now attempt, in the three following particulars.

I. The justice which punishes sin, as it exists in the divine mind, is an exercise of goodness.

II. The execution of justice produces the best effects in society.

III. It treats the sinner according to his true character and deserts.

I. It is amiable as it exists in the divine mind, because it is an exercise of goodness. The justice of God, which inclines him to punish, is part of his goodness. Tho' it produces different effects, in the condition of the creature who is punished, from what would be by the exercise of grace; still as it exists in the infinite mind of God, it cannot be distinguished from his glorious love to himself and his holy kingdom. God hath the same motive to punish some sinners, as he hath to forgive others. The whole divine rectitude moves towards one ultimate end or object, and neither his counsels or works are divided in their final tendency. One great design runs uniformly through his eternal counsels, and the execution of them by creation, government, redemption, the glory of his saints, and the punishment of sinners. This design is to make the most happy universe—the greatest sum of holy felicity. The punishment of sin, like all his other works, leads directly to this end. So that justice, as it exists in God, is goodness. Punitory justice is as necessary to make him a being of infinite goodness, as his disposition to forgive and glorify repenting sinners. This infinite goodness and justice hath no private end, or partial desires. He sanctifies and forgives such as the general good requires; and leaves and punishes some for the same end. If God's general motives be the same, in the exercise both of punishment and of grace; his character is as amiable in one as in the other. To omit either would be an infringement on his rectitude, and he would not be a God of eternal holiness.

The inhabitants of heaven, represented in the Vision of John, had this apprehension of punitory justice; or they would not have broke forth, in a rapturous anthem of praise, on seeing the seven angels go forth, to execute the seven greatest plagues on a guilty world.

II. The execution of justice, in the punishment of sin, produces good effects in society.

It is the good effects or consequences which come from punishment, which cause infinite love to choose it. The benefit of divine judgments, in such a state as the present, are very apparent. If there were no punishment, the earth would be filled with violence.—Sinful men, who are not drawn by love to think of God and seek him, would soon forget and give themselves up to every vice.—Every thing would be directed, by the outbreaking passions and appetites of wickedness; and a sense of moral obligation, either to God or men, would be almost wholly effaced from the mind.—The condition of things would be wholly unfit for a state of probation.—It is probable, if there were no punishment here, but what is found in the very exercise of sinful passions, men would be more miserable through an excess of their passions, than they now are with all the judgments inflicted by a righteous God; so that considering the nature of sin, the present punishments of God, do on the whole lessen the quantity of unhappiness in the world. This is done by punishment and the fear of it, acting as a restraint on those sinful persons who have no love of God and his law.

But we ought not to confine our view of the subject within these limits.

The prophet Hosea saith, "*Thy judgments are as the light that goeth forth.*" By judgments are here meant punishments. They are a light in time, and will be through eternity. A light, without which, the full excellence of holiness can be neither known nor felt by creatures. They are a light to teach the holiness of God—the determined rectitude of his nature—his abhorrence of sin—his determination to support his moral law and government, by which myriads of creatures are made blessed. They are a light to show the evil tendency of sin, for a great part of the punishment, flows immediately from its very nature and exercise. The greatest happiness in the created universe, is made by seeing the true character of God; but how could this be seen, if he did not punish sin. If punishment were separated from sin, it would go far to involve the moral system in darkness, and thus take away the greatest means of intelligent blessedness.

If any suppose, that the punishments of another world, are designed only to gratify some passions of the Supreme mind, similar to the vengeance of sinful mortals; they have indeed formed a debasing opinion both of God and his government. These punishments are designed to be a shining light through eternity, and will be necessary for the best good of society, on the great scale in which it subsists.—Admit the existence of sin, and this is a fact which cannot be denied, and punishment is necessary for the general glory and good; and the justice of God who inflicts it, is an amiable part of his character. There never will be an inſtance of puniſhment in the divine government, that is not ſolicited by the moſt benevolent motives. When the attention of men is arreſted by the mighty power of GOD, they will ſee this truth ſo fully, as to ſilence thoſe objections which now riſe againſt divine juſtice. Though the heart may remain in full oppoſition, the tongue will have no argument to plead; and it will be one great ingredient of miſery to have a heart oppoſed to the Supreme government, without a reaſon to ſhew how it is wrong.

III. THE puniſhing juſtice of GOD treats the ſinner according to his true deſerts.

IT is known, that if the ſinner did not deſerve puniſhment, the divine character would not be amiable in executing it; but there is a full deſert of all, that is or ever will be endured by the wicked.

THE ſinner is oppoſed to that holy temper, law, government and practice, which are abſolutely neceſſary to make the univerſe moſt happy. All the principles of ſin are oppoſed to ſocial good, and we can conſider the ſyſtem of intelligence in no other view, than a great ſociety, under the government of an infinite king. So much abhorrence, as is due to a ſet of principles, which have a natural tendency to deſtroy all happineſs; the ſame is due to the principles of a ſinner's heart. And how ſhall this abhorrence be expreſſed, by a good mind and a good governor, except it be by puniſhment? Let the man, who can ſhow any other way, come forth and teach the world.

BUT it may be inquired, is it poſſible the principles of ſin ſhould go thus far? Do ſinners mean this by their vices? Have they this enmity againſt God and the univerſe?——Let ſcripture anſwer. *The friendſhip of the world is enmity with God; whoever therefore will be a friend of the world, is the enemy of God.* James iv. 4. Supreme love of the world and of ſelf, is enmity with God.—Is not this ſupreme love of ſelf and the world natural to men, or do they love God more? Let their actions tell. Let their daily appearance, their devotion to time and forgetting of God tell. Let their prayerleſs lives and oppoſition to the kingdom of Christ tell. Let a review of their hearts and the ſubjects which have occupied their meditations tell.—Let them conſiderately, and in the fear of the Moſt High, anſwer this queſtion; Have I loved God more than all other things with the chief ſtrength of my heart and mind?—It is enmity and an injury to God to deny him that which the infinite perfection of his nature deſerves, or to love the world and ourſelves more than we love him; and there needs nothing but an extenſion of theſe bad affections in the heart, to wiſh and attempt the higheſt rebellion againſt heaven.

But do ſinners mean this in all their evil actions and affections? It is poſſible they may not think of this in all they do; yet they mean to do that, which ſcripture and conſcience tell them to be wrong.—They will purſue this, ſo long as it promotes their own deſigns; and add opportunity and power to their hands, there would be no check to the immoral diſpoſition. A luſt to injure another, is the very principle which ends in killing; and a denial of one divine right, implies a denial of all. Hence the apoſtle James ſaith, *He that offends,* againſt the law, *in one point is guil-*

ty of all. This is the nature of an unholy temper, and that evil heart which is natural to man. No one will deny that it deserves punishment, and who can show that eternal punishment is beyond the desert? When we consider, that it is a temper directly aimed against an infinite and eternal good, no less than the whole happiness of God and his kingdom; that it never stops in its claims; never gives up the throne to God, to whom it is due, but repines and is uneasy; never ceases coveting, nor can cease, until a universe is swallowed up in its desires; that no motive of reason or equity, no new light of doctrinal information will alter this disposition; these things being conceded, who can describe the greatness of the sinners desert of punishment? Desert of punishment, doth not consist in a certain quantity of revenge being due to a certain quantity of sin; but it arises from the sinners relation to a holy God, and the great kingdom of intelligence.—By sin he hath lost all claim to good and is exposed to evil: and the evil deserved, is just so much, as general good requires. When we attend to the nature of sin to destroy the greatest good, and the infinite object against which it is levelled; human imagination cannot conceive a greater or more durable punishment, than the public good may require, and God who knoweth all things, hath been pleased to tell us it is without end.

On these grounds, it is supposed that the justice of God which punishes sin, is an amiable perfection. It is an exercise of divine benevolence; produces the best effects in society; and is according to the sinners true deserts. The scriptures bear abundant testimony, to the excellence and amiable glory of God's justice. They call on men to love and serve him—to exercise confidence and trust—to fear and praise him—

because he is a just God. Indeed, if the justice of God could be rightly impeached, in the smallest instance, it would overthrow the foundation of creatures happiness.

A serious improvement may be made of this subject.

1. It teaches us the danger of sin, and the certainty of punishment on those who do not repent.

It shows that God doth not speak capriciously in his threatenings, nor act under the influence of such passionate hatred as men often feel. If this were the case, sinners might hope he would relent and passion subside; but as the case now is, all the evidence of his being good may be adduced to prove the certain fulfilment of his threatenings. Goodness, infinite goodness is the same justice; which threatens, condemns, and will execute. To what can the sinner appeal? If he flies away from justice, to some perfection of Jehovah which he thinks more mild; infinite love will answer, it is I who am executing this, and if I should desist, I could not be good to myself, and the immense creation around me. My justice, with which you are rightly terrified, is that goodness which spread the heavens, founded the earth, peopled the universe, and governs for their happiness. There is no perfection in God more mild than justice; no compassion different from it, to which the sinner who is finally condemned, may address himself for escape.

Further, when the sinner comes to see all these truths, as they will at last be exhibited; it will fix the severity of that part of his punishment, which arises from self-accusation, and will complete his despair of a remedy. Tho' he cannot see the beauty of holiness, as it is seen by God and holy minds; his reason will be convinced it is the goodness of God which passed the sentence, and that the rectitude which condemned him is the foundation of heavenly bliss. As the evidence of God's goodness increases to his knowledge, which will probably be the case thro' eternity; it will at the same time be evidence of the perpetuity of his own sentence. The accusations of conscience accompanied with despair, in such a case, must be extreme misery. It is a fearful thing to fall into the hands even of a good God, when he comes forth as a condemning judge; and the terrors grow in proportion to the infinitude of his love. In view of this, God in the character of a Saviour addressing himself to prisoners of hope, exhorts us to immediate repentance, and without delay to escape for our lives.

2dly. To assist our self-examination, it becomes us to inquire, whether the justice of God appears to us an amiable perfection; and if we think it doth, on what ground?

God's whole character appears amiable to the holy. They are not disposed to separate his various perfections in respect of beauty, as men conceive and speak of them under different names. His justice, his sovereignty appear as lovely as his grace. Finite creatures must consider an infinite mind by parts, and all the parts to a sanctified soul appear lovely alike. He doth not say, this perfection I admire—of another I am some afraid —and a third, I wish were removed from the supreme nature. Any thing of this kind in our feeling, shows a want of conformity to God, and that his spirit doth not dwell and reign in us.

The saints of God love his justice, because it is necessary for his glory and the good of his kingdom; for tho' it may diminish their own happiness, it increases the whole.

If we think ourselves friendly to divine justice, let us enquire on what ground our friendship stands?—The heart is very deceitful, and sin hath a blinding power. We may have a very strong hope, that our own sins are forgiven, so that justice will never injure us, and that all its effects will fall on others while we are safe. If this, be the only reason of acquiescing in God's justice, we are hypocrites. A holy approbation of justice is not altered by any selfish consideration; but can cheerfully say this is a glorious attribute, and will forever remain so, whatever its effects may be in my own case.

3dly. It is necessary sinners should submit to the justice of God in condemning, and see the fitness of the sentence he hath passed, before they can be benefitted by the grace of the gospel, and accepted thro' Christ. They must come as penitents and mourners for sin, and they never can be true mourners for sin, until the justice which condemns them appears right and amiable, and worthy of an infinite and perfect God. Coming to God and Christ, in the gospel way, is a friendly exercise of the heart—friendly to God himself—to the Mediator—to his law and gospel—and to his government. The object to which we are friendly, whether it be divine or human, appears amiable. Sinners do not come to Christ the Saviour, until he appears glorious in all his perfections; in his justice, as well as his grace. The rising of our hearts against the sentence of our own condemnation, not only proves our want of holiness, but a want of that renovation, which muſt precede our coming to CHRIST in a ſaving way. When ſinners have ſeen the fitneſs and the excellency of juſtice, they will loathe themſelves—will mourn for ſin—will be pleaſed with the goſpel plan—and with the character of Chriſt. They will come, receive, truſt, and glorify him; and none of theſe exerciſes can take place, until there hath been a reconciliation of heart to the juſtice of GOD. By theſe obſervations, we may bring our hearts to very ſtrict examination; and all will do it, who have true apprehenſions of the conſequences depending.

4thly. How great will the glory of GOD appear, after the concluſion of the preſent ſtate, when all moral agents in the creation, of whom we have any knowledge, have received their portion!

How glorious in all his attributes—in creating goodneſs—in redeeming grace—in his patience and forbearance with a world of ſinners—in forgiving, ſanctifying and glorifying the guilty—and alſo in the execution of juſtice. Juſtice is the attribute with which men are moſt ready to contend, for they are afraid of it; but it will in the end appear both glorious and good. Enough is now ſeen to fix deep guilt on the tranſgreſſor, and more will be ſeen in the progreſs of divine government; ſo that the ſong of Moſes and the Lamb will be forever ſung. It will be ſeen, that to be juſt is to be good; and in the adminiſtration of GOD, theſe two names of his character are never ſeparated. All holy creatures will agree in this, not becauſe they delight in pain, or have a pleaſure in natural evil, for this is far from their hearts.—It is becauſe they delight in good, and ſee the glory of goodneſs and juſtice to be the ſame.

5thly. The description that hath been given of divine justice, shows the perfect harmony of the law and gospel.

It is very common for men to fall into the unscriptural notion, that the law and gospel of God are in some way opposed. The reason of such an opinion is, that the law condemns sinners and the gospel pardons them. This is truth, still the gospel doth not pardon them in a way, which opposes the law. Grace doth not abound, in such a manner, as accuses the nature of justice. *Mercy and truth have met together, righteousness and peace have kissed each other.* Where is the glory of condemning justice, so fully proved, as by a gospel of grace? If justice had not been amiable, God would not have given his son to sanctify its claims. If Christ had not seen an amiableness in the justice of God and the law, he would not have borne the curse on the cross. The gospel is a most full display of the glory of the law, and the forgiveness of free grace magnifies condemning justice. Thus God glorifies all his perfections! Thus grace and justice will ever harmonize! Thus both the salvation and punishment of sinners will make God to be adored forever and ever!———Amen.

SERMON IV.

The sovereignty of GOD.

LUKE X. 21.

In that hour JESUS rejoiced in spirit, and said, I thank thee, O Father, Lord of heaven and earth, that thou hast hid these things from the wise and prudent, and revealed them unto babes: Even so, Father; for so it seemed good in thy sight.

THE sovereignty of GOD in the dispensations of nature and grace, is one of those truths in which all who are good will rejoice. The virtuous delight in it, the evil are opposed to it. The virtuous choose a sovereign GOD; the evil wish him to be removed from the throne. This prejudice against divine sovereignty, shows both the wickedness and folly of sinners.—It shows their folly as much as their wickedness; for the only possible hope of transgressors stands upon the sovereignty of JEHOVAH; and if he were not such, it would be eternally impossible, that a guilty creature should ever come to the holiness and glory of heaven.

THUS our Saviour viewed the doctrine. In sight of it he rejoiced in spirit, for he saw it to be right, and he always rejoiced in right things; he saw it to be for the glory of GOD, which was dear to him; he saw it to be the broad, the sure foundation of sinners redemption, and that a scheme of grace could stand and be executed, on no other truth.—For these reasons he rejoiced in spirit, and said, *I thank thee, Father, that thou hast hid these things from the wise and prudent*, in their own opinion; from those who take on themselves to judge better than thy word, and to know by their own reason what the Lord of all the earth may and will do; from those, who trusting to themselves and their own works, cannot submit to the soul humbling terms of the gospel. I thank thee, Father, that thou hast revealed these things unto babes; unto those who are weak, ignorant and guilty, and in every sense without strength; for such are all, whom the sovereign mercy of GOD saves, before they are sanctified and enlightened by his spirit.

CHRIST might also have a special reference to the character of the disciples, who had then received him. They were babes in all external, worldly advantages, compared with the scribes, pharisees and spiritual lawgivers of the jewish nation, from whose eyes, the glory of CHRIST and the gospel was hidden by their own sin. To the disciples there was a revelation, through the renovation of their hearts, of the spiritual glory of GOD—the preciousness of CHRIST, and the fitness of his gospel, to redeem sinners.

Even so Father for so it seemed good in thy sight. ——These are words of great emphasis and meaning, in CHRIST's address to the Father.—In the preceding clauses he had acknowledged a divine efficiency in hiding from some and revealing to others, and had praised GOD for this efficiency; and in these words, he traces up the distinction that was made between men, to the sovereign council of GOD, and acknowledges the fitness of it.—Those who see the divine character right, will know it to be a fit and desirable thing, that GOD should act sovereignly in all his appointments, and in the distinctions made between men, in the present and future dispensations of his government.

I shall attempt to illustrate the following truth.

The sovereignty of GOD, in all cases, is glorious for himself, and a reason of rejoicing for creatures.

The following definition may be given of the divine sovereignty.

It is his all-powerful acting, according to his own will, and by motives derived from within his own mind.

To his purpose and acting there can be no effectual resistance, for he is Almighty in all things; and the ineffectual resistance that is made to his will by sinners, arises from his permission, is wholly under his control, and managed by him, in all respects, as he pleaseth.

That GOD hath in fact this sovereign action, and that creatures ought to rejoice in it, are truths to which the holy scriptures bear the most full testimony; and they are truths which arise from the nature of an infinite being, who is the sole creator and preserver of finite existence.—To suppose the contrary, would be the same as to conclude, he is not the sole creator.—The Lord in his word, every where claims this sovereignty to himself. *The counsel of the Lord standeth forever ; the thoughts of his heart to all generations.— For God is in the heavens ; he hath done whatsoever he pleased.—I form light, and create darkness ; I make peace, and create evil : I the Lord do all these things.—Who worketh all things after the counsel of his own will.* God challenges a supremacy over the whole creation—the luminaries of heaven and the earth—the seasons—the laws of nature—kings and empires—the minds of men and angels—the good and the bad—the past the present and the future. He speaks of these as his agents, which are pursuing the destination of his councils ; and represents in the most forcible language, his high independence of any thing external to himself.

He asserts the fitness that this should be the case, and assigns, " *Thus saith the Lord*" as sufficient reason, for the highest creature both to believe and obey.

In comforting his people, he assigns his own sovereignty, as a reason for their trusting and rejoicing in him forever more ; and represents their blessedness, standing upon the independent goodness of his nature.

Also in threatening sinners with punishment, its certainty is urged, by his being a sovereign, and by the impossibility of any release from his hand, or foreign influence on his determination.

The whole law and gospel harmonize in these ideas of divine sovereignty—take this away from the divine character, and it breaks the obligation of the law, and disunites the doctrines of the gospel scheme, so that they must become inefficacious for salvation.

The absolute supremacy of God, is one of those doctrines, against which the unholy heart naturally rises.—Pride is mortified; a wicked selfishness is crossed by it; and the sinner sees that his only safety depends on the entire submission of his will. Further, this sovereignty shows the absolute necessity, either of choosing what is not loved, or remaining under God's displeasure; so that the doctrine becomes alarming to his fears.—Hence, as might be expected, hath arisen many objections and misrepresentations of the doctrine; especially, that it gives a gloomy and unlovely view of the divine character, and makes him more an object of dread than of delight.

To dispel the mistake; silence the objections of a bad heart; and more fully show, that God's sovereignty is glorious for himself, and a reasonable ground for creatures to rejoice, the following things concerning it ought to be considered.

1. The sovereign determination and acting of God is not without motive and system, nor is it the excess of bad passions.

Indeed, we cannot conceive, that intelligent beings should, in any case whatever, act without motive; but they may act without system.—By acting without system, I mean acting from the impulse of present passion, without a regard to what is rational and right.—This, in a great measure, is the case with all sinful beings. In using the word sovereign, we should distinguish between its meaning, when applied to guilty sinners, and when applied to an infinite and holy God.—

Sovereignty, in the hand even of a holy creature would not be defirable, becaufe he cannot have knowledge to direct its operations.—Let his heart be ever fo good, it would be dangerous to the univerfe, through a want of knowledge and power to exercife it in the beft manner.

Sovereignty, in the hands of an unholy creature, is dreadful in all refpects; for he hath neither underftanding nor a heart to do wifely. Such fupremacy as evil men often exercife, hath raifed a prejudice againft the word in fome minds, who would rejoice in the afcription of fovereignty to God, if they underftood it right in this high application.—In the fupremacy of guilty men, there is tyranny, oppreffion, a wanton exercife of power according to the prefent impulfe of paffion, abfurdity and mifery. Reafon is difregarded; right is forgotten, and jealoufy, enmity and rage act in the place of calm deliberation.—There can be no confiftency in fuch a fovereignty as this. Thofe who act under it know not how to obey or pleafe; or whether they fhall meet the capricious fmile or the warrant of death. There cannot be the order and confiftency of fyftem, in the paffions of fin. They flow from a felfifh fource, and act from the paffion of the prefent moment.—If omnipotence and infinite knowledge were given to a finful mind, he could not reduce the exercifes and practice of fin to a confiftent and fafe fyftem of action. He never could gain perfect happinefs. Perfect happinefs, arifes from the enjoyment of an object, commenfurate to the capacity of enjoying; but the finner never can find this in himfelf, nor in all the creatures, though they were by an infinite power, fubordinated to his wifhes.—The nature of minds and of the creatures doth not admit it. The sovereignty of a sinful creature must necessarily be dangerous to others, disappointing to himself, and without rational design.

Far different from this, is the glorious sovereignty of Jehovah. He is a God of order and system—proposes to himself the highest object, an object reaching thro' an eternity past and to come—and in all his actions and commands, keeps this object in view, so that the infinite energy of his working is here centered. There is the most perfect order and system in his sovereignty, and the same forever. His moral character; his supreme object, and all his counsels leading to this supreme and ultimate object, have the whole harmony of reason and order in them. There is nothing that answers to the idea of passion and caprice, as they are applied to men.

Remove imperfection and sin from the word sovereign, in its high application to Godhead, and it goes far to show that his sovereignty, is glorious for himself, and ground of rejoicing for creatures.

2. The sovereignty of God is infinite goodness.

The glory and desirableness of the divine supremacy, depends entirely upon his being a good and holy being. If God were an evil being, his sovereignty would be the most gloomy and ill-boding doctrine, that could be set before his intelligent subjects; but in the same proportion as we have evidence of his holiness, it is matter for rejoicing.

Goodness delights in doing good—in doing the most good—in doing the most good with the least degree of evil, that is compatible with the object supremely sought—and in doing good to the greatest number of individuals, that can be admitted as sharers without detracting from the general sum of blessedness. All this will doubtless take place under the government of GOD. There will be the greatest good or sum of happiness with the least evil, and extended to the greatest number of partakers, that the nature of things admits. This goodness of GOD, will be assisted by infinite power and knowledge.

To such sovereignty, what can be objected, or what is there in it unamiable? By this description, it is in the best and most powerful hands, and here every honest and good mind will choose it should remain. Evil minds have no right to object. Good minds will not wish to object. They choose sovereign power to be in such hands as will make the best use, and apply it to the most good; so that the sovereignty of GOD is the ground of their rejoicing.

3. THE sovereignty of GOD is exercised without partiality and respect of persons, and therefore glorious for himself, and safe for the rational universe. In exercising that power over creatures, which the holy scripture compares to the power of the potter over the clay, making one vessel to honor and another to dishonor, GOD is moved by motives of general good. In choosing some to holiness and salvation thro' free grace, and justly leaving others to perish in their sins, he acts like a good GOD; and the general cause of holiness and happiness, is as much promoted by leaving some, as by pardoning others. In this sense, he is no respecter of persons; that is, doth not treat them differently, thro' any previous or sinister attachment to one and aversion to the other; for he grounds his different treatment on

a general utility, which includes his own greatest glory, and the highest good of the creation, considered as a collective and intelligent system. Creatures ought to praise GOD for this sovereignty.

4. THERE is no injustice done to any creature by the divine sovereignty.

THE impenitent are not treated contrary to justice. The redeemed ones of GOD, are accepted by free grace, in a way consistent with the justice of GOD and his government. Those who are left are rewarded, in all respects, as justice requires; according to their temper, and their actions, and as the good of society requires; so that the sovereignty of GOD, hath all the glory of infinite goodness and infinite justice. If creatures cannot rejoice in this, it shows their hearts to be bad, and opposed to right.

5. THE ignorance which there is, in unholy minds, of the glory of this doctrine, and their being unable to rejoice in it, is no evidence against the truth advanced.

So long as the mind is altogether unholy, it is unable to see the true glory of any divine perfection or moral truth. A rational conviction of truth doth not discover its glory.—The apostle says, "*If our gospel be hid, it is hid to them who are lost.*" He here means the glory of the gospel, and of GOD's character in this manner of treating men.

IT is not to be expected that unholy persons, will either see the glory of GOD's sovereignty or rejoice in it. They cannot rejoice, because they are opposed to it; neither doth the mind ever see amiableness, in a truth, an event, or a char-after to which it is opposed. So long as sin abounds in the world, it must be expected, persons enough will be found, to deny the glory of the doctrine advocated; and if it were not thus, sin would contradict its own nature. Let all men be made holy, and conformed to God in a gospel temper, the praise of divine sovereignty would be constantly on their tongues; and the supremacy of the divine government, would be the highest ground of their joy.

6. The sovereignty of God was defined to be " His all-powerful acting according to his own will, and by motives derived from within his own mind."

It is evidently implied, in the sacred representations, that his motives for acting as he doth, are derived from within himself. It is in such expressions as these, " according to the counsel of his own will—according to his own good pleasure—because it seemed good in his sight"— with a vast multitude of similar passages, which carry the human mind, to conceive all motives of divine action, originating in Deity himself. And whence could God's motives arise, unless, it be from within himself? Antecedent to all existence beside his own, there could be nothing without himself, to influence him by way of motive. Certainly, therefore, he must find the motive within himself to create; to create such a system as he hath; such creatures as exist; and all the circumstances of their existence. If any thing existed independent of his creating fulness, and beyond the reach of his governing control, he might have motives to action, external or without himself; but so long as it is allowed, that all are dependent on him in the most absolute manner, it must also be allowed, that all the motives to his sovereign action, are from within himself. His sovereignty, therefore, is of the most perfect and absolute kind; and the more absolute, the more glorious for himself, and the greater reason for creatures to rejoice.

HERE the proud heart objects.

CAN this be cause of rejoicing, that I am in the hand of a most absolute sovereign? Is this consistent with my dignity as a rational creature, and a free agent?——Truly it is. If thy reason be exercised right, all its dictates will be in conformity to the sovereign counsel and acting of GOD.—If thy heart be opposed to infinite reason, or prejudices thy reason, it is the depravity of thy heart, and not the sovereignty of GOD, which degrades, and takes dignity away from thee.— Neither is thy dignity as a free agent lessened. Art thou not as free in sinning, as the holy angels and holy men are in loving and obeying GOD? Is not sin thy choice? Dost thou not sin because thou lovest sin? The sovereignty of GOD will never destroy thy freedom as a rational agent, but an evil use of this freedom hath made thee base, and without repentance, will be the means of thy misery forever.

6. THE sovereignty of GOD, is the ground of all our blessed hopes of forgiveness, and complete redemption.

THE holy scripture always traces back the salvation of guilty sinners to the free, rich and sovereign mercy of GOD, and to the riches of goodness within his own mind; to the purpose which he purposed before the foundation of the world.

—They speak of God, as being moved to exercise kindness for his own mercy's sake, and his own name's sake; and not for the sake of those who are forgiven.—All hope for sinners arises from the divine sovereignty.—Take this away, and the foundations of the gospel are overturned. Where else can the hopes of a guilty sinner stand? Does he deserve salvation? Hath he merited deliverance by such costly means, as the gospel reveals? Can he save himself by paying a price? Can he sanctify himself? Can he make any claim, or say it would not be just in God to leave him in the misery of his sin? All these questions must be answered in the negative; so that nothing but the sovereignty of divine goodness remains, as a reason for hope. Well might Jesus Christ rejoice in spirit, considering the sovereignty of God, which hath revealed truth and grace to the babes of his flock.—Well may the church sing the praise of God's supremacy, and say, *The Lord reigneth let the earth rejoice, and let the multitude of the isles be glad. Not unto us, O Lord, not unto us, but unto thy name give glory, for thy mercy and for thy truth's sake. Our God is in the heavens; he hath done whatsoever he pleased.*

The sovereignty of God must therefore be considered, as glorious for himself, and matter of rejoicing for creatures.

We may improve what hath been said on this subject, to try the state of our own hearts.

1st. Can we rejoice in the divine sovereignty, and say as our Saviour did, I thank thee Father, for so it seemed good in thy sight!

If the sovereignty of God be according to reason; if it be holy, just and good; if it seeks the greatest sum of happiness in the kingdom of intelligence; if it be all the hope of fallen and guilty creatures, every good heart muft rejoice in it, and all feelings of oppofition difcover a criminal badnefs.

By this rule of trial the holy and unholy heart, will come into view. In examining ourfelves we ought to let the rule have its full extent. Our fubmiffion, to be a gracious one, muft extend to all events of the divine government.—An unholy heart may rejoice in its own gain and pleafure, and of courfe in a fovereign providence; which in all things gratifies a worldly ambition and love.—Our Saviour faid, *If ye love them who love you, what reward have ye?* What evidence is this, that ye are delivered from the felfifh corruption of human nature? So we may fay, with refpect to fubmiffion. If ye cheerfully fubmit to that fovereign providence, which gratifies all your earthly wifhes, and fubmit no farther; what evidence is this of a holy love to GOD, or a delightful reverence of his nature? Gracious fubmiffion extends to all events; both to profperity and adverfity; to afflicting evils, and the frowning difpenfations of heaven; to pains, reproaches and poverty, if it be GOD's pleafure to appoint them. Thefe trying events are as much the direction of infinite rectitude, as earthly bleffings are; they are as right; they are as neceffary for GOD's glory, the good of his creatures, and the beft government. He appoints them, not through a pleafure in looking on affliction, feparately confidered, but becaufe they are right and beft; and the fame reafons which influence his righteous will to appoint, will make a righteous creature rejoice in his fovereign determination.—If our hearts are good, the fovereignty of GOD, in its whole extenfion, will appear to us glorious for him; and best for the universe; neither will afflictions change our sentiments, or ruffle our hearts.

This opens to our understanding, one of the many reasons, why a God of infinite wisdom hath appointed so many afflictions to his people. —It assists them in examining their own state, and if they be sincere, gives strength and peace to their hopes. The day of affliction is much the best time for self-examination, and is commonly a season of most lively exercise in grace. Therefore the apostle saith, " *We glory in tribulation also, knowing that tribulation worketh patience; and patience, experience; and experience, hope; and hope maketh not ashamed, because the love of* God *is shed abroad in our hearts, by the Holy Ghost which is given unto us.*

2. If our hearts are opposed to the sovereignty of God, it shows us to be in a state both sinful and miserable.

It must be sinful, either to resist or distrust a sovereignty that is always right. It is also a most miserable state to be in. What more miserable, than to be opposed to that irresistible counsel and power, by which the universe is governed? To feel a will, rising against the divine will; which cannot be changed or successfully resisted? Do we not all know there is misery in a disappointed will, and in beholding a supreme government, in all its operations acting counter to our desires? This must be the misery of those who oppose the sovereignty of God; neither can they avoid the unhappiness. They are in his hand; they depend on him for their all; their resistance hath no efficacy with it, further than he suffers them to go. If they appear for a little time to succeed, he can in a moment disarm them of their weapons, and cover them with confusion. A conscioufness of these truths, must make the minds of sinners very miserable. This is one of those sources of sorrow which are thick planted, in the nature of things, of society, and of the human mind, for the punishment of sin. There is room enough in the nature of things, as they at present exist, for GOD to inflict a punishment on transgression, equal to all the threatenings of his word; and observing this natural preparation for punishment, is a strong argument for the truth of revealed threatenings.

3. To object to the sovereignty of GOD is an implied rejection of the whole gospel plan of salvation.

ALL our knowledge of gospel redemption, is derived from the holy scriptures, which uniformly represent this deliverance to be from the sovereign mercy of GOD. *He hath mercy on whom he will have mercy. By grace ye are saved,* and a gift of grace must be at the sovereign option of the giver, and by motives derived from within himself.

MEN are often willing to have some gospel benefits, if they can attain them without those doctrines from which they flow. The benefits would be agreeable, while the doctrines and duties from which they come are undesirable to their hearts. But is it not folly, to attempt a separation of these things, which infinite wisdom hath joined together; or can we expect success in the attempt? The gospel is a most glorious scheme of wisdom and goodness; a superstructure which stands on many pillars, one of which being taken away the whole falls.

If we place human merit in the room of an atonement; or deny the necessity of personal holiness; or the need of the spirit to sanctify; or the sovereignty of God thro' the whole work of deliverance, the true gospel scheme is broken in pieces, and the hope of salvation thro' a Redeemer falls with it. All must soon appear before God, and all wish to come into his presence, with the best hope of acceptance; and is it not folly to mutilate the scheme of divine wisdom, when by this, its whole efficacy for redemption is destroyed. Many who are willing to be christians on their own terms, shrink back from the sovereignty of God, and do not seem to consider, that by thus doing, they cut themselves off from the benefits of grace, and that it is out of man's power to give a new gospel, or change from the letter of scripture, which is already given. If God's sovereignty be right, he will not be argued out of his own prerogative, or suffer the purposes of his counsel to be moved by the darkening of words.

Calling the doctrine a hard and uncomfortable one, will not alter the case. We know that it is uncomfortable enough to the proud mind; to the sinful heart; to the unholy man under whatever description of vice he falls, to think he is in the hand of a God sovereignly holy. But whence doth the uncomfortableness arise, from his own unholy self, or from the holy sovereignty of God? Doubtless from the former. Let his reigning sin be removed, and the doctrine will be uncomfortable no longer. Reigning sin being removed he is become a christian indeed, and greatly rejoices in a gofpel of fovereign grace, and that JEHOVAH will forever be fupreme.

4thly. THE fovereignty of GOD, is neceffary to make the gofpel redemption fafe and certain, for thofe who receive it.

THE certainty of falvation now ftands on GOD's own nature, and his acting by motives derived from within himfelf. This being rejected, there is no other fo fure ground of fafety. Placed on the creature's own goodnefs it would be unfafe indeed. Placed on an action, which is to be guided by motives derived from the creature, is making it equally unfafe. After the moft thorough examination, we can find no other fafe ground of hope, but the fovereignty of GOD. In this therefore, let us rejoice; and if we do not rejoice, let us know that our hearts are wrong. May GOD continue to reign, and bring us to be glad in his government.——AMEN.

K.

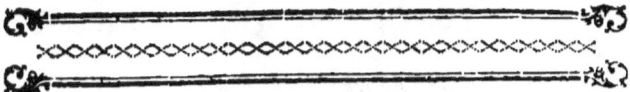

SERMON V.

On God's acting for his own glory.

ISAIAH xliii. 7.

—*For I have created him for my glory, I have formed him; yea, I have made him.*

THE subject to which these words apply may be learned from the seven first verses of the chapter, which I will repeat.

But now, thus saith the Lord that created thee, O Jacob, and he that formed thee, O Israel, fear not; for I have redeemed thee, I have called thee by thy name; thou art mine. When thou passest thro' the waters, I will be with thee; and when thro' the rivers, they shall not overflow thee: when thou walkest thro' the fire thou shalt not be burnt; neither shall the flame kindle upon thee. For I am the Lord thy God, the holy One of Israel, thy Saviour: I gave Egypt for thy ransom, Ethiopia and Seba for thee. Since thou wast precious in my sight thou hast been honorable, and I have loved thee: therefore will I give men for thee, and people for thy life. Fear not; for I am with thee: I will bring thy seed from the east, and gather thee from the west; I will say to the north, Give up; and to the south, Keep not back: bring my sons from far, and my daughters from the ends of the earth; Even every one that is called by my name: for I have created him for my glory, I have formed him; yea, I have made him.

THE whole passage is a promise to the church, and one of the most glorious recorded in holy scripture; in which GOD declares himself, to be the creator, redeemer and protector, of his people. The title of creator, which GOD here claims to himself, particularly applies to the forming of his church, and the sanctification of those individuals who compose it. It does not mean his original creation of the universe, but that new creation which sinners must experience before they belong to the true Israel or church of GOD: The word created is used in the same sense, as by the apostle in the following passage—" *For we are his workmanship, created in* CHRIST JESUS *unto good works.*" The change in mens hearts by the spirit of GOD, is often compared to the original creation of the universe, and the making of light, where before, there was darkness.

IN the passage recited, GOD declares his own special agency in forming his church, *thus saith the Lord that created thee*—his right in those who belong to it, *I have called thee by thy name, thou art mine*—he promises efficient protection, *when thou passest thro' the waters I will be with thee, when thro' the fire thou shalt not be burned; fear not I am with thee*—he also promises a great increase both in extension and numbers to his church, *I will bring thy seed from the east, and gather thee from the west; I will say to the north, Give up; and to the south, Keep not back; bring my sons from far, and my daughters from the ends of the earth, even every one that is called by my name.* In my text which immediately follows, God declares his design in this great and wonderful work, *For I have created him for my glory.* I have formed my church, and the moral character of those who compose it, for my glory.

It is clearly a scriptural truth, that all which God does, is for his own glory. For this he created the world, made angels and men, and governs the whole. For this he introduced the glorious scheme of redemption, and will carry it into full effect. Therefore he told Israel, when he promised deliverance and sanctification; *Not for your sakes do I this, saith the Lord* God, *be it known unto you. But I had pity for my holy name; which the house of Israel had profaned among the heathen whither they went. Therefore, say unto the house of Israel, thus saith the Lord* God, *I do not this for your sakes, O house of Israel, but for my holy name's sake.* In granting the promised favor, God wrought for his own glory.—To display *the riches of the glory of his grace,* is often mentioned as his design in the work of redemption.—When he comes to close the state of trial on earth, and judge the world, it will be done, that he may " *be glorified in his saints and admired in them that believe.*"— There is no need of repeating texts, to prove all that God does is for his own glory, for the diligent reader of the scriptures must have noticed them.

Further, creatures are directed to seek the glory of God in all they do. *Whatsoever ye do, do all to the glory of* God. *For ye are bought with a price: therefore glorify* God *in your body, and in your spirit, which are* God*'s.* Though Christ suffered for the salvation of sinners, he still describes his active obedience and his suffering to be for the glory of God. All holy exercise in God himself, in the Redeemer, and his people, agree in being designed for the divine glory; and this may be a rule, for the trial of our gracious sincerity in all we do.

It is doubtless true, that in all God hath done, or ever will do in the creation and government of the universe, he seeks his own glory; and for justifying any part of his conduct, it will be sufficient to show, he was glorified thereby. In doing thus he is not a selfish being, as creatures are, when they seek themselves only; but does it in infinite benevolence to himself, and the intelligent created kingdom, which flows out from his will. In seeking his own glory, he pursues the most direct means to make himself happy, and give the greatest happiness to creatures; so that there is nothing of the nature of selfishness in the supreme mind, though the action of his government is calculated to glorify himself. This is a subject worthy of most serious attention, both as it shows the reasonableness of divine government and law; and convicts sinners of great guilt in denying to glorify God, and in murmuring against him when he glorifies himself.

I will attempt an explanation of the following points.

I. What is meant by God's doing all things for his own glory.

II. I will explain the reason, why God makes his own glory the rule of his action.

III. The divine acting for his own glory, is the only possible exercise of infinite goodness.

IV. The great truth, that God in all things acts for his own glory, gives us a high conception of the amount of happiness there will be in the intelligent universe, in GOD himself, and the creation under his government.

I. WHAT is meant by GOD's doing all things for his own glory.

THE glory of GOD sometimes means his essential glory, or the unchanging fulness and perfection of his nature, which hath been the same from eternity, and can never be increased or diminished.

AN infinite glory, or fulness of perfection both natural and moral, is essential to the supreme JEHOVAH. He hath power, wisdom and goodness to the greatest degree. And if he had not these, at all times, he would not be GOD. Is the same yesterday, to day and forever; and as great and good in one period of duration as in another. This is the essential glory of GOD, and cannot be altered in any sense by the services of creatures.

GOD does not any thing to increase the essential glory of his nature, but all his counsels and works flow out from that glory, and are an expression or notice by which it is made visible to his creatures. Therefore in saying GOD hath done all things to promote his own glory, it is not meant to increase his own essential greatness, or fulness. Independent of all, he ever hath and ever will exist, the most blessed and glorious JEHOVAH. The things that have been, that now are, and that will be, are GOD's eternal fulness of glory exercised in a wise creation and a holy government.

AS GOD doth not increase his own essential glory, by his wonderful works and Almighty action; much less can creatures do it. If by any of our services, we expect to increase divine blessedness, or the honor of his majesty existing in himself, we are greatly deceived, for no such thing can be done.

2dly. By the glory of God, the scriptures most commonly mean his declarative glory.

The declarative glory of God is the display of his essential glory, and it is this which he seeks by all that he does in the works of creation, providence and redemption; also it is this, which holy creatures seek, in all their words and actions. The Lord God made the worlds, he governs them, and he redeems guilty sinners to display himself, and the fulness of power and love, which are essential to his nature. The heavens declare the glory of God. They do not increase the essential fulness of his nature; but display or manifest it. His essential glory is the cause; the created heavens are the effect, and the greatness of the effect, manifests the greatness of the cause. This manifestation, is glorifying God declaratively, and is done by all his works.

Natural creation shows the fulness of the creator's nature, and his providence is a continuation of the same display. The work of redemption glorifies God more than creation, by containing a fuller display of what he is; the plenitude of his goodness, and the nature of several perfections, which are all comprized in this general name. The more plainly divine truth, justice and mercy are evidenced to the understanding of creatures, the more God is glorified; and this is principally done, by the purchase and application of redeeming grace. This great work of love brings the essential glory of Godhead into view of the intelligent univerſe with the greateſt clearneſs.

It is the declarative glory of God which creatures are required to ſeek. Our obedience, love and praiſe, are a declarative acknowledgment of God's infinite fulneſs, by which he is entitled to the ſervice of creatures. Thus the Lord acts for his own glory in whatever he does; and this is the motive of all holy exerciſe in creatures. To glorify God, is the thing moſt deſired by holy beings; and tho' ſinful creatures do not ſeek this; through his overruling wiſdom, their exiſtence and all which they do and ſuffer, will be made to promote this end. The manifeſtation of God's eſſential glory will increaſe thro' eternity, and thus a foundation is laid for increaſing bleſſedneſs in the univerſe of holy creatures.

II. I am to explain the reaſon, why God makes his own glory the rule of his action.

The reaſon God ſeeks his own glory in all he does, is to make his own happineſs, and the happineſs of the created univerſe the greateſt it can be. Seeking his own glory is an exerciſe of infinite benevolence to himſelf and his kingdom; and as truly to his kingdom as to himſelf. The phraſe, *making his own happineſs the greateſt it can be*; is not meant to imply an increaſe of divine bleſſedneſs, as the diſplay of his nature increaſes, neither doth it mean a defect of happineſs in any paſt period of duration, for God hath been infinitely bleſſed from eternity in the knowledge of himſelf, and in the foreknowledge of thoſe diſplays, by which he doth now, and ever will, con-

L

tinue to spread happiness around him. Though the infinite blessedness of God, and the greatest happiness in his intelligent kingdom, are not practically separable, as will appear further on; yet it may assist our weak minds in conceiving so great a subject, to consider them separately. I will begin with the happiness of creatures. When we have seen how God's seeking his own glory, in all he does, makes the greatest possible amount of created good; it will lead us better to conceive, how it constitutes his own infinite blessedness.

1. God seeks his own glory in all he does, that he may make the greatest possible created happiness.

Let it be kept in remembrance, that seeking his own glory, means his declarative glory; that it is displaying, manifesting, or acting out the internal glory of his own nature.

Without this, there could have been no creation; no existence of finite minds, to know and be happy, for all creation is the fulness of God acted out. So that our being, our power of acting, our capacity for knowing and becoming happy, depend entirely on God's glorifying himself. There could be no happiness of creatures, without an existence to perceive, to feel, to act and to receive.

Further. The happiness of creatures, depends on having an object of enjoyment; and this could not be, unless God glorified himself, or made a display of the fulness in his own infinite nature.

In acting for his own glory, God hath made innumerable objects and set them before our understanding. God himself, is the only object adequate to the utmost desires of the created mind; and he is known, only by his acting for his own glory, by which he manifests his essential fulness. So that all created happiness, depends in the most absolute sense, on God's seeking his own glory. If he had not done this, or brought his eternal fulness, into action and communication, there would have been no created being, or knowledge or object of enjoyment. The objection, which sinful men feel, against his acting in the most sovereign manner for his own glory, if it could succeed, would extend further than they wish, and stop in nothing, short of the utter extinction of created being.—All divine works of creation, and redemption, through time and eternity, will be a display of the glory and essential fulness there is in the Supreme Godhead. Enmity against this display, is in fact, enmity against God and the universe; against existence, knowledge and happiness. The evil of such a temper must be the greatest possible.

2. In doing all things for his own glory, God hath a primary regard to his own happiness.

The essential moral glory or fulness of God, consists in love or communicative goodness. His benevolence to himself, is in proportion to the measure of his nature, and must therefore be infinite. Being good in his own nature, and a disposition to do good cannot be separated, or perhaps they are the same thing; for doing good is an exercise of being good.

How can a being of infinite perfection, benevolence and energy in action, do good to himself?

It cannot be by increasing his own fulness, for that is already infinite, and admits no increase. Doubtless one way of doing good to himself, is by communicating from, or acting out his fulness, in the existence, knowledge, holiness and happiness of creatures. This communication of himself is acting for his own glory. The bestowment of good around him, is doing good to himself, because it satisfies his benevolence; and the satisfaction of his benevolence is his happiness. His own happiness in communicating good is as much greater than all the happiness of created minds in receiving, as the infinitude of his glorious nature, exceeds the collected quantity of their finite existence. So that it follows, God is always doing good to himself, and satisfying his own benevolence, which is his happiness, when he communicates good to others; and the proportion of good which he doth to himself, is according to his infinite nature. God's doing all things for his own glory, implies and is the very exercise of his infinite benevolence, to himself and to created existence—displaying his own glory, is the only way in which his benevolence can act for its own satisfaction; and without the display he would deny his own blessedness, and there would be no creatures to exist and be happy.

We therefore see why God always seeks his own glory. It is to perpetuate his own blessedness, and enjoy his own fulness. He doubtless ought to have the highest and a primary regard to himself in this, because he is an infinite being; and the preservation of his own happiness is the greatest possible object, which can be sought by a holy love.

It also appears, that the blessedness of Godhead and the greatest happiness of creatures never can be separated.

Though we can conceive and speak of them as distinct, and it assists our weak power of conception to do thus, they cannot be practically separated; for the blessedness of God consists in doing good to himself, by the communication or display of glory from his own fulness, thus making happiness around him; and the happiness of creation consists in beholding, adoring and enjoying the display. It is thus, that benevolence makes an unchanging and eternal union, between Jehovah and his holy creatures. They are united in character or temper; they are united in the love of happiness; they are united also in the means of happiness, for the means by which God enjoys himself, are the only means by which creatures can be happy.

III. The divine acting for his own glory, is the only possible exercise of infinite goodness.

The heart of man, in its natural unholy state, is opposed to the glory of God. There is a dislike of him because he glorifies himself, and an enmity against the command which enjoins all creatures to seek his honor, in whatever they do.

It has been said in contradiction to truth, that to represent God doing all things for his own glory, is describing him to be a selfish being.

Those who make this representation in order to disgrace a truth, which either they do not love, or understand; show great ignorance, in what benevolence and selfishness consist, and that they have not yet attained just ideas of this high and glorious subject. They judge the nature, and measure the quantity of divine benevolence, on the scale of their own selfishness and pride. Such persons, generally, have not a true idea of what is meant by GOD's doing all things for his own glory; but suppose it to be something that is similar to their own engrossing temper. They feel their own finiteness, and wish to extend their quantity of existence, their power, influence and possessions; they seek great things for themselves above their worth; their actions are all for personal exaltment. This is selfishness indeed, and this they transfer from themselves to GOD; and then call it reproachful. They do not see the reproach in themselves; but after it is unjustly ascribed to the divine character, they can see it to be wrong. Such ought to be instructed, that GOD's acting for his own glory, is wholly another thing.

HE knows his own fulness, and cannot wish it to be greater. Neither the quantity of his being, nor his power, nor influence, nor possessions can be increased. Infinite cannot wish an addition to itself, nor a higher rank, nor a greater plenitude of glory than is possessed. The divine acting in all things for his own glory, is acting out or communicating from his own fulness. This is directly contrary to engrossing or selfishness. It is giving of his own, to others, both their existence and their happiness; and not taking from them, for the purpose of self-advancement, what was independently theirs.

BUT, replies the objecting heart, by seeking his own glory, GOD makes himself happy or enjoys himself, and this is his principal motive; and is not this selfishness? I answer, is it possible to please a heart which can make this objection? The objector will doubtless allow, the quantity of GOD's existence, his energies of action, and his capacity of blessedness to be infinite, and therefore greater, than the sum of created existence and its felicity ever can be. He must also allow that happiness in Deity is as valuable as in a creature. Consequently God's own happiness, ought to be his principal motive; and no reasonable objection can be made against it, unless from the manner of his happiness.

And what is the manner of his happiness? It is not by engrossing, but communicating; not by taking to himself, but giving away. It is by giving to the objector his existence, and capacity for being happy; and if he will accept it, the eternal glory of heaven. Dost thou still object, and call God selfish in making himself supremely happy by doing good? If thou dost it shows the bitterness of thy heart, and an implacable hatred against all happiness that is not thine own. The objection shows the exceeding sinfulness, and irreconcileable and destroying nature of sin, and that it is as the apostle teaches, *Enmity against* God. While sinners endeavour to hide their enmity, and often deceive themselves so as to think they have it not, their caviling against God and his government prove its existence. The objection, that by seeking his own glory, in all things, God is selfish; is so far from having truth or force, that this is the only way in which he can be benevolent. If he did not communicate good from his own glory, and enjoy himself in doing it, he would instantly be called malevolent or selfish. He does it and is infinitely happy, and still the same objection is continued. There is no way to please the sinner, but by joining his own endeavours to put himself in the place of God.

IV. The great truth, that God in all things acts for his own glory, when it is justly understood, gives us a high conception of the amount of happiness there will be in the intelligent universe, in GOD himself, and in the creatures under his government. Our conceptions, on this subject, must fall below the reality; and language must fall below our conceptions. GOD's complacence and delight in the fulness of his own being; his benevolence to his own nature; his happiness in communicating and doing good, whereby, if the expression may be used, his own eternal fulness is multiplied to himself; all prove his infinite blessedness.

THE communional blessedness of the Father, Son, and Holy Ghost, in the divine fulness, and in the ocean of good, which diffusively flows from himself in the production and blessedness of created existence; is a subject on which the finite mind can but feebly look. The blessedness of GOD is as incomprehensible as his nature.

How great must be the amount of happiness in the holy intelligent creation! We can learn its greatness better from considering GOD, than from any speculation on the nature of creatures. Looking on the nature of creatures, how imperfect and dependent! On the nature of men, how undeserving and guilty! Confine the view here, without going higher, all is gloom, weakness and wretchedness! But raise the prospect higher, and as the Creator and Redeemer come in sight, the light beams, and glory and blessedness spread over the holy creation, whether it be composed of those who retain their primeval rectitude, or such as have been new created by the spirit of CHRIST.

FROM the fulness of GOD let us learn the fulness of created bliss. The happiness of creatures is made by GOD, made for himself, made worthy of his infinite fulness, made worthy of being the means by which he enjoys his own plenitude of love. How astonishing then must the sum of created peace be! A sum eternally increasing! Tho' it can never be infinite, it is that, by which, infinite goodness is expressed, and infinite benevolence enjoys itself. GOD's benevolence to himself, is the proper measure of that amount of blessedness, to which the holy creation is ever approximating; and tho' a fixed period can never be assigned, in which it will become strictly infinite, yet the subject, in this vast extension, is as really incomprehensible by us, as the nature of GODHEAD.

THIS is the consequence of our Lord's doing all things for his own glory. It is the natural fruit of benevolence, by which he is disposed to grant, and actually enjoys himself in communicating good. Consider the excellent nature of benevolence! Compare it with malevolence or selfishness; for selfishness and malevolence are really the same both in their nature and consequences, and as men commonly use the words, there is no difference, except in the strength of evil exercise.

SELFISHNESS grasps all for itself; it knows no good but self-advancement; takes no delight in communicating or doing good to others, but envies their blessedness and hates their prosperity, unless a personal advantage be derived from it. This is the depravity of human nature, and the embryo of those future torments prepared for all the ungodly.

SELFISHNESS is malevolence; and malevolence, in its increase, by the most unalterable laws of nature, goes far in conſtituting the miſeries of the world to come.

TURN from this, and behold the excellent nature and fruits of that benevolence, which is the moral fulneſs and bleſſedneſs of GOD himſelf, and the holy creation. This holy love, in the firſt inſtance, enjoys all its own internal fulneſs, and then enjoys itſelf again in a diffuſive communication, which is made without leſſening its own ſtore. Few perſons have conſidered this ſubject ſufficiently to ſee how benevolence multiplies happineſs. Take, as an example, the mind of a holy creature, filled with the ſpirit of love from GOD. Tho' he be in himſelf frail, of limited powers and knowledge, and a limited capacity of perſonally receiving divine bounties; ſtill how amazing the field of happineſs, opened before him. Firſt, his own perſonal wants are completely ſupplied—every thing, which his rectified heart deſires, is given in the utmoſt fulneſs, he can receive. He can ſay, my nature, my whole heart and mind is filled—the veſſel can perſonally hold no more good, than GOD hath poured into it, and will continue to pour thro' eternity. It will be allowed, this is a happy creature, and that taking into conſideration, the eternity thro' which all his wants will be ſupplied, his ſituation is bleſſed indeed. But is this a juſt or complete deſcription of his bleſſedneſs? By no means. His benevolence ſtill multiplies happineſs to him. He loves the happineſs of his neighbour as his own, and in beholding his good, re-enjoys all the bleſſedneſs a finite mind can receive; and in traverſing an immenſe creation of holy beings, every one he meets, like a glaſs, reflects back on his heart, a good which he enjoys, equal to the ſatisfaction of his own perſonal wants. How different is the meeting of two envious, or of two benevolent minds?

The envious spontaneously kindle into all the rage and torment of hell. The benevolent reciprocate a divine blessedness, and each brings with him, an ingredient of heaven for his brother—each is happy in his own supply—equally happy in his brother's good. They join in transport on beholding the Redeemer's kingdom. They behold JEHOVAH, whose name is love, pouring forth from himself an ocean of felicity. An infinite nature! Infinitely happy in doing good to himself, by the communication of good.

THESE are the prospects set before the children of GOD, who are redeemed from among men by the blood of CHRIST, and sanctified by his holy Spirit. It hath not entered into the heart of unholy men, to conceive this blessedness. Their own want of benevolence, disqualifies them for conceiving the length, and the breadth, and height of the love of GOD. All this is prepared, and freely offered by sovereign mercy to his repenting enemies; prepared for them while enemies, and hating both his character and government. O the astonishing love of GOD! The greatness of the riches of his grace! Looking on the guilty character of men, we are ready to say it is impossible such grace should be; but it is by looking on GOD himself and the gift of his Son, that we see the possibility of salvation. I shall conclude this discourse with some inferences.

1. NONE but a most wicked heart, can be opposed to GOD's doing all things for his own glory.

AGAINST this doctrine of revelation men have a natural enmity. Many do not obtain just doctrinal knowledge of the truth, and are thus exposed to be carried away with the cavils of error. A multitude more, will increase in opposition as the truth comes into sight. Where there is a wrong heart, doctrinal knowledge will not change, but increase the bitterness of its exercise. Selfishness and benevolence cannot agree. They are two masters of the heart, of opposite natures and tendencies.—One is darkness, the other light; one is the principle of heaven, the other of hell. The divine acting for his own glory, in all things, has been shown to be an exercise of benevolence; so that every good heart must rejoice in it. The enemy of this truth, is the enemy of happiness—he is the enemy of God's happiness, which consists in acting out his own love—the enemy of true happiness in creatures, which arises from beholding and receiving the communications that issue from the uncreated fountain of goodness.—What is more wicked, than to be thus the enemy of God, and the best interests of the creation. No plea can justify, no pretence can excuse this temper. The sinner's own mouth must be shut, when the whole truth, in this point, is seen.

WHEN men are convicted of a selfish temper, or of an unwillingness that GOD should seek his own glory; it is surprizing with what security they will answer, selfishness is natural to man, and none are free from it. This is allowed to be true, and a very threatening truth it is to sinners; but to what doth it amount? Is it a justification? No. Is it an argument there is any right or any safety in this temper? Not at all. It amounts to a condemnation of all men; is a confession of their demerits; a justification of GOD in condemning; and an avowal of the first principles of eternal misery, in every mind of man, unless sovereign, sanctifying power is pleased to deliver.

2. If God doth all things for his own glory, we have no right to think ourselves in a safe state, until our hearts and actions are governed by the same motive. A right to salvation stands in a covenant union with Jesus Christ, which always implies a union of moral character, and conformity to God in holiness. The Spirit of Christ gives to his people *grace for grace ;* gracious affections corresponding to his infinite moral perfections. God and his people, love the same objects—have similar desires—promote the same interests, and have a common source of happiness. To make them his people, he communicates from his fulness, a benevolence like to his own, and a desire to promote his glory, as he has to glorify himself. If we have not this desire to promote his glory ; if it be not a principal motive with us in our actions, we are not real christians, and he will not in the end own us for his. The disciples of Christ love their master's glory, more than their own earthly pleasure ; and when it is seen how his honor and the interest of his kingdom may be promoted, without consulting flesh and blood or a corrupt heart, they immediately set themselves to glorify their Father in heaven. Men may go a great length, in the visible duties of religion, without any intention to glorify God. They may act wholly with the servile design, to escape the worm that dieth not, and the fire that is not quenched. With this view, they may give alms of all they possess, and beggar themselves to feed the poor, while they never mourned in secret for the dishonor done to God in the world. Those who think they are christians, and going fast to heaven, if they have not often put the question to themselves, will this action be for God's glory ? Or how can I dishonor him less and glorify him

more? are not such christians as will bear the trial of the judgment day. To see the glory of God displayed will be a heaven to the holy—the more it is displayed the more joyful their heaven will be, and if his glory be now forgot, it demonstrates them destitute of the preparative principles of eternal glory. A visible life of religion is necessary evidence of being in a safe state; but if any think they have this and do not feel an ardent desire to glorify God, they are as a sounding brass and a tinkling cymbal, and all their works will profit them not. The people of God, feel a most sensible pleasure in the promotion of God's glory; and they can endure trials with great patience, and even glory in tribulation, that the divine name may be honored. Let us examine and prove ourselves by this rule. If there were more examination and prayer, there would be fewer weak and doubting christians, than we now find. The sincere would gain new evidence by the increase of their graces; and many who think themselves safe, would detect their own hypocrisy. Let all rejoice that God reigns to glorify himself, and may this be our blessedness. AMEN.

SERMON VI.

Man's depravity.

ROMANS iii. 9, 10.

—For we have before proved both Jews and Gentiles, that they are all under sin; as it is written, there is none righteous, no, not one.

THE depravity of mankind, is a truth very clearly revealed in the holy scriptures. There is also a general conviction of natural conscience that this is the case; a conviction which extends far beyond any knowledge of the christian revelation, and among nations of every religion, which hath been received by any considerable number of men. This shows the christian revelation, to agree with the natural notions of men, and with natural conscience. Whoever, will take pains to examine the heathen systems of religion, will find they are not confined, to such doctrines and services as only imply praise; or to such parts of prayer, as imply only praise and a sense of dependence, which would be the case if they had no consciousness of sin. Their religion, also, includes something that is designed for expiation—to appease an injured being and make peace with him. This shows the natural sense of conscience, that men are sinful and guilty creatures, to be deeply written on the mind. The few scattered instances, of men whose consciences are seared as with a hot iron, can be accounted for, on natural principles, without discrediting the general truth; and the scriptures of God do fully account for them.

We have, therefore, the highest evidence, that men are under a moral depravity, which is common to the race. It is testified by scripture, by our own consciences, and the general conviction of the world. Infidels, who deny the truth of revelation, may talk as much as they please, of superstition, and the prejudices of education; but they cannot make it appear, probable or possible, as human nature is, that the general opinion of depravity should arise from such causes. Self-love will be allowed common to human nature. From this comes a love of their interest and private rights, and a love of their reputation not less than their interest. Superstition and the prejudices of education are allowed to have great power, over both the sentiments and practices of men; but they have not a power to resist the general impulse of self-love. It will not be pretended, that they have a power to make men generally, renounce all their worldly interests, and private rights. The acknowledgment of depravity is an acknowledged loss of reputation, and it is not to be supposed there would be a general confession of this; unless there be the powerful testimony of natural conscience, that it is the case.

It is a matter, of the greatest importance, to understand the nature of this depravity, or in what it consists; for without such knowledge, we can neither know the extent of our sin, nor the most suitable means of deliverance. Men may be conscious of sin, they may feel themselves guilty, may be afraid to come before God, and fly to many services as means of appeasing him, while their notions of depravity, are very indistinct. This is often the case thro' inattention to the subject, or from not faithfully searching the holy scriptures, which give us the best light. I believe, also, that depravity itself, indisposes men to acknowledge the thing in which it essentially consists.

In considering this subject, it will be proper;

I. To collect evidence from the holy scriptures, that all men are in a state of depravity and sin.

II. Inquire, in what this depravity consists, and how the several powers and faculties of the mind are affected by it.

III. Compare the description which will be given of our original and common depravity, with the apparent character of mankind; their conduct, and their treatment of God and creatures in all ages; by which we shall see the scriptural account of this moral corruption to be a just one, and entitled to our most serious belief.

I. The sacred history of human nature, gives us an account of the introduction of sin, soon after the creation. If there were no account of this and the point were wholly in the dark, it would not disprove the depravity of mankind, which is discovered by so many facts in general experience. Still, the account of the introduction of sin, by which our first parents and all their natural offspring became depraved and guil-

N

ty creatures, is a circumstance which adds great credibility and consistency to the divine story.

AFTER the apostacy, GOD brought the offenders to trial, and pronounced sentence on their disobedience. Effects of the sentence have been found in every age; pain, distress, misery, and many calamities. In the history of the ages immediately succeeding the apostacy, GOD charges all men with being sinners, and proves the charge by their works. The earth was filled with violence, until the honor of GOD required him to cleanse it by a deluge. Tho' this was a necessary chastisement, to stop the progress of vice, and bear a testimony for the moral character of the supreme governor; it did not regenerate human nature. The nature of man remained the same after the deluge as it was before; and the corrupted heart proved itself by corrupt actions.

AFTER this, GOD selected a particular family and nation, to be the repositories of his word and a written law; as the most eligible way of resisting the torrent of vice and spiritual ignorance, and of preparing the way for a kingdom in the world, glorious in divine knowledge and holiness. This was the beginning of the written word, which is now compleated in the canon of scripture.

THROUGH the whole, there are frequent allusions and direct references, to the first apostacy, as the source of those evils with which the world is filled. Men are represented sinful and guilty —departed from GOD—ignorant of his glory— indisposed to honor him—without a love of his holy nature and government—serving themselves and the creatures in the exercise of divers' lusts —hating, biting and devouring one another, when left to the practice of their natural temper.

The historical part of scripture confirms this representation, by innumerable facts, concerning nations and individuals; so that the total depravity of human nature, is a fact most strongly proved by the sacred history of mankind.—This history hath in it, all the marks of sincerity and truth, and the visible sins of both Jews and Gentiles, are traced back by the omniscient writer, to an evil heart that is common to men. This is the common story of the Old Testament historians and prophets; and in numberless addresses, instructions, reproofs and warnings from GOD, the universal depravity of man is assumed as a fact, that is indisputable.

WHEN we come to the New Testament, which particularly unfolds the method of salvation by the grace of GOD; the whole scheme of doctrine, and the evangelical duties required from sinners, are grounded on the previous fact, of a total depravity in men. On this account a divine atonement became necessary; also the influences of the Spirit of GOD, to create men anew, and raise them from spiritual death to a holy life in CHRIST JESUS. If the scripture be true, the utter sinfulness of men in the sight of GOD must be allowed. Those who attempt to receive the scriptures, or the gospel, as being of infinite value, on any other ground than this, are bringing together two schemes of sentiment, which can never agree. The sacred writers in proving the need or showing the offices of the gospel, either pre-suppose, or prove the depravity of all the earth.

PAUL considers this subject largely, in the beginning of the epistle to the Romans, preparatory to his stating our justification by the free grace of GOD through JESUS. He divides mankind into two great classes, Jews and Gentiles. The former were God's professing people, of the seed of Abraham, to whom his law and the oracles of grace were committed. Under the latter name of Gentiles, it is well known, that in the scriptural use of the word, all other people, beside the Jews, were included; so that Jews and Gentiles inclusively contain all mankind.

In the first and part of the second chapter, he considers the universal character of the Gentiles, and enumerates the sins, which were a proof of the state of their hearts. He says, concerning them, *That when they knew God they glorified him not as God, neither were thankful, but become vain in their imaginations, and their foolish heart was darkened.—That they did not like to retain God in their knowledge.—That they are without excuse.—That they changed the truth of God into a lie, and worshipped and served the creature more than the Creator;*—together with many other expressions descriptive of the greatest depravity.

The second chapter includes the Jews also under the same sentence of total sin. *Therefore thou art inexcuseable, O man, whosoever thou art that judgest: For wherein thou judgest another thou condemnest thyself; for thou that judgest doest the same things.—Behold, thou art called a Jew, and restest in the law* (i. e. a revelation, or the ritual law) *and makest thy boast of God. &c.—Thou therefore which teachest another, teachest thou not thyself? —Thou that makest thy boast of the law, through breaking the law dishonorest thou God? For the name of God is blasphemed among the Gentiles through you.*—Afterwards, in the third chapter, the apostle puts the question, *What advantage then hath the Jew?* What benefit do they derive from being the professing people of God, if they be not as a people delivered from the depravity of human nature? The answer is, *Much every way, chiefly be-*

cause to them were committed the oracles of GOD. Their advantage, is doctrinal instruction in the nature of sin and the way of forgiveness; but they came into the world with sinful hearts, as the Gentiles do, and remain under the condemning guilt of sin, until sanctified and justified by the grace of GOD.

FURTHER on, he comes to our text as a conclusion of the discourse.—*We have before proved both Jews and Gentiles that they are all under sin; as it is written, there is none righteous, no, not one:*—And he also adds, *There is none that understandeth*—*there is none that seeketh after* GOD—*they are all gone out of the way*—*they are together become unprofitable*—*destruction and misery are in their ways, and the way of peace have they not known.* This is Paul's description of Jews and Gentiles, including all mankind.

I WISH it to be remembered that a great number of positive testimonies, for the total depravity of all mankind, and which might be pertinently introduced here, to prevent repetition will be reserved to the next branch of the discourse, when we shall inquire in what this depravity consists.

WHEN the scriptures speak of good men, or of any exercises in the human heart, that are pleasing to GOD; they ascribe them to an origin, perfectly consistent with the doctrine of a total, moral corruption of human nature. The question is not, whether there be any holiness in any of mankind; but whether, there be any in them naturally, previous to the gospel renovation and forgiveness? We know there is a degree of holiness and conformity to GOD in some minds; but whence doth it come, and is it the natural char-after of any man? It comes wholly from the sanctifying grace of GOD thro' JESUS CHRIST, and had no existence until produced by divine power. All those sacred passages, therefore, which ascribe the existence and every degree of holiness, to the renewing spirit of GOD, and such passages are very numerous; are as much a testimony for the original depravity of men, as they be for the need of sanctifying grace. The whole Bible, may therefore be adduced, as evidence in point for the moral corruption of mankind, and that they act wholly under the influence of it, except so far, as a sovereign GOD is pleased to redeem and change them.

THE history of the apostacy; the history of nations and individuals in every age; the history both of bad and good men; the history of redemption, in its progress, purchase and application; the description of the spirit's operation, and the evangelical graces of good people; the history of the divine government, and its terminating in a state of eternal rewards; do all suppose and prove the depravity of human nature. It is in vain to say, we need a greater number of particular texts, affirming this fact, concerning every creature who is born into the world; for we have enough such, and if the number were increased tenfold, and expressed in the most pointed manner, the evidence arising from these particular assertions, would not be equal to the general testimony of scripture history and doctrine. All these agree in this point, that man is a creature totally depraved and dead in trespasses and sins.

II. WE are to inquire, in what this depravity consists, and how the several powers and faculties of the mind are affected by it.

The understanding, is that capacity of the rational mind by which it perceives truth, and judges the relation between different truths. The will, is that power of the rational mind, by which it chooses or refuses, receives or rejects, such truths as are perceived or known by the understanding. Choosing or refusing always imply love or hatred of the proposed truth. Choosing a truth or an object, is loving it; rejecting, is hating it. Hence, the will, the heart, and the affections, may in most moral and evangelical discourses, be used as words of the same meaning. A holy will is a holy heart, and a holy heart flows out in holy affections, towards holy objects.

1. The primary seat of depravity is in the heart, will, or affections; so that if this be made right, a rectification of whatever is wrong in any other power or faculty of the mind, will of course follow.

This depravity, is so essentially seated in the heart or will, that no kind of address or acting on the other faculties, will remove sin from the soul. The regenerating power of GOD, acts directly on the heart or will, and the most powerful or long continued action, on the understanding, will not change the heart. A temper, disposition, inclination, taste or relish which are right or wrong, mean the same as a heart or will, that is right or wrong.

The word heart, most commonly is used in the scriptures, denoting the will and affections, and seems to be uniformly considered as the seat or source of holiness and sin. There are a multitude of passages which show this.

The law of holiness given by Moses and by CHRIST is, *Thou shall love the Lord with all thy heart*—that is, choose and cleave to him with the strongest affection. When GOD describes his own sanctifying action on the mind, he says, *Then will I sprinkle clean water upon you, and ye shall be clean. A new heart also will I give you, and a new spirit will I put within you; and I will take the stony heart out of your flesh.* Those who hear the word aright, are such as receive it into *good and honest hearts*. Holiness is described, by a clean, a right, a pure, a wise, and an understanding heart; and sin by the contrary, such as an evil, and a hard heart. In describing the antediluvian corruption, GOD says that mens *hearts were to evil only, and that continually*. The prophets and JESUS CHRIST describe mens rejection of the truth, to their hearts being waxed gross. The apostle ascribes mens spiritual ignorance to the, *hardness of their hearts*. GOD charges mankind with having an *evil heart of unbelief*. CHRIST in enumerating the practical sins of men, says, *they come out of the heart*. It is said of men, that *Their hearts gather iniquity to themselves—are corrupted—are hardened—that they commit all manner of sin in the heart—that they imagine mischief, study destruction, and are mad in their hearts*.

SOMETIMES the word *will* is used denoting the same, *Ye will not come to me that ye might have life*, that is, your hearts are opposed to coming. The sensible exercises of the heart and will are what we call the affections, such as love, delight, rejoicing, hatred, enmity, mourning, and all these are exercises of the heart.

MENS depravity is often described by their love of what is wrong, and their want of love or enmity to that which is right and good. They love sin—delight in departing from GOD—choose not his ways nor his law, and endeavour to put far away his character and the duties they owe him. They prefer or love their own will, more than his holy will. The law of holiness is to *love the*

Lord with thy whole heart. The depravity in sinners is *a love of themselves and the creatures,* with the whole heart or supremely; and hence it comes that *the friendship of the world is enmity against God.* And that, *the carnal mind is enmity against God; for it is not subject to the law of God, neither indeed can be.* Enmity to God, his law, and government is the necessary consequence of their supreme love being turned on themselves. The natural structure of the human mind is such, that a want of love to God, terminates in a supreme love of himself, and the creatures as they are adapted to gratify the lusts of a sinful heart. Let a love of God cease from the heart, and enmity to his character, his law and government, and the whole system of holiness will of course follow. So that the heart must be considered as the primary seat of man's depravity. Here it entered —here it reigns—and from this fountain it corrupts the soul. And as all the effects of the first apostacy, on other powers of the mind, proceeded from a corrupt heart; so it is upon the heart that the power of God is exerted to bring us into a right state. Therefore the change of regeneration is called *being renewed in love,* a renovation of the will and affections, whereby there is a supreme delight and choice of holy objects.

God is love. His love is his holiness. The highest sum of happiness in his own infinite nature, and in the intelligent kingdom he hath created, is the object of his love. He loves himself in union with his kingdom, and his kingdom in union with himself; so that both make but one object. The creature, who is perfect in holiness, hath the same object, and regards himself only as a part, subordinated to the glorious and eternal object of holy affection. He loves, desires, and acts for an end infinitely greater than himself. In sight of this the perfect saints loose sight of themselves, and know their own worth only in union with GOD and his pure family. This holiness exists in the heart and affections.

THE depraved sinner can love, but it is his own happiness in solitary distinction and actual opposition to the happiness and glory of GOD and his kingdom. The holy and the depraved mind have, therefore, objects of love, entirely distinct; so that there immediately springs up an opposition of interests, and this in its natural operation becomes enmity against GOD, and a hatred of his law and of religious duty.

2dly. THE word of GOD doth also describe the depravity of man, by ignorance, darkness and blindness. If the will or heart be the primary seat of depravity, what is meant by these expressions, and how is the rational intellect or understanding affected? In answer to this inquiry I reply,

1. THAT by the ignorance or blindness ascribed to sinners in the word of GOD, is not commonly meant doctrinal ignorance, or any incapacity in the natural intellect to perceive truth, or judge of the relation between different truths.

HOLY and depraved men, can alike perceive the truth or falsehood of propositions which are placed before the understanding? They can receive evidence, and infer one truth from another. This is a natural operation of the mind, which was not destroyed by the apostacy, and doth not prove, either the existence or want of holiness. If men had not the natural powers of understanding, and of receiving doctrinal knowledge, they could not be sinful. As an instance, If men had no doctrinal knowledge, of GOD's existence or of his law, or the intellect was incapable of receiving it, they would not be guilty for actions of disobedience. CHRIST told the Jews, *Ye have both seen and hated me and my father.—If I had not come and spoke to you, ye had not had sin, but now ye have no cloak for your sin.* Both these passages, refer to doctrinal knowledge, and the persons who saw, and who heard CHRIST speak, were in the depth of that blindness, which is essential to depravity.

THERE are millions of sinners, at the present time, who have just doctrinal knowledge, and much clear speculation on the gospel; who labor under the genuine blindness of sin, to as great a degree as the heathen. All unsanctified persons are under that ignorance and blindness of sin of which the scripture speaks.

I WOULD not be understood, that there is as much doctrinal light among sinners as there would be if they were holy. The indulgence of their intemperate lusts, by injuring the body, may enervate the mind and the vigor of natural understanding. Also by the opposition of their hearts to truth, they are indisposed to seek for it; they neglect means and do not study to be informed. From hence comes an amazing degree of doctrinal ignorance, in those who have the word of GOD and the best means of instruction. It is surprizing to see this ignorance in multitudes, who know that the blessedness or misery of eternity is at stake; and it shows the prodigious dislike of their hearts to the truth; a dislike so strong, that it pains them to see doctrinal light, and they fly away from it as disagreeable. Still, even this ignorance, is not the thing, of which GOD's word most commonly speaks, in describing the sin of human nature. Doctrinal or spiritual light and ignorance, are distinct things; and it is spiritual ignorance which is essential to the nature of depravity. Where there is the greatest doctrinal light, there may be the greatest spiritual blindness. Doctrinal light, is seeing the truth by means of evidence presented to the understanding; and when seen, it may appear either glorious or hateful; according as the moral state of the heart shall be. Spiritual light is seeing the glory of truth; it appears amiable, excellent and lovely. Seeing the glory of truth implies a good heart. Spiritual ignorance is seeing no beauty and glory in truth, and nothing in GOD which makes him to be desired. Doctrinal ignorance may be removed by the instituted means of instruction; but spiritual ignorance can be removed only by the power of GOD renewing the heart, and all means of instruction are here ineffectual. When GOD acts to enlighten spiritually, he does it, not by a revelation of truth which was before unseen by the understanding, or giving any new power to the perceiving faculty; but solely by changing the heart. In the heart there is a new creation, new moral qualities infused by the holy spirit, and this is regeneration. When the heart is made holy, the beauty and glory of holiness is perceived; and until there be this change of heart, the sinner whether he lives in a heathen or christian land, is in total spiritual blindness.

THIS blindness is meant in the following passages, and many others. *Being grieved for the blindness of their heart.—Having the understanding darkened, being alienated from the life of* GOD, *thro' the ignorance that is in them, because of the blindness of their heart.—And knowest not that thou art blind.—If our gospel be hid, it is hid to them that are lost: In whom the God of this world hath blinded the minds of them that believe not, lest the light of the glorious gospel of* CHRIST, *who is the image of* GOD, *should shine into them.—For* GOD *who commanded the light to shine out of darkness, hath shined in our hearts; to give the light of the knowledge of the glory of* GOD, *in the face of* JESUS CHRIST. The hiding, the blindness, the light shining into the heart, which are mentioned in these passages, applies solely to spiritual light and ignorance. *Having the understanding darkened, being alienated from the life of* GOD *through the ignorance that is in them, because of the blindness of their heart.* This blindness, which is most dreadful to human nature, is one under which men will remain, until GOD is pleased to sanctify them for himself; and all the means of instruction in the christian world, have no power to remove it, unless the renewing spirit of GOD accompanies his own means.—For this reason, the depravity of human nature, in the word of GOD, is traced to the heart as a fountain. —There must be a conformity of the heart, to the moral character of GOD and to the truth, in order to see his glorious loveliness, and the satisfying beauty of virtue.

IT hence appears that depravity doth not originate in the understanding, but hath its primary seat in the will and affections; and when these are perfectly rectified, the whole mind ministers to holiness.—There are a great number of useful inferences from this subject, all of which, except the two following are deferred to a succeeding discourse.

1. THE preceding description of man's natural corruption, shows that the use of means alone can never remove it.

MEANS may instruct and act powerfully on the understanding to give doctrinal light; and this is the whole of their efficacy, the whole for which they were appointed, by a wife GOD.

Let us consider what the means of religion do, and their action on the mind of man.

They fix our attention; set the character and law of God before us; make us acquainted with our own character, and wants, and with the nature and consequences of holiness and sin; and generally, they give doctrinal information; but beyond this, it is not conceived they have any power.—If the depravity of man consisted in doctrinal ignorance, the means of instruction might set him right; but this is not the case. The supposition, that means, by the most diligent use of them, will remove the corruption of human nature, implies that the heart is previously right; and that all sins are no more than pitiable mistakes, arising from doctrinal ignorance—Let this idea be followed in its genuine consequences, and it really denies the sin of human nature. The heart, the will, the moral taste can be changed only by the power of God.—Hence the scriptures speak of a new birth—a renovation—a new creation—a new heart—and the necessary action of the Holy Spirit to make the change. This may be illustrated, in the instance of seeing the divine character. The ignorant sinner has doctrinal knowledge to a certain degree, and to that which is seen of God his heart is opposed. Let his doctrinal knowledge, by the use of means be doubly increased. Will this enlarged view of what he disliked, make him love it? Common sense would determine quite the contrary. Those who depend on the use of means to change their hearts, are denying the power of God and resisting the Holy Ghost; and there is no reason to expect he will help until they feel that they are in the hand of sovereign power and goodness—and that he must work to save them. Means were instituted to instruct the understanding, and fix the attention on truth. The Holy Spirit is appointed to renew and sanctify, and the spiritual enlightening which he gives, comes from his prior action on the heart. But is there not a greater probability that those who diligently use appointed means, wil be sanctified by divine power, than if they omit the use? Doubtless there is, and those who omit the use, have no reason to expect that GOD will sanctify and forgive. In the salvation of his people, he does honor to all his own institutions—he may give the Spirit to whom he pleaseth, and he will not give to those who are regardless of his appointments—we ought therefore very diligently to use appointed means, and be at the same time sensible, that it is the sovereign power of GOD which changes the heart, removes the power of original corruption, and gives a beginning preparation for heaven.

2. THE description that hath been given of man's natural depravity, shows that the ignorance of which the scriptures speak is no excuse for sin.

DOCTRINAL ignorance may, in some cases, excuse from sin. Thus the heathen who never had CHRIST preached to them, are not guilty for the neglect of receiving him; while in those who have the gospel, the want of faith is a great sin. If men did not know the moral law, either by a natural or revealed evidence, this would be an excuse for those things in them which are now sinful.—All men, have sufficient doctrinal knowledge of the moral law, to render them inexcusable in the sight of the judge.

THAT spiritual ignorance which I have largely described, in no sense or degree, is an excuse for sin.—It all comes from sin in the heart, and is in proportion to the degree of sin. The more sinful the more blind.—This blindness, instead of being an excuse, is the index of an evil character, and the degree of blindness measures the degree of guilt; hence the word of GOD considers mens blindness as their sin and threatens it with punishment. When sinners come before the bar of GOD, if they plead, that they saw nothing in his character which delighted them—no glory in his truth and justice—nothing amiable in his law—nothing lovely in CHRIST's purity, and the holy doctrines of his gospel—no excellency in the christian temper and obedience—no pleasure in the duties of worship and the company of GOD's people; the judge will answer that on this very evidence, they are guilty and righteously condemned. And should we not my reader in a similar case, judge the same? Suppose an unholy son, pleading as an excuse, for his undutifulness and his disobedience to the reasonable laws of a just and good father, that the character of the father disgusted him, and he could find no pleasure either in his character or law; would this excuse his disobedience? Nay, would it not be the aggravating proof of his depravity?——It certainly would. Let none therefore think, because religion doth not appear amiable to them, that this will be any excuse. So far to the contrary, the more blind they find themselves to the spiritual glory of divine things; the more alarmed they ought to be for their situation.—This circumstance shows them to be exceeding sinful, and far removed from the kingdom of heaven.

MAY the Lord change all our hearts to delight in himself. AMEN.

SERMON VII.

Man's depravity.

ROMANS iii. 9, 10.

—*For we have before proved both Jews and Gentiles, that they are all under sin; as it is written, there is none righteous, no, not one.*

IN a former discourse from these words, evidence was collected from the holy scriptures, that all men are in a state of depravity and sin.

INQUIRY was also made in what this depravity consists, and how the several powers and faculties of the mind are affected by it. The understanding; and heart, will or affections were defined. From the word of GOD, it appears that the heart or will including the affections, is the primary seat of moral depravity; and the understanding is consequently affected, but not in such manner, that the ignorance of sinners is any excuse for them, or that doctrinal instruction will have any power to remove the disorder. It was the heart which apostatized, and by this means, the underſtanding was made dark. It will continue dark while the heart is wrong; which muſt be changed by the holy ſpirit, to illumine the ſoul with the glory of God, and the beauty and delights of holineſs. As this blindneſs comes entirely from ſinful affections, God treats it as ſinful; and the degree of a creature's ſin may be known by the degree of his blindneſs.

The diſorder, in the ſinner's heart, is a miſplaced love. His chief affection is taken from God; from the general good; from ſeeking the greateſt glory and happineſs of the intelligent ſyſtem, and placed on himſelf. For himſelf alone he lives, deſires and acts. The object of holy affection, is the happineſs of God and his kingdom in union. The object of ſinful affection, is ſelf in a ſtate of ſeparation from God and his kingdom; and this ſtate of ſeparation runs directly into a ſtate of oppoſition and enmity, from whence come all the ſins of men againſt God and his creatures, nor is there any perception of glorious beauty in holy objects.

The third thing propoſed, in conſidering the ſubject, is to compare the deſcription that hath been given of our original and common depravity, with the apparent character of mankind; their conduct; and their treatment of God and creatures in all ages, by which we ſhall ſee, the ſcriptural account of this moral corruption to be a juſt one, and entitled to our moſt ſerious belief.

Before I proceed to a compariſon of the doctrine, as it hath been deſcribed, with the actual conduct of mankind in all ages; it is neceſſary that ſeveral things be premiſed, to explain ſome appearances, which may, otherwiſe, be relied on as evidence, in favor, either of the purity of human nature, or of a partial depravity.

By the total depravity of man, is not meant, that the heart breaks out into all poffible enormity of vice.

We know this is not the cafe. An inward enmity may rife higher—finful objects may be loved more—and vifible crimes may be multiplied. It is not meant that finners are as wicked as they can be, or as they will be, in fome future time, if they remain impenitent; but it means they have no holinefs, and all their affections, fo far as they have a moral character, are finful, without any mixture of true holinefs.

Two finners of the fame natural capacity, may be entirely finful, and ftill one of them may be more finful than the other. The fame finner may be totally finful, at two different times; but more finful at one than the other. In this world, the wills and affections of men are under the reftraint of God, out of favor to his own kingdom, and the ingathering of fouls to Christ. If all men acted out their hearts, in the full extreme of finful paffions and actions, it would difqualify the world for a place of probation. Thro' mutual injuries, there would be no time for reflection, or opportunity to ufe fuch means, as the fpirit accompanies for falvation. But this reftraint is not holinefs; neither, is there in it, any thing that approaches towards the moral nature of holinefs. The reftrained perfon is ftill totally depraved; that is, all which is in his heart is finful, and nothing holy, and without holinefs no man can fee God.

When evil men hear themfelves charged with total depravity, to appeafe confcience they often argue, in the following way.——There are fome defirable things in the world which I have not coveted;—fome things I have coveted, which I might in a more wicked manner have taken by violence; therefore, I am not totally depraved. Allowing this to be true, it is no difproof of total depravity; for the queftion is not, whether the finner be finful to the greateft extreme of exercife, but whether there be in him any thing that is morally good or holy?

FURTHER, in moft cafes, there muft be fome profpect of fuccefs to bring into exercife fenfible defires of the heart.

MEN may not defire to walk acrofs the ocean, only becaufe they know the thing to be impoffible; whereas, if a poffibility appeared they would defire it inftantly. So the finner may fay, I never defired to deftroy the GODHEAD and fit on the throne of the univerfe. I will allow, it is poffible, that no fuch fenfible defire hath ever paffed in the finner's mind. Still I muft inquire of him, whether he never repined, or thought he was hardly treated by providence, or that things might be ordered better? All thefe are exercifes of the fame heart, which would defire to dethrone GOD, if the thing might be probably effected. Total depravity doth not imply the greateft poffible degree of unholy exercife or action; but it means the whole want of what is morally good—a total deficiency of a right temper and affections, fo that the man, fo far as he acts, is altogether a finner.

THRO' the ordering of fovereign wifdom, the circumftances under which finners exift, make a great difference in the weaknefs and ftrength of the affections. In the prefent world, things are ordered to reftrain fin, and keep the energies of its action within certain limits. The prefent good of GOD's kingdom requires this. In another world, it will be different, and divine glory may require all reftraints to be taken off, that the odious nature of sin may fully appear. This will be awfully the case.

2dly. The state of things is so ordered in this world, that many actions, which produce visible good effects in society, proceed from a heart and from motives, which are unholy.

A heart altogether selfish, is totally sinful; but men with such hearts, may do things which are for the present benefit of society. Ambition, pride or avarice may make them diligent in their business, fair in their dealings, humane to their neighbours, or intrepid defenders of the public weal, while all is for themselves. Both the public and their neighbours, would be injured and hated, if from a change of relative situation self-interest required it. How many fair words are spoken from a heart of bitterness. How many friendships stand on party alliances, which are sinful in their nature and design. How often do sinners patronize one another, carefully watching over their mutual reputation and interest, solely to keep themselves in countenance, or to find companions agreeable to their taste, or to secure some good to themselves. The world itself would not contain the books which might be written describing civil actions—neighbourly actions—actions apparently humane and just, which come from a heart and motives altogether unholy in the sight of God. It is thus, God uses hypocritical sinners, to preserve such a state of order in the world, as the purposes of his own eternal counsel require. He makes use, even of the destructive actions of sinners, to build up his own kingdom. But let it be remembered, that the civility of mankind is not holiness, if the heart and its motives be wrong.

THIS description may be extended, even to the visible services of religion. Men may pray—hear the word of GOD—read the scriptures—in some sense keep the Sabbath, and regard gospel ordinances, while in a state of total depravity. There was no holiness in the Pharisee, who said, *I thank thee, Lord, that I am not as other men, for I fast twice in a week;* nor in the young man, who told CHRIST concerning the commandments, *All these have I kept from my youth up.* There was no holiness in these persons, therefore, they were totally depraved. They did all thro' selfishness—thro' a love of themselves only, and a dread, rather than love of GOD.

If ye love them who love you, said CHRIST, *what reward have ye?* It is altogether sinful. Performing a visible duty, only thro' dread of divine punishment, is the same as doing it wholly from a love of ourselves, without regard to the excellence of GOD. So that the performance of many visible services in religion, is no evidence against the doctrine advocated.

ALSO pity, compassion, a love of our country, a zeal for its good laws, and many other things, which in the common language of men are called social and political virtues, may be found, for a season, in creatures who are totally unholy. All these may arise from some real or supposed benefit to ourselves, while there is no love of moral excellence.—We know the most depraved may love their children because they are their own.—For the same reason, they may love their country and its laws, and in many instances pity the distress of a fellow-creature. The wonderful wisdom of GOD is seen, in managing the wicked selfishness of the human heart, and making it the means of preserving a certain degree of order in the human state, so long as he is gathering his own people into the kingdom of holiness.

3dly. IN comparing the description of human depravity, with the appearance and conduct of men, we must also consider; that many have been reclaimed from the reigning power of their natural sin, by the sanctifying grace of GOD.

WHEN infidels attempt to depreciate a revelation, by setting up the powers and attainments of reason; it is their custom to ascribe to reason, much of that knowledge which originated in a revelation. So those, who attempt to prove, either the natural purity or partial depravity of human nature, claim as evidence, all the good which there is in the hearts and actions of men, without giving any credit to the sanctifying grace of GOD thro' JESUS CHRIST. There are many pious people—there is some degree of holiness in many hearts; but whence did it come? Was it natural to these persons, or hath it been excited by the action of the holy spirit? Ask the sanctified, for they are the best judges, and their answer will be; that if they have any holiness, it is in small degree, and this small degree was not natural to them. These good persons, are the first to allow their own total depravity by nature, and give all the glory of what there is right in them, to the sovereign and renewing mercy of GOD. If these who appear the nearest to purity, in their temper and actions, claimed this as their natural character, it would give some colour of objection to the doctrine; but they are the first to cry out unclean, totally unclean, in the sight of GOD.

The advocates for a natural purity, or partial depravity, are found among such as appear to be farthest removed from it; and tho' some of them may be regular in their lives, they give no evidence of an ardent love of God—delight in the fpirituality of the divine law—pleafure in a life of prayer and devotion, or eminence in any of the exercifes which fhow a very fanctified heart. The truth is, they have no great fenfe of fin, and therefore think human nature pure, or but little debafed.

These remarks will fully account, for fuch appearances in the character and conduct of men, as fome' may ufe to evince but a partial depravity. They teach us, that the doctrine of total corruption by nature, is not rendered doubtful by a comparifon with matters of fact.

I shall now mention fome things, in the general appearance of mankind, which fhow a heart by nature totally depraved.

1. There is a natural and general forgetfulnefs of God; and the few thoughts of him, which men have, appear to be excited by terror and not to flow from a heart filled with love.

Alarming providences, dangers, wants, pains, the inftituted means of inftruction, impel men fometimes to think of God. The ways of divine providence, and inftituted means are wonderfully calculated, to remind us of the divine character and government. All nature around us—all daily events, our mercies and our trials, are defigned to make us keep God in fight. With all this provifion of means how little is he thought of? The defires of the heart reft on the gift, without afcending to the giver. Mens thoughts ftop on fecond caufes without rifing to the great firft caufe. All their difcourfe and actions prove, that other objects are more agreeable to the heart; and that it is with a kind of reluctance, they are brought to think of JEHOVAH. His pure character—his holy law—and moſt juſt government, are not pleaſurable ſubjects. As young minds open to the evidence of GOD's being and perfections, this doth not correct the evil diſpoſition. Objects of ambition, intereſt and pleaſure engage all the attention. They look to the things around them for happineſs, and on theſe their diſcourſe turns. Unleſs the providence or ſpirit of GOD ſpeaks, with uncommon energy, they go on in deep ſecurity, devoted to themſelves and the world.

COULD things be ſo if there were any love of GOD? The law of reaſon and revelation require a ſupreme love of him, and who dare deny the juſtice of the requirement? Could things be ſo, if any, even a partial love of GOD, or as much as we have, for ourſelves and the creatures, were natural to us? They certainly could not. Nature impels us to think of the objects which we love. The heart is inquring and following them; and if the love be ſupreme it makes haſte to find them. No pains are too expenſive, and no watchings too laborious to find the objects we love; and when found every action and word is expreſſive of joy.

Is this ſeeking GOD natural to men? Do they come into the world, grow up and go thro' life with it? When providence brings his character into view, do they rejoice as in ſight of a beloved object? Do they peruſe and re-peruſe his image drawn in his law, or appear to be ſearching for him in the glorious works of nature? Whence ariſes the natural dread of his preſence, and of coming before him by death, if his character be loved, when it is a law of our being to ſeek the preſence of a beloved object?

If there were not, a total want of delight in God, and a natural oppofition of heart to his holy nature and government, men could not be fo forgetful of him, by whom they are clothed and fed, and of whofe infinite perfection, there is fuch clear evidence. When we add to this the high crimes which are conftantly happening, and the actual fins of which every man is confcious, it gives great ftrength to the conclufion. The character given of mens natural ftate, by the word of God, fufficiently accounts for this ftate of things.

2dly. The conduct of men in all ages proves them to be felfifh creatures, and that their natural love is only to themfelves.

Can thofe who have thoroughly confidered human nature, and read the character of man in his actions—in the conduct of individuals and of nations, in every age, have any doubt of this? Is not this generally confeffed, by the watchfulnefs and guard men exercife for themfelves over all others? Do they not feel it, until a change takes place in their affections, which, after they have experienced, they are willing to afcribe to the fanctifying power of God? This felfifhnefs or finful felf-love, is the very effence of a total depravity, and there needs nothing more, when all reftraint is withdrawn, to make moft complete wickednefs.

It is a dictate of common reafon, that all rational beings and objects, and all the interefts of intelligence ought to be loved according to their excellence. The glory and happinefs of Godhead is of more value, than all creatures—of many creatures, more than of one—of the whole, more than of a part. Thefe obfervations point out to us the moral law of holinefs, as confifting, in a benevolence proportioned to the value of the object. Selfishness or a sinful self-love is contrary to this. The selfish creature wishes the whole to be subordinate to himself; or if such a wish hath not passed in his heart, it was prevented by the apparent impracticabilty of the thing. This selfish heart shows itself in all that takes place around us—in mens grasping desires—in their feelings and actions to others. They wish to be first in influence, in esteem, in property, in power. To this the heart is continually reaching. Dear self-advancement is at the bottom of action. By this rule, measures and events are judged—parties formed—worldly friendships cemented—and animosities kindled. By this, the man in his natural state, is excited to those exertions which have many laudable effects on present society—he often advances the interest of others as the most direct way of advancing his own—does beneficent actions to advance his reputation—adds the weight of his influence to the energy of good laws, that his own person and property may be safe in a world of violence—lets others enjoy some things, which he hath power to take, lest the spirits of the multitude, selfish like himself, should be exasperated and wrench from him his all. He loves his family, because they belong to himself. If those children, which are the idols of affection, belonged to another, with the amiable qualities they now possess, he would have no affection either for their bodies or souls. For the same reason he may love many other individuals, his neighbours and his nation. He may also be liberal, for who more liberal than the tyrant often is—but observe how he is liberal! Only to administer to his own safety and pleasure. He is liberal to the flatterer who sooths his pride; or the defender of his safety; or to the subordinate sinner, who is in some way necessary for him; or perhaps his liberality is from fear rather than love.

NATURAL conscience reminds him of the day of judgment, and he does many good actions gladly, to purchase his own safety; but selfishness still is his predominating temper, and with all these he is totally depraved. This alone is the hinge on which his affections turn, and he hath no love of GOD for what he is in himself, nor of the divine rights, nor of a universe of creatures, for the real value of their intelligence and happiness. If he had this love it would be holiness, and such as can with certainty find some degree of it in themselves, may hope that GOD hath had mercy on them.

THUS the appearance and the conduct of mankind, considering all circumstances in this world of probation, as we may reasonably suppose they would be ordered by a GOD of infinite power and wisdom, confirm the scriptural account of a deep and total depravity, which is the natural character of men; and that this depravity is seated in the heart, will or affections. This withdrawment of supreme love from GOD and his intelligent kingdom, which are the only objects of a holy love, and resting in himself, will account for all the wickedness that can ever be practised by creatures. It will produce enmity to the divine character, law and government. It will produce every crime of heart and practice against GOD and man. It will cause an ignorance of the beauty of holiness—and it is justly exposed to all the threatened punishments of this and another world.

1st. THIS description of depravity, shows that men may do many actions which are useful in the society of this world—may be visibly free from crimes—may attend on the public institutions of religion—and difcover great zeal for right actions, while they are in the gall of bitternefs and under the bonds of iniquity.

Paul tells us this—*Though I fpeak with the tongues of men and angels—though I have the gift of prophecy, and underftand all myfteries, and all knowledge; and though I have all faith, fo that I could remove mountains—though I beftow all my goods to feed the poor, and though I give my body to be burned, and have not charity, it profiteth me nothing.* And what is this charity? It is love divefted of felfifhnefs. It is a love of character and truths, for their own excellence and value. It is a love in which felf is fubordinate to general good, to the glory of God, and the greateft fum of happinefs in the intelligent univerfe. This is gofpel charity, the chriftian holinefs. There is great danger of reliance for falvation, on fuch attainments, and vifible obedience, as may come from a heart deftitute of charity. This is the moft common mode of felf-deception. Immerfed in the amufing and bufy fcenes of life, and without ferious confideration, pains are not taken to fearch deep into the heart.—It is not a pleafing employment.—Such do not know their total felfifhnefs in all they do.—Though confcious of fin, they hope it is partial, and that there is fome little good in them.—Perhaps they are moral in their vifible actions—may be kind neighbours and fair dealers.—On comparifon with the moft abandoned finner, they find their characters much more fair, and hence draw the conclufion that they are not totally depraved.—They determine to make fome amendments, and hope God will accept them.—Such perfons become prejudiced againft the doctrines of divine fovereignty—a total corruption of human nature—and the need of being regenerated and made new creatures.

Thus, they go wholly off from the true gospel scheme, and while they rely some on CHRIST; they rely more on themselves, and in their own opinion are going to a holy heaven, though destitute of that renovation spoken of in the scriptures. Persons in this situation, have never seen the sin of their own hearts, nor the true distinction between a holy and depraved temper. Thus their hopes may be considerable, and every action, the matter of which is right, is eagerly seized as evidence of their own safe state.—Self-love, and fear may produce many such actions. They may even love GOD from a supposition, that he loves them, while selfishness is the central point of all their affections.—In this way hypocrites are made.—Thus, mere moralists are easy in their situation.—Thus, the thorough doctrines of the gospel become unpleasant to their hearing, because the selfish ground of their hopes is overturned, and they wish a bible and a preacher more tender to the selfish affections.—It is for these reasons, self-examination becomes so unpleasing, and so difficult a work for fallen sinners.

IN addition to these objections, it is also added by the selfish mind, I can see no kind of beauty in such holiness, as these remarks imply to be necessary.—This is a fact which must be allowed; but blindness to this beauty proves their criminal condition, and it can be removed, only by a renovation of the heart.

2d. WE may infer, that the opposition of mens hearts is to the true character of GOD, and not to a misapprehension of him. He is opposed to their selfish wills and affections, and they see him to be thus, which is the very reason of their sin.

So long as they conceive him friendly to their selfish affections, they are friendly to him; because, it appears as though he had made himself and his government subordinate to their will.—They love GOD in this case, from his supposed subserviency to their interests. This sinful love of GOD is founded upon a misconception of his character; for the moment his true character is seen—that he requires self-consecration and a complete submission to his own will, the opposing heart breaks out in enmity and disobedience; so that the opposition of men's hearts is to the true character of our most holy Lord. Those who suppose a little increase of doctrinal light will remove it, have overlooked the fountain of corruption, and not seen their own hearts truly.

3d. THIS confirms the doctrine of CHRIST, *Except a man be born again, he cannot see the kingdom of heaven.*—*That which is born of the flesh, is flesh; and that which is born of the spirit, is spirit.*—*Which were born, not of blood, nor of the will of the flesh, nor of the will of man, but of GOD.* Fallen creatures have no better principle, than this depraved self-love; and it must be the work of the Holy Spirit, to create them to new and holy affections. To resist or deny the Spirit of GOD, is shutting the door of the kingdom of heaven, and destroying to ourselves the efficacy of the gospel. All those, who deny this work of the Spirit, make the gospel as inefficacious for their own salvation, as if they were to deny CHRIST himself. Between these two kinds of infidelity, either denying CHRIST, or denying the Holy Ghost, how many shut themselves out from the kingdom of heaven. May a GOD of sovereign mercy have compassion to open their eyes before it be too late. AMEN.

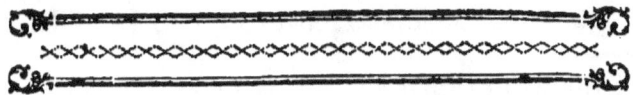

SERMON VIII.

Sinners under present condemnation.

JOHN iii. 18, 19.

But he that believeth not, is condemned already, because he hath not believed in the name of the only begotten Son of God.—And this is the condemnation, that light is come into the world, and men loved darkness rather than light, because their deeds are evil.

THE evangelist, in this chapter, relates a discourse of our blessed Saviour, in which some great and important gospel doctrines are brought into clear view. The conversation was with Nicodemus, a master and teacher in Israel, who tho' he was in that station, was ignorant of a divine renovation of the heart, as necessary for salvation.—CHRIST explained the doctrine to him, and most plainly asserted the need of such a change—the impossibility of being saved without it—and the power and agency of the Holy Spirit by whom it is wrought. He said that this change is not of blood, nor of the will of the flesh, nor of the will of man, but of God.—The Spirit of God is the author of it.—We shall not reason ourselves into a holy temper, nor gain it by any means or endeavours, unless the Holy Spirit works; so that to deny his agency, or to grieve him away when he comes to assist, is most effectually shutting the door of divine grace against ourselves.

Being born again further implies, a holy principle from God put into the soul, by which it is enabled to relish, and taste the excellency of all holy things.—A principle of moral likeness to God where there was none before, nor any thing which bore a moral resemblance of him.—It comes from God, and makes those who receive it, in some degree conformed to him.

Having stated the need of being renewed, Christ proceeds, also to describe the necessity of a saving faith, which is that exercise, by which a renewed soul receives Christ for his Saviour, and thus becomes entitled to the gospel promises of forgiveness and final redemption.—Faith is here called believing in name the of the Son of God. And Christ illustrates this grace by comparing himself to the brazen serpent, which Moses lifted up in the wilderness, to which the wounded Israelites looked for healing. The illustration is very instructive. The Israelite felt himself mortally wounded, and in danger of immediate death. So the sinner, before he will look to Christ, must feel the mortal wounds of sin—that his spiritual disease is a fatal one, threatening the worst of deaths, and without a remedy in his power.—After the Israelite felt himself wounded, the cure was effected only by looking.—So the wounded sinner, finds no efficacy to ease a pained conscience in what he does. All his own works leave him under condemnation of the law.—The virtue which heals is in JESUS CHRIST, and he finds benefit by faith alone, which beholds, receives and chooses the Saviour and his salvation. Whoever thus looks is no longer condemned, being forgiven through JESUS CHRIST, who has suffered and become a ransom for all those who are his.

HAVING stated the way of salvation in the important doctrines of the new birth, and a saving faith, in our text, he describes the unhappy case and the extreme danger and guilt of all such as have not been changed unto holiness, and believed in him, *But he that believeth not, is condemned already, because he hath not believed in the name of the only begotten Son of GOD.—And this is the condemnation, that light is come into the world, and men loved darkness rather than light, because their deeds are evil.* Among many important truths, which these words contain, there are three, which I shall consider.

1st. ALL, who have not a saving faith, are in a state of present condemnation. There is not simply danger they will be condemned, in some future time, but the sentence is already passed.

2dly. THE light which is come into the world, and the means which GOD hath used and still continues to use, will greatly aggravate their guilt, and make his justice in condemnation, very glorious.

3dly. The only reason, those who have the means of information do not come to this light, and derive saving benefit from it, is the corruption of their hearts. They do not choose such salvation as the gospel offers.—*And men loved darkness rather than light, because their deeds were evil.*

1st. All who have not a saving faith, are in a state of present condemnation.

The words of Christ are so express, there is no way of placing on them any other fair and natural construction—*He that believeth not is condemned already*—the sentence is passed, and agreeable to this the holy scriptures say, that God is angry with the wicked every day, and his wrath abideth on them.—When he looks on them, as he doth every moment, and sees their sin—a wrong temper—a wrong practice, and a want of love to him, his displeasure is perfect.—The original threatening was, *in the day thou eatest thereof thou shalt surely die.*—After sin was committed, justice appeared and pronounced sentence upon the sinners, from which moment, they were in a state of condemnation.—All of us are in the same situation naturally, under the same sentence, and there is only one way of being delivered from it, which is by a holy faith in Jesus Christ.

It is true, there is a short reprieve from complete execution of the sentence, granted to us all; but we should very carefully distinguish between a temporary reprieve from complete execution, and a reversal of the threatening. The reprieve extends to all men for a season—the reversal is only to those who have become vitally united to the Saviour of men, the Son of God. If the reprieved person go to Christ, in the prescribed way of humility and repentance, divine grace will declare him free from condemnation, and until he doth thus go, the sentence remains in full force as it would be, if there were no Redeemer. Also, it remains most certain, that after a short delay, execution will commence on the impenitent, without allay. The reprieve consists in two things.

1st. THE extremity of the sentence is not yet executed.—Men are now suffering much punishment for their sins, but it is not the full punishment.—God has placed them in a state of trial. The full punishment of sin is probably so extreme, as to be inconsistent with consideration and trial, and would so distract the mind, that it could not hear the calls of divine grace, in the manner it now may. Therefore, we find a partial suspension of wretchedness, and only so much is suffered, as warns and teaches us, that the wages of sin are indeed sorrow and death. It ought, by no means, to be concluded, that the penalty doth not contain something vastly more bitter than what sinners feel in this world. When the state of trial ends, extreme punishment will be inflicted, for infinite wisdom will no longer have a reason for suspending.

2d. ANOTHER thing contained in this reprieve, is an opportunity to escape to the only begotten Son of GOD for an eternal deliverance, and complete reversal of the sentence of condemnation.

GOD is now warning us of our danger—inviting us to come to him by repentance that we may live—and to begin a life of holiness and true grace, and taste how sweet and soul-satisfying it is. Of those who truly come none will be rejected—GOD will forgive their sins, for the sake of his Son, and never bring them to suffer such punishment as they have deserved.

THE whole state of things, in this world, is evidence, that those who believe not are condemned already. There are innumerable punishments actually taking place, and if execution is begun, it shows that sentence is passed. In how solemn a situation does the conscious sinner stand, if sentence be already passed—if execution be begun—and only a few days are to intervene before the full weight takes place. It is in sight of these truths, divine mercy becomes so importunate in its calls to a secure world, and says, in the most pathetic language of pity, *Why will ye die, O house of Israel?* It is in sight of these truths, God speaks so plain to us in his holy word. The case is so urgent, that infinite wisdom sees it to require the most plain dealing—the most plain address to conscience—and the most explicit description, of the endless ruin that will follow a misimprovement of this short season.

CERTAINLY the great and infinite GOD, who upholds so august a universe as this, and is the parent of reason, cannot be a passionate and capricious being. Neither is it supposeable that he would try to terrify us with groundless fears. And he tells us expressly, that all who have not come to JESUS CHRIST are already under sentence of death. The awful sentence of the last day will not be a new one, but only a repetiton of that which is passed already, with this aggravating circumstance, that the state of reprieve is ended. Mercy will never again come forward and try to save the guilty, sentenced creature. O that all might feel the reality of the truth I am now urging. A long observation of human nature gives me right to say, that until they feel themselves to be condemned already, they will never take one step towards a life of thorough religion. Until they feel this, they will be as secure, and as full of vanity, as if there were no eternity before them—no heaven to obtain—or no state of endless punishment to escape. Among all the strange things found in a sinful heart, it is one of the strangest that sin closes the eyes, on the danger attending it—on the need of an immediate escape—on the certain truth of God in what he hath told us, and on the awfulness of going into another world, without that preparation which the gospel declares to be necessary. And there is not only a present blindness, but so strong a desire of remaining blind, it gives a great displeasure to see or hear any thing, which has a tendency to awaken conscience.

2d. The light which is come into the world, and the means which God hath used, and still continues to use, will greatly aggravate their guilt, and make his justice in their condemnation very glorious.

This is the condemnation, that light is come into the world, and men loved darkness rather than light. The meaning of this part of the text is, that the surprizing clear light which shines, if misimproved, will greatly aggravate the condemnation and misery of impenitent sinners. It is the same truth as Christ expressed in the following words.— *If I had not come, and spoke unto them, they had not had sin; but now they have no cloak for their sin.* They would not have had so great sin, nor would their conduct have been so criminal as it now is.

A vast number of men in the christian world, who do not live christian lives, speak of their privileges with great pleasure. They place great dependance on their light and opportunities, tho' they do not make any use of them, to obtain a real conformity of heart to God himself, which is the only thing for which their privileges were given them. Still, it is a solemn truth, that misimproved privileges will only increase condemnation. This is one of those truths, which CHRIST often brought into view. He told the Jews, it should be more tolerable for Tyre and Sidon, and even for Sodom and Gomorrha, in the day of judgment, than for them. The reason was, because they sinned against greater knowledge, and better means to do their duty, than the people of those devoted cities had. The gospel, which originated in infinite love, and offers salvation to sinners who are sensible of their wants and their guilt, carries with it nothing but terror to its condemned and selfish opposers. Therefore the apostle said explicitly, on this subject, that the gospel which he preached, was a favor of life unto life, unto those who obeyed; but of death unto death to those who perish. If it did not save, if it did not sanctify them, it would increase the weight of their guilt. If they refused it, in its saving and sanctifying call, it must make them more guilty creatures, than they would have been, had no gospel been published.

GOSPEL calls and warnings—the searching admonition of the spirit—the clear shining of truth from GOD, in whatever way they come, never leave men as they find them. These things, either leave us made better than we were, and forgiven by GOD; or they leave us hardened, and much more guilty than before.

When the unclean spirit is gone out of a man, he walketh through dry places, seeking rest, and findeth none. Then he saith, I will return into my house from whence I came out; and when he is come, he findeth it empty, swept and garnished. Then goeth he, and taketh with himself seven other spirits, more wicked than himself, and they enter in and dwell there: and the last state of that man is worse than the first. The meaning of the representation is this.—When by the clear shining of light, either immediately from the spirit of GOD, or by means, men are brought to some consideration—are attentive—show a hearing ear, and go no further, they become more guilty. They only walk in dry or comfortless places. They do not their whole duty and repent, and believe in JESUS, and therefore find no peace in what they do. As they continue to sin against increased light, they are constantly becoming more hard, and finally resolve to sit down again in security. A man thus returning to security, finds his house empty, swept and garnished. He has quieted himself with a few visible regulations of amendment; but it is his house and not his heart, that is garnished with love as it ought to be. The awfulness of such security, and the increase of sin and guilt, are most solemnly represented—*he taketh to himself seven other spirits more wicked than himself, and the last state of that man is worse than the first.* He is become sevenfold more guilty in the sight of GOD. Misimproved light has greatly increased the weight of his condemnation.

THESE words are the doctrine of JESUS CHRIST and of the holy scriptures. And can we say a word against the reasonableness of the truth? Do not our own common sense, reason and conscience confirm the truth? Does common sense dictate any thing more clearly, than this, that the man who sins against the clearest light is the most guilty creature? Must we not allow, that for sin, in the face of such light as we have, we are more guilty than the heathen, who have no scripture instruction—no knowledge of a Saviour—no means of grace—and no description from GOD's own revelation of the nature of a holy life and a holy reward? Must we not allow, that after GOD's spirit has warned us by the instrumental-

S

ity of our consciences, we are more guilty in every sin committed, than before such warning was given? If, in full information of truth and our own duty—of offered redemption through JESUS CHRIST—of his death, to show the holiness and love of GODHEAD, we still neglect, our mouths will be shut in self-condemnation. This is the very circumstance, which in the plainest manner, shows the exceeding sinfulness of a sinful heart. It is this, which at the last day, will in the clearest manner prove, the unreasonableness of sin, and the glorious wisdom and righteousness of GOD in being opposed to it. The most aggravated part of the condemnation will be, *that light is come into the world, and men loved darkness rather than light.* They acted not from mistake, but according to the taste of their hearts; and they ought to reap the fruit of that, which they chose.

3dly. THE only reason, those who have the means of information, do not come to this light, and derive saving benefit from it, is the corruption of their own hearts, by which cause, they do not choose such salvation as the gospel offers.— *And men loved darkness rather than light, because their deeds are evil.*

CHRIST knew the human heart, better than any man, and he expressly assigns this as the cause. It is *because their deeds are evil;* because there is something wrong in them, that they do not savingly rejoice in this light, and love such a Saviour and such salvation with their whole hearts.

LET us be very candid on this subject. If no other cause can be found, then every one must allow, that the cause assigned by JESUS CHRIST, is the true and great one.

1st. CERTAINLY it is not for want of information.

THE means and nature of this salvation are most clearly described. The temper, the affections, the practice, the duties of religion, cannot be told more plainly than we find them to be, in the word of GOD. Religion is a holy love of GOD, with a correspondent practice, in which there can be no mystery. Men well enough know, what it is to love the creatures and themselves; and love to GOD is like this, only turned to him and his holiness as the object of affection. The cause, therefore, is not any mysteriousness in the nature of religion.

2d. I THINK, also, it is certain, we must have a doctrinal conviction that religion, in the long run of things, will be for our interest.—No man seriously doubts this.—Though he may think it will militate against some worldly interest, which he wishes at present to preserve; still, he cannot but think it will be for his interest, in the long run of things and as he stands a candidate for an eternal existence. Let these two things be granted, that we have a doctrinal knowledge what religion is; also, a doctrinal conviction that it will be for our interest, to become savingly religious; I think no other cause remains to be assigned, but a disrelish of heart to the salvation itself.—There is a want of love to such salvation as we need—to such light as shines in the character of JESUS CHRIST, and in the holy character and law of GOD. Therefore, if men do not come savingly to this light, some evil in their deeds, and deeds always betray the heart, is the cause of their delay. If there be blame, it falls on themselves.—I know the mighty power of GOD's Spirit is necessary to save sinners—to make them truly religious and bring them to JESUS; but it is an opposition of heart to the salvation itself, which makes the necessity. So that the reason men do not come savingly to this light, is because their deeds are evil. They disapprove so holy, so pure, so GOD exalting, soul humbling a light as that which shines in the gospel.—This is that guilty state of human nature, which JESUS CHRIST solemnly described in the words of our text.—May the Lord, who is infinite in mercy and sovereign in his goodness, have compassion on us all; and draw us by his power to the true light, that we may be saved from our sins and made forever blessed. AMEN.

SERMON IX.

The connection between sin and misery.

ISAIAH lvii. 21.

There is no peace, saith my God, to the wicked.

THOSE who practise sin are seeking happiness. None love their own peace better, though they are going directly away from it. Among all delusions, it is one of the greatest, to hope sin will end happily; yet, it appears that evil men act under the influence of such hope. In many cases, they seem to expect, what they know to be impossible; and after a thousand experiments which have ended miserably, rush again, with high expectations, into the same disappointing scenes.

WE have the greatest evidence, that sinners, while they remain such, cannot find a satisfying happiness. There is the word of a true and infinite God, who created all things, gave a particular nature to every object, and appointed the laws by which all things material and intellectual exist, act, perceive and feel. All things are, and ever will be, in his hand. We have the evidence of experience that he is true; also, it may be inferred, from such other perfections of an infinite nature, as he clearly possesses. If there were no evidence, beside his word, of the connection between sin and misery, this would be sufficient to conclude the point; and every sinner, ought to depend on being wretched, until his heart is changed. But in this case we have other evidence. We need not depend on abstract speculations, drawn from the nature of GOD; nor need we depend solely on his word, for nature with which we are acquainted, the laws of existence under which we act and feel, and experience which gains strength every day, confirm the truth of revelation, that, there is no peace for the wicked. They have no present peace, and there is no foundation, in the existing nature of things, for them ever to obtain it. *To be carnally minded is death*, or misery. The death is begun —it hath been felt by every sinner, and must continue until sin is taken away. So that the unholy are, as much, acting against the appearances of nature and experience, as they be against the word of GOD. This necessary exposure to unhappiness, is not confined to such as perpetrate the most atrocious crimes, nor to such as give themselves away to indecent appetites; but is common to sinners of every description.

By the wicked, the text means all unholy persons—all who do not love GOD and his law—all who have not been delivered by sanctifying grace, from their natural depravity. In the verses before the text, GOD describes himself to be the giver of all true peace. There is, also, a description of those, who are capable of receiving, and to whom it is given. *Thus saith the high and lofty one that inhabiteth eternity, whose name is holy, I dwell in the high and holy place ; with him also that is of a humble and contrite spirit, to revive the spirit of the humble and to revive the heart of the contrite ones.—For the iniquity of his covetousness, was I wroth and smote him.—He went on frowardly in the way of his heart. I have seen his ways, and will heal him : I will lead him also and restore comforts to him, and his mourners. I create the fruit of the lips ; peace, peace to him that is far off and to him that is near, saith the Lord, and I will heal him.* It is the humble and contrite heart, that is healed by God, and receiveth happiness. Then immediately follows a description of sinners.—*But the wicked are like the troubled sea, when it cannot rest, whose waters cast up mire and dirt. There is no peace, saith my God, to the wicked.*

The image is both forcible and just. As the pullution of the turbulent sea, is cast up by its own waters, and comes from its own bottom ; so the sinner's want of peace, and his misery comes from the state of his heart. I will illustrate the following truth.

There is a necessary connection between sin and misery, so that all unholy minds fall short of the happiness they seek, and plunge themselves into eternal misery.

By necessary connection, I mean a certainty from the condition of things, and those natural laws under which they exist and act. To have it otherwise, another constitution must be given, to intellectual moral and material existence, which is perhaps impossible, and certainly not best. None can expect the certainty of a connection between sin and misery, to be made plainer, than it is told in the word of God ; but it may be useful to inform the sinner, that all nature around him, and his own experience, if he would obferve it, confpire with the fcriptures, to warn him of his forlorn cafe, and urge a fpeedy repentance, left the day of grace fail, and he fall under the wrath, from which there is no deliverance. We may go through the univerfe, and everything fhows the certain mifery of finners, and that there is no continuing peace to the wicked.

1. LET me begin by appealing to the finner's own feelings, and inquire of him, whether he hath ever found the peace and happinefs which he fought. He may fay, he hath found fome happinefs. This I will grant, and fhall afterwards fhow, that it doth not militate againft the truth I am urging. Can any finner fay he hath found contentment—found a fatisfying portion, with which his heart was placed at reft, fo that he wifhed nothing more, than a continued enjoyment of his attained good. The unholy perfon hopes to do it, in his own way; but whether he hopes, and whether he hath obtained, are two queftions. He hath been, and ftill continues hoping vainly, and the continued difappointment is mifery.

LET us for a moment, fuppofe a thing which cannot be. That it was lawful, and no divine anger would rife againft the attempt to put himfelf and the creatures, in the place of GOD, and love them fupremely. This he hath done in the face of a divine threatening; but we will fuppofe the threatening taken away, and no fear of an offended GOD. Does he find in himfelf a fund of enjoyment? After he hath loved himfelf as he ought to love GOD, doth he find his own nature or any thing in himfelf, an object commenfurate to his defires. With his whole felf for a portion, doth he not find an emptinefs, a want, a diftreffing thirft for fomething more? Suppofe, that with fuch a nature and mind as he hath, he were placed at an infinite diftance from all other objects, to contemplate, to know, to enjoy himfelf without moleftation ; his folitude from other objects, and confinement to felf-companionfhip, would be a hell to him. A creature, who is the GOD of his own affections, if the cafe hath been ftated truly, in himfelf, hath a miferable idol. The mind of man was formed by the all-wife creator to be happified by the love of meet and glorious objects without itfelf. There is no proportion, between the whole quantity and excellence of a created mind, and its powers of loving and defiring. No object, lefs than infinite, can fatisfy the heart of a finite creature. This confinement of the affections to himfelf muft therefore entail mifery on the depraved mind.

2dly. IF we take in all the creatures as objects of enjoyment, thefe alfo are infufficient to fatisfy, and the unhappinefs remains. King Solomon made the experiment, fo far as can be done with the greateft advantages, and as the nature of the creatures admits, and having made it, wrote the univerfal motto, *Vanity of vanities, all is vanity.* Men often look forward in expectancy, to certain bounds of obtainment, and promife themfelves, with thefe to be happy. Indeed, this delufion is the finner's happinefs, and when it ceafes his happinefs will ceafe with it, and defpair take the place of all his expectations. He thinks, if he could attain to fuch a point of honor, wealth, or means of fenfual gratification, he might have peace, and fay to himfelf, as the fool recorded in revelation, *Soul, thou haft much goods laid up for many years, take thine eafe, eat, drink and be merry.* But the finner, who faid this, had not attained contentment, for his barns were ftill to be pulled down, and larger ones built. Before this was done, his naked ſoul was called away from the whole. So it ever is. Life is not long enough to obtain happineſs in the creatures, and if it were an eternity, the difficulty would not be removed. There is nothing in the nature of the creatures, to ſatisfy that ſenſe of want and emptineſs, which purſues the ſoul after it is alienated from GOD. Therefore, we find by experience, the world cannot take away the miſery of an unholy heart. Something is ſtill wanted. There is no contentment—ſome unſatisfied wiſh, and generally a thouſand of them remain. Something is feared; and if not of men, there is a dread of GOD, a dread of futurity and another world. If power be given to the graſping mind, beyond certain limits, perſonal ability to act ceaſes, and others muſt execute. Here jealouſy ariſes, ſo that the thirſt for power, and the ſuppoſed poſſeſſion of it, become a ſcourge. If riches become immenſe, the care of watching them is ſtill more immenſe, and a great evil. There is nothing in all theſe things to remove the want and miſery of a ſinful heart. Nature itſelf forbids an intelgent ſpirit to be made happy by the creatures of this world. The ſinner is alienated from his GOD, and his affections are terminated on himſelf. As this is not an object to ſatisfy, his luſts rove abroad among the other creatures, thinking thence to ſupply the want. Theſe, beyond the ſupply of natural wants, are empty alſo, and the tranſgreſſor remains miſerable. He, who might be happy by giving back his heart to GOD, and by contentment with ſo much of the world as would ſupply the real wants of his nature, is daily ſuffering the death of miſery that follows a carnal mind. The penalty of the law hath taken hold of him, and in many reſpects he feels the beginning of eternal death. Every unsatisfied sinner is a living witness of JEHOVAH's truth, when he said, *In the day thou eatest thereof, thou shalt surely die.*

3dly. A GUILTY conscience is the natural consequence of sin, and becomes a fruitful source of misery. There must be an inward struggle, between the affections of the heart which are depraved, and reason and conscience, which forbid sin. Evil men have evidence of truth and duty—they feel a natural conviction of what is right—how they ought to treat GOD and his commandments, and of the divine authority over them. The word and providence of GOD is continually reminding them of their duty, and their obligation to obey. Their hearts resist this information, and go abreast to the rational judgment. A conflict is raised in the mind, so that the man is divided against himself; his heart against his reason and conscience, which must be a state of wretchedness. This unhappiness of a guilty conscience is often great in this world, and we have reason to suppose, that in another it will be the gnawing worm that never dies. By a guilty conscience the sinner becomes an accuser, a judge, and an executioner to himself. He forms the charge, is the witness, and is unable to plead not guilty. This part of his punishment is inbred, and must be coeval with his existence, unless removed by the sanctifying grace of GOD. *The spirit of a man may sustain his infirmities; but a wounded spirit who can bear?* An innocent sufferer feels a fortitude to endure, and his conscious integrity gives him a strength almost above mortal. The guilty are deprived of all natural fortitude, and sink in despair under the weight of their wretchedness. No flight is possible, either from an injured God, or from themselves; and after the prefent day of grace is paffed, there will be no alternative of peace, and all the pain of being confcious finners muft be endured.

Further, fundry of the finful paffions include pain in their very exercife. This is the cafe with impatience, fretfulnefs, anger, malice, hatred, and fundry other wicked affections of the heart. To hate or to be impatient is to be miferable, and muft thus remain.

Alfo, the difappointment of finners, muft make them unhappy. So long as God reigns, the devices of the wicked fhall fail, and their pride be confounded, fo that they cannot attain their defires. We all know the pain of difappointment. When the finner is brought to his final punifhment, the pain of difappointment muft be extreme.

3dly. The focial nature and relations are an inlet of great peace, or of an aggravated mifery.

The finful, can have no peace in the focial relations and affections, after all reftraint is taken off from their evil hearts. To anfwer the prefent purpofes of redeeming wifdom there are many reftraints on the unholy. Acting from felfifh principles they now form fome alliances, which have a degree of peace, and fome hours of harmony. But let finners be removed to a condition of exifting, which doth not admit of alliances formed on felfifh motives, and there will be a total end of harmony. All will be difcord, oppofition, enmity, and mutual injury.

The prefent miniftration of finners to their mutual comfort, arifes from the fingular nature of the ftate in which God hath placed us, and not from any natural tendency in finful affections to unite and do good. Let wicked fouls be taken from these bodies, and from this worldly state, in which they can be mutually advantageous, and placed in a condition where they have no personal benefit to expect; there will be no friendship, no mutual aid—no comforting expressions of benevolence. We may learn this from the events of time. The union of the wicked is short. Self-interest unites them, excites their zeal, their protestations of fidelity and love; and in the revolution of events, self-interest again separates and fills them with enmity, even to a thirst of blood.—We need no other proof, how unholy minds are united. The apostle James gives us this idea, when he says, *From whence come wars and fightings among you? Come they not hence, even of your lusts. Ye lust, and have not: ye kill, and desire to have, and cannot obtain: ye fight and war, yet ye have not.* That the wicked can have no peace, in social relations and affections, after all restraint is taken off from their hearts, is evidenced by the nature of depravity.

4thly. The wicked are made miserable by their knowledge of God's true character.

They may be pleased with him, thro' a misconception of what his character really is. They may think him such an one as themselves; that he will approve the things they love; protect and bless them abundantly in all the designs of their hearts, so that through his providence they expect to rise higher, than they could by any other means.—But all these pleasing contemplations arise from a false opinion of his nature and will. A sight of his true character, always makes the wicked miserable; for it discovers him opposed to their whole temper, their desires, their actions, and the objects of their love.—God prescribes one rule of right, one object of chief affection; the evil heart another. A direct opposition arises to the divine character, and every attribute of his nature is dreaded. Even his goodness is disliked, for having an object different from the sinner's wishes.—His justice and righteousness are dreaded.—His knowledge and power insure success to a government, conducted on principles, which are disapproved by the heart.—His immutability makes it certain, that his government and purposes will always be the same.—Thus every divine attribute is feared. The certainty of being always under the control of an infinite being, who is disliked; the certainty of his displeasure, and of perpetual disappointment, will fix the soul in deep despair. This character of God is now set before the unholy, both by natural and revealed evidence. The evidence will be forever increasing, and the point of opposition between a holy God and wicked creatures coming into more distinct view; a view glorious for him, and confounding to them. I might go much farther, in describing the misery of wicked minds, which necessarily arises from the construction and laws of created existence, as they are, at present, brought to our knowledge by experience.

5thly. To place the matter beyond all doubt, God hath assured us there is no peace to the wicked; and that the connection between sin and misery which now appears, shall continue forever.

He who created and upholds the universe, and knows his own purposes, can neither deceive nor be mistaken. How presumptuous! How unfounded in respect of probability, and how much without excuse, is the hope of the wicked to prosper in sin. The word of infinite truth forbids the thing; and when we see all nature prepared to fulfil this word, and actually doing it every moment, the delusion appears like madness. The wicked in heart, may turn to their own experience in self-enjoyment, and in an enjoyment of the creatures; to their own experience in the social relations; to their own knowledge of GOD, and find a confirmation of sacred truth, that a fearful punishment is prepared for all who disobey. There is every reason to suppose, that as the divine government progresses, new sources of sorrow to the sinful will be opened.—The scripture plainly intimates one which I have not yet mentioned. By an immediate act of divine power, GOD will impress a sense of his displeasure on the guilty. It will be *a fearful thing, to fall into the hands of the living* GOD.

To all this, the wicked may object, that they have found some happiness in the principles and practice of sin, and therefore the preceding arguments do not absolutely exclude their safety.

LET us attend to the kind of happiness sinners may now have, and why it is permitted by a holy GOD, for a short season.

THE greatest part of their happiness is in hope or expectation, and not the peace of enjoying a present good. Their expectations are contrary to nature, and the fulfilment of them impossible. Their happiness therefore, is all a delusion, and must cease in the light of eternity. GOD now suffers it, that the blinding, deceiving nature of sin in the heart may appear; but it will not continue in the world of retribution.

THE unholy do also enjoy worldly happiness, they are fed, have animal pleasure, the waters of a full cup are often poured out to them, they enjoy sinful objects, and sport themselves with their own deceivings. Infinite wisdom hath a reason for suffering this. If the condition of sinners did not admit happiness of this nature, the world would not be fitted for the ingathering of CHRIST's church, as infinite wisdom designed it should be. We have before shown, that in all this, there is no enjoyment which amounts to true peace of mind. It is not a happiness from moral qualities of the heart, delighting in excellent objects; but solely from the particular structure of things, in this transitory world, and when taken from it, their quiet will cease. When divine long-suffering hath ended, other scenes will commence, and the divine prediction have a complete fulfilment, *there is no peace to the wicked.*

1. THIS subject teaches us, how much the word of GOD is confirmed, by the established laws of nature. In the present day, many either really do or affect to disbelieve the holy scriptures. Some speak of them with great levity; and many disobey in the most careless manner. They especially try to reject the representations of misery that is coming on sin. Such persons are strangely deluded. Their eyes are as much shut on nature, as on the word of GOD, and they do not know what a task they have taken on themselves in attempting to overturn revelation. To do it, they must first overturn nature itself, that is, the established laws under which minds exist, act, and are acted upon, in the intelligent universe. Many doctrines of GOD's word are proved by reason and experience. If the holy scriptures, contained a scheme of truth, which appeared, in all respects, unfounded in nature and experience, it would be a hard thing to prove their certainty; but this is not the case. Nature and experience confirm the being of a GOD—they confirm many things concerning his character, which the scrip-

tures teach—they fhow us the fitnefs of the moral law—the tendency of a virtuous temper and practice to produce happinefs, and of fin to produce mifery. They teach us a connection between fin and mifery. When we read divine threatenings againft fin, and then look on the human mind and a focial ftate, and behold a natural preparation to fulfil thefe threatenings; it muft be a great evidence of truth. Thofe, who feel a fixed unholinefs of heart, and a rifing oppofition to the doctrines of revelation, are hoping for fafety againft all probability. If they will firft overturn the preparation in nature to punifh them; we will then give the fcriptures up to their rage. If they will make the creatures fatisfying to the foul; if they will make the felfifh depravity of the heart confiftent with focial happinefs, and deftroy its tendency to mifery; if they will convince us a fight of GOD's true character, may give peace to an unholy heart, there will be fome room for them to contend with the fcriptures of GOD. Until thefe things can be done, though all written threatenings were deftroyed, the danger of mifery is not removed, nor its caufe in any degree taken away.

SOME great truths of revelation will not admit natural evidence of their certainty. Such, are the way and means of falvation by JESUS CHRIST, and for evidence of their certainty, we muft depend wholly on the revealed word. Other truths do admit a natural evidence from reafon and experience; fuch, as the connection between fin and mifery. When we find reafon, experience and revelation, perfectly harmonious, concerning all truth which admits both kinds of evidence; we may thence determine, that revelation may be firmly trufted, in all things which admit no

U

other kind of evidence. A creature muft be mad indeed to reject their united teftimony.

2dly. The natural connection between fin and mifery, fhows the folly of men, in hoping fo favorably of their ftate, while deftitute of evidence, that the reigning power of fin in their hearts is broken.

Law and gofpel harmonize in the fame fcheme of holinefs. What avails a gofpel to fuch hearts as are oppofed to the gofpel fpirit? If mifery muft be connected with fin, what avails a gofpel to thofe, who are as much under the power of fin, as they ever were? It follows, that they are as much under the power of mifery as they ever were; and have no releafe from the curfe. So long, as fin reigns in the heart, the curfe will reign over the whole man. So long, as fin is fupremely loved, the penalty is in execution, tho' not to the extreme degree, it will be after a day of grace is ended.

There is a clafs of perfons who believe the fcripture—who believe that impenitent fin will be punifhed—who alfo confefs they have no reafon to think their own hearts changed; and ftill they are in perfect fecurity. I requeft fuch to look on their own conduct—to confider and mark it well, and fay if it be not ftrange. A rational creature, with knowledge of his danger, a danger for eternity, and yet not taking a fingle ftep to efcape it. Living without any anxiety, without prayer, and fpending in ufelefs amufement the only time, which was given for preparation. All this is done, againft the admonition of God in his word, and in full knowledge of the miferable end to which fin is coming, and even under the beginning execution of the penalty, for fuch are all the pains and diftreffes of the finner's life.

By this security the folly of sin is proved, beyond what we could suppose possible if we did not see it.

3dly. Those, who fall under final punishment will not be able to plead, that they have come to an unhappy end without warning.

God hath warned them in his word, in his law and in his gospel. He warns them every day of life. All the miserable fruits of sin in this world—all our pains of body and mind—all dissatisfaction of the heart in its present worldly attainments—all the stings of conscience—all the painful feelings of sinful passion—all the mutual enmities and hatred of wicked men—all the dread of God's presence—all these are warnings that the wages of sin is death. With what remorse and self-condemnation must the mind look back, on its present blindness and security.— This conviction will stop the mouth, though it will neither change the heart, nor remove its pains. May the view we have taken of the natural connection between sin and misery, excite us to repentance and to seek deliverance from our own unholiness.—Let us bless God for a way of escape opened in the gospel, and pray for his Spirit to accompany the means of grace, and to draw us to the blood of Christ for cleansing from all sin. Amen.

SERMON X.

Regeneration.

JOHN i. 13.

Which were born, not of blood, nor of the will of the flesh, nor of the will of man, but of GOD.

IF man, by nature, be wholly depraved, and unlike to GOD, it is neceffary he fhould be changed, before his falvation and bleffednefs in the divine prefence is poffible. There muft be a moral conformity of temper for the happinefs of communion. The want of this conformity makes finful creatures oppofed to GOD's pleafure, repine againft his government, and feek their own happinefs in fuch a way as his foul hateth. This is the real cafe with men, and even with feeking finners before their hearts are renewed. The falvation which they feek is not the fame falvation, which the gofpel offers, and the heaven they defire, is effentially different from the glorious life of communion enjoyed by the Saviour and his people. The two doctrines, of man's total depravity, and the need of regeneration for eternal life, stand or fall together. Jesus Christ expresly taught both of them, and on their truth depends the need of his incarnation and atonement.

The doctrine of regeneration is much opposed in a sinful world, and among those who confess it, many endeavour to explain away the spirituality and greatness of the change. One reason of their opposition is, that the need of regeneration, implies the natural and total wickedness of the heart; a charge which they are unwilling to own, and a condemnation to which they do not intend to submit. Another reason of opposition and doubt, is ignorance of their own hearts. Conscience is asleep, reason is blinded by appetite, worldly interests and sensual pleasures possess all their thoughts, and they very little consider God, their own character, or eternity. In this state they feel no disease, and therefore no need of a change; no guilt, and therefore no need of forgiveness; no sense of moral obligation, and therefore no fear of God's anger.—When the Holy Spirit comes to convince sinners, they have new apprehensions on these subjects; and tho' conviction of sin doth not imply holiness or a new heart, they are made sensible of a threatening law, and an angry God. Also, though they have no just idea of the gracious exercises and peace which follow regeneration, they still suppose there must be some change, before they can be happy.

We are told in the verse before the text, that *as many as received Christ, to them gave he power to become the sons of God, even to them that believe on his name.* The text, which follows, describes these persons by the change of their hearts. *Which were born, not of blood, nor of the will of the flesh, nor of the will of man, but of God.* This teaches us, that none but regenerated perfons, have received CHRIST and become the fons of GOD, fo as to receive eternal life. All others are expofed to the curfe of the law and wholly unprepared for death. Their anxiety for falvation, if they have had any, their ufe of means, their doctrinal belief, and every other poffible attainment fhort of a new and holy heart, has left them in the miferable ftate of unpardoned finners. The heart of man cannot be brought into conformity to GOD by any pains ufed, or any means fhort of a fpiritual renovation. Fear and other caufes which may check the excefs and fenfible out-breakings of fin, do not change the temper of the foul.

THE Holy Spirit is the great and immediate agent in renewing the heart, and without his work in applying, deliverance is impoffible.—Therefore JESUS CHRIST reprefented fin againft the Holy Ghoft, as the moft dangerous of all fins. And it becomes thofe who think lightly of the Spirit's work in redeeming men, to examine the fubject, left they fall under the guilt of unpardonable fin. I will

I. EXPLAIN what kind or defcription of finners, are commonly the fubjects of a gracious regeneration by the Holy Spirit.

II. IN what regeneration confifts.

III. MENTION fome holy exercifes or affections which follow a renovation of the heart by the Spirit of GOD, and are evidence of the change.

I. I AM to explain what kind or defcription of finners, are commonly the fubjects of a gracious regeneration by the Holy Spirit.

Doubtless it is those who are convinced of sin, and in their own apprehension slain by the law. I am sensible it doth not become us to limit the gracious power of God, and positively to say, he never changed the heart of a person in deep security; but still we have no right to think it is the case. Such an opinion is not encouraged either by scripture or experience; also it is dangerous to entertain it; and has a tendency to fear the conscience and sink unholy men into deep stupidity and the worst of crimes.

Sinners feel no motives but fear and a love of themselves, to seek religious instruction, and if on the testimony of others they suppose a change of their hearts to be necessary; still, if they think those who are in a state of security to be probable subjects of God's renewing power, they will neglect all means to obtain religious instruction or to discover their own sin and guilt.

Neither does there seem to be a preparation for the exercise of grace by the renewed heart, which hath been previously insensible of sin, of guilt, of enmity against God and his law.—Such a mind would see, neither the wonderful love, nor sovereign grace of God in sanctifying and forgiving, nor the bitter opposition there was in the heart before its change, nor be sensible of the diametrical opposition there is between sin and holiness, in their nature, desires, and end of action. Christ tells us *it is sinners*, doubtless meaning, anxious, convinced sinners, *whom he calls to repentance—that it is the sick who need the physician.* The apostle says, *The law is a school master to bring us to Christ.* That *without the law* men think themselves *alive*, or whole, and we know one use of the law is to convince of sin in heart and life, and make us very concerned for deliverance.

THEREFORE, we have no reason to expect that secure sinners, who give themselves no trouble about sin, escaping it, and the salvation of their souls, will be renewed by the Spirit of GOD while they are in this state.—Should it happen it would be a strange thing, and the subserviency of one part of personal experience to another, would be lost. Nor have we reason to expect any will be changed, who are insensible of a sinful heart, as appears to be the case with many, who will yet allow they have committed visible transgressions.—Such secure persons are eminently in the broad road to ruin. They are not earnestly attempting any thing for their own salvation; nor is there any intimation that GOD ever designs to save them. If we saw them awakened by his action on their consciences, though their hearts are enmity against him we might hope, that by his mighty power their hearts would yet be changed, and that he is preparing the way for a rich display of his power; as, he who awakens can also renew. The security of such persons chills our hope for them.—They are blind, and know it not; in peril, and fear it not; and GOD is leaving them in ignorance of their disease and death. This deep security concerning personal salvation, and this ignorance of a heart naturally estranged from GOD, are most dark omens concerning the persons, places and times in which they happen; for when the Spirit of GOD in his convincing and sanctifying operations is withdrawn, the doctrines and institutions of the gospel will have no saving effect.

THERE cannot be religion without feeling, deep feeling, and such feeling as makes every thing in this world appear small in comparison with our eternal well-being. Therefore CHRIST directs us to watch and pray, to strive and agonize that we may enter into the kingdom of heaven. Those persons are building on a sandy foundation, who suppose, if they keep themselves free from visible crimes, and live what is commonly called a moral life, their state is safe enough, without any anxiety concerning another world. It is true that all who have the gospel morality are safe, for this is the same as evangelical holiness, and includes, faith, repentance, a love of God, mourning for sin, self-denial and watching against the motions of sin, much examination of the heart and prayer to God for his assistance. If this be meant by a moral life, it is through the grace of God connected with salvation. Every thing short of this may be found in those, who have not been taught their own miserable state; and though men cannot accuse them of crimes, they are in a secure ignorance of God, their own state, and eternity. Neither is there any prospect, of their ever becoming the subjects of a gracious regeneration, until they are in another manner convinced of sin and misery, and the danger of enduring the wrath to come. An effectual conviction, of these truths, will make people serious and temperate, and it is easy to discover the deep inquiry of their minds, *What shall we do to be saved.*

In the conviction of sin, which usually precedes a gracious change of heart, the sinner is made deeply sensible of the following things.

God's displeasure against sin of every kind, both of heart and life, of omission and commission, and that his anger rests on those who are not forgiven; so, that it is strange they are not consumed by his punishment. The reality of the divine law, and its penalty, together with the certain danger of sin; and under a sense of this danger, he is furprized at his paft life of fecurity, and wonders how he made himfelf eafy, when fo often told of his expofed ftate.

He fees a life full of fins, of which he formerly had no fufpicion. The fecurity for which he ufed to juftify himfelf—his contemptuous neglect of God—his prayerlefs life—his injurious reflections on thofe who were anxious for falvation—his mifimprovement of time—his profaning the holy fabbath and neglect of God's word, are now a heavy burden on his confcience.

He is alfo led to look within, and find an inward fountain of tranfgreffion. Sinfulnefs of heart, before this, was a hearfay thing to him; but now he finds, a heart that is hard, and a will unbroken. He fees thofe inward lufts, which like a fountain flow forth in ftreams of tranfgreffion. When crouded by the terrors of the law, he finds enmity againft the commandment and God who gave it, and though he dare not contemptuoufly avow fuch feelings, a confcioufnefs of them, convinces him of the depravity of his heart. A rational conviction of the fin in his heart, of divine juftice, and the certain penalty of the law, affure him that his ftate is deplorable. He now feels a truth which was never realized by him before, which is, that he fhall remain a finner, miferable, and under the curfe of the law, if God doth not deliver him by his own mighty power. Once he fuppofed it was an eafy thing to become religious indeed, fo as to attain a confcioufnefs of pardon; now, it appears to him a thing impoffible without help from God, which he has no right to claim. He finds an oppofing will and hard heart, to be the unmanageable enemies of his falvation, which none but God can remove, and thus defpairs in himfelf. This despair in himself takes place, before he has any delight in the truth.

It is usual for God, to produce this conviction of sin, and self-despair, before he graciously changes the heart. There is a fitness the creature should know his own spiritual impotency and guilt in the divine sight, before he receives mercy.

But though I have urged the need of these convictions, in order to show secure men, there is no probability of their receiving divine grace, in the present condition of their minds; it is proper for me to caution all, against expecting their inquiries, convictions and duties will renew their hearts.

True holiness, flowing out in the exercises of faith and repentance, is a fruit of renewing power—a fruit of the spirit's sanctifying operation in the heart. On the one hand, it is dangerous to deny the need and use of these convictions; so, on the other, it is a dangerous error to suppose the inquiring, convinced sinner is gradually becoming holy, and in a slow manner acquiring a moral conformity to God; or that his reigning temper, is not as fixedly opposed to holiness as it ever was in any period of his life. It is true, that the out-breakings of a sinful heart, may not be so visible to mankind; but why is it so? Only through the restraint of fear. In this case, the sinner himself, when convinced, will allow his heart to be growing in hardness. It is also true, that his case appears more hopeful to all pious beholders, who are acquainted with God's usual manner of recovering sinners, but why is it more hopeful? Not because his terrors, convictions, and efforts for deliverance make him more worthy of mercy; for in all these efforts, he has been moved by unholy motives. Not because these things have begot a small particle of holiness, or made one begin to grow which was natural in the heart. They have not begotten a small particle of holiness; nor is there any one natural in the fallen heart. Grace or holiness, when begotten in the heart by the spirit of GOD, is a thing entirely new; a thing of which there was no degree, or to which there was any likeness, before a divine renovation. The superior hopefulness of the sinner's situation, arises entirely, from the tendency of inquiry and conviction to bring the mind into such a state, as GOD chooses guilty creatures should feel themselves to be in, before he in sovereignty grants renewing grace. He renovates, of his own good pleasure, and acts by motives drawn from within himself, and from the nature of his government.

THE purpose of infinite wisdom, in the progress of this work, is to teach the guilty creature he is a sinner, which he never feelingly apprehended before; to show him his impotency, that he has a heart guilty, opposed to GOD, and which he cannot change. That the impossibility of changing his own heart arises from the stubbornness of his will, or the excess of sin that is in him; and also to prepare him for the exercise of holy affections, when GOD is pleased to give them.

WHEN public teachers or private christians, are called to instruct anxious souls, it is a matter of great importance, to teach them the danger of relapsing into security, by which their deliverance, will be rendered improbable; also, to assure them there is no holiness and compliance with the gospel, and that they are not becoming more worthy of forgiveness by any thing done in compliance with their fears, and solely to escape from danger. An endeavor, either to quench these convictions, or to make any believe they essentially alter the moral state of the heart, is, in the striking language of the prophet, daubing the wall with untempered mortar, and sewing pillows under the arms, to give security where conscience ought to be kept awake.

Our text is very explicit in ascribing a gracious change of heart to the direct and immediate power of God—*which were born, not of blood, nor of the will of the flesh, nor of the will of man, but of God.* This sacred description not only excludes means, as having any efficiency of any kind, in changing the heart; but also goes much further, and assures us that the change is not according to the sinner's own will, that is, he doth not desire such a change as this is. The terrors of a miserable end, which have been thrown in his way by the providence and Spirit of God, have made him wish for some change, for some escape from misery, some deliverance from the pains of a wounded conscience; he is also convinced that whatever the change be, God must be the author; but all his pains and fears have not brought him to will or choose such a change as the gospel regeneration is, therefore it is *not according to the will of man.* And it is doubtless true, when God renews an unholy soul, which hath been asking much of him, the particular favor granted is an unsought one, and granted by sovereign grace.

II. I am to describe in what regeneration consists.

In describing this change, the word of God makes use of the highest expressions, denoting both the special power and action of God, and the newness of the thing produced. It is not the modification of any moral principle, which previously exifted in the mind, but the production of one that is new. It is called a renewing by the fpirit —being born of incorruptible feed—born of the will of God—a new birth—a new creation—old things pafling away, and all things becoming new —a new heart, with a multitude of other expreffions, the ftrongeft poflible, denoting the immediate agency of God in the production of a new moral principle, or a new heart.

The heart or the will and affections are the feat of this change; therefore, the increafe of doctrinal or fpeculative knowledge, be the degree ever fo great, hath no tendency to regenerate a perfon. Doctrinal light hath its feat in the underftanding, and it is contrary to all experience, that more knowledge of an object, to which the heart or will is for its very nature oppofed, will change the oppofition into love. We may know this from the objects of love and hatred, which daily occur in the experience of life. If the tafte of mind be oppofed to the very nature of an object, the more the object is feen, the more an oppofing tafte will exert itfelf.—The divine action in regenerating an unholy foul is, therefore, on the heart, or the will and affections.

What we call a new moral principle, may alfo be called a new tafte, relifh, temper, difpofition, or habit of feeling refpecting moral objects and truth. Words are not effential if ideas be according to truth. In the holy fcriptures, the words heart and will, mean the fame power or faculty in the mind, and it is that faculty in which holinefs exifts, and on which God acts in renewing finners.

The manner of divine acting in this inftance of creation, is as much above our conception as it was in the creation of the worlds. It is only the effects of his action, which are sensible to the person who hath experienced it. He finds in himself a new principle of moral love—a new relish or taste—a new temper—new feelings towards moral objects. He hath not done it himself. Though through fear of punishment he wished a change, he finds this to be another kind of change from what he wished, and infinitely more excellent. He feels, that it is above the power of means or any thing he hath done, to make such an alteration in his heart.—That it is a great change and worthy of God to make—that his moral feelings are indeed become new. The objects and the sins he once loved are now his aversion, and God himself, truth and duty, in which he had no pleasure, are become agreeable to his heart. This change of moral principle or taste, is that renewing by the spirit, or new birth which our Saviour declares to be necessary for seeing the kingdom of heaven, and of which he says, *The wind bloweth where it listeth, and thou hearest the sound thereof, but canst not tell whence it cometh, and whither it goeth ; so is every one that is born of the spirit.* That is, the manner of divine acting is unknown, the moment of divine acting is unperceived, the creature is passive in his change ; but by the effects of the change, after he hath had opportunity for deliberate self-attention, he knows it hath happened. All the dispute, which some have raised concerning the direct agency of God, and a kind of regeneration partially effected by the creature's previous endeavours to become right, will cease in those, who have became real subjects of the change. Feeling what it is by its effects, and comparing them with what they were before, as effectually convinces them of an Almighty moral creator ; as a consciousness of their own existence, and the surrounding creation doth of the natural creator.

REGENERATION is that change from which holy exercises proceed, and is therefore the beginning of spiritual life in the soul. It is the beginning of that moral conformity to GOD, which is the true preparation for heaven and its blessedness. Though many, who have never experienced regeneration, think they wish for heaven; the real object of their wish is an ideal heaven, which never existed, and is essentially different from that holy state and place, which GOD will forever fill with his glory.

THERE will always be a strong temptation, with unholy minds, to deny the need of this change; and such a denial, in most cases, is the first step towards infidelity. There is a greater and more present temptation, to deny the need of an efficacious work of GOD's spirit renewing the heart, than there is to question the need of CHRIST's atonement. This doctrine of a new heart, more directly brings home the charge of depravity and the necessity of our immediate departure from all sin, to escape the punishment of GOD; which becomes a present and a strong temptation to deny the need of a change. A willingness to escape misery is common to men both good and bad; but it is only the sanctified, who are willing to leave sin; and though the effectual means of deliverance are purchased, it is natural to resist and deny the need of their operation. To guard ourselves against such fatal resistance, we ought to remember the words of CHRIST, which accord with the whole tenor of scripture, *Verily, verily, I say unto thee, except a man be born of water and the spirit, he cannot enter into the kingdom of GOD.*

III. I SHALL next mention some holy exercises or affections, which follow a renewing of the heart by the spirit of GOD, and are evidence of the change.

It is of infinite importance that we judge right of the state of our own hearts. Considering the great consequences that depend, the bare possibility of a mistake should make us examine; but in this matter, there is more than a bare possibility. The word of GOD tells us that many shall be deceived. There is great difficulty in knowing the heart, not because the nature of holiness is uncertain or badly defined, in the scriptures; but from the deceitfulness of the heart itself. There are powerful temptations, to make us think our state good when it is really bad; and we have reason to fear multitudes will be deceived, and go with closed eyes into the eternal world. To prevent this, we should acquaint ourselves with the nature of those holy affections, which evidence a change.

GOD *is love, and he that dwelleth in love dwelleth in* GOD—*He that loveth is born of* GOD—*Love is of* GOD, *and every one that loveth is born of* GOD, *and knoweth* GOD. Love, is the most appropriate as well as comprehensive name of gracious affections, which is used in the holy scriptures. Holy exercises are a conformity to the law, which saith, *thou shalt love* GOD *with all thy heart, and thy neighbour as thyself.* Every one who is born of GOD loves the divine character, as exhibited in his works and word, and wishes well to his being, blessedness and government. He is more pleased that GOD is blessed and glorious, than with any personal advantage.—He chooses that every thing should be subordinate to the divine will and the exaltment of GOD, and when he begins to pray, forgets himself until he hath said,

Father glorify thyself. Although an unholy man may think he loves God, his love, whatever it be, on examination is found to terminate in himself; and he loves Jehovah, only because he is his own acknowledged God, has kept and done him much good, and will bless and save him in time to come. The love of a new heart, feels the perfection and excellence of God to deserve praise, exaltment, adoration and the most perfect obedience. He knows it is reason enough for a whole universe of creatures to exist eternally, that such a Lord may be thereby glorified, and bless himself in the fulfilment of his will. He sinks in his own apprehension, into less than nothing and vanity, and the highest value of his own existence, appears to him, to arise from his subservience to the divine purposes.

He loves the providence of God, because it is the providence of eternal right and wisdom. A sinful love of God is fitted only for days of personal prosperity. While this continues, it can cry hosanna to the Son of David; but when it ceases, crucify him, crucify him. A holy love is not afraid of an adverse providence—can suffer and praise—can be humbled and adore—can feel the rod and kiss the smiting hand, and say, these painful strokes are one reason why God ought to reign in absolute sovereignty. If it will glorify God, if it will advance the majesty and goodness of his government, let him lay me waste, let him smite and slay me. I cannot pray, I cannot even wish the rod should cease, so long as God is glorified and the interests of his holy kingdom are promoted by the continuance.

Beloved let us love one another: for love is of God, and every one that loveth is born of God. The renovated person loves his brother and neighbour as himself. And cannot the unholy sinner love his neighbour? Doubtless he can, but only so far as his neighbour's good conduces to his own. It is a love of himself acting through the prosperity of his neighbour, and it grows no longer than some personal advantage is the root of nourishment. From this root, grow many of the neighbourly and civil alliances and amities of the world. It may serve, in this life of trial, to make a midway state, between a heaven of glory and the place of perfect torment. God admits no such selfish alliances as the basis of heavenly peace. The born of God can love a brother without regard to personal advancement. A brother's happiness is, in its nature, so valuable an object, there is no need of selfish inducements to love and seek it. The holy soul, placed in a situation to derive no advantage, except it be the happiness of acting rationally and doing good, beholds and seeks the happiness of others with most ardent desire. This benevolent love of men is an exercise peculiar to the new heart.

Whoever is born of God repents of sin. There is a self-loathing on account of past sins, and our liableness to a future relapse. This loathing doth not arise from a fear of punishment, for if there were none, sin would not be less loathed by the holy soul. The tendency of sin to injure the rights and diminish the happiness of social being, is reason enough why it should be loathed; though we are personally placed in safety from its consequences. The penitent, doth not loathe sin less, for having been the sinner who committed it, or feel any desire for self-justification. How deep this mourning and sorrow becomes, in view of the excellent glory of God, and the injury done to him, can be conceived only by those, who have felt it under the sanctifying action of the blessed Spirit.

Those who are born of God can say—*O how I love thy law, it is daily my delight—on thy precepts do I meditate day and night.* The law of perfect holiness is an image of God. We cannot do without it, either as a rule of duty, or as the most direct means of teaching us the infinite and glorious rectitude of Godhead. That commandment, from which sinners turn with aversion, both on account of its holy requirements and its penalties, is the portion of the godly; and by looking on this image of their heavenly Father they daily grow in conformity to him.—Give them the written law for instruction, and the privilege of prayer as a means of communion with their God, and they are ready to say, I am as rich as I can be on this side heaven.

But how shall words describe that glory of God in the face of Jesus Christ and in his gospel, which is seen by new-born souls, and by no others. The glory of the gospel is hid to those who are lost, who were never renewed by the Spirit. They see no excellence in its moral nature and tendency; and the best they can consider it, is, as undesirable means of saving men from a more undesirable end. A regenerated heart perceives a fountain of glory in the gospel which was before unperceived—a display of moral perfection in God—his glory in the face of Jesus Christ—the holy nature of his government and kingdom—and the highest benevolence in communion between the unsearchable Jehovah and his holy creation. The method, in which the gospel delivers from sin and misery, adds blessedness to heaven, by such a discovery of God to created minds, as could never have been without it. After renovation, the moral glory of the gospel, of its author, and of the whole plan of grace, breaks in on the mind, in such succession, as its parts can be viewed by a finite understanding. The soul is drawn to God, in this new way of approach, by the irresistible cords of love. There is no pause, to deliberate whether it is best to receive or reject such a God. There is no longer a deliberation between going and staying. The voice of the heart is, let me go if I may. The torments of eternity, prepared for rejecting sinners, are at such a moment forgotten, and are not the motive for choosing God. A sense of guilt and unworthiness is the only impediment, and though this be great, it does not prevail.—Drawn by divine glory the humble penitent approaches, thinking, perhaps he may be accepted; and if punishing justice should meet and repel him, still, if he may continue to behold this God and Redeemer, it will be a support under any possible pain. Thus the soul is united to God through Jesus Christ.

This firm and delightful approbation of the Mediator, his character, the whole plan of grace, and the most humbling doctrines of the gospel, is one principal evidence of a changed heart.

It is to holiness sinful men are opposed. It is holiness, which God means to display and promote by the gospel. Sinners will be pleased with the doctrines of divine grace, so long as they can understand them, in accommodation to their own evil disposition.—Approving gospel doctrines is no evidence of a good heart, unless these doctrines are understood, as a dispensation, from first to last, promoting holiness of heart and life. It is the holiness of the gospel which a good man loves.

PATIENCE, humility, meekness of spirit, self-denial for the glory of GOD, perseverance in good works sincerely practised, and an observance of positive religious institutions, so far as they are known to be such, are also contained in the evidence of being born of GOD.

FROM what hath been said on this subject we may infer, the unhappy state of sundry descriptions of persons, which in collection amount to a very great number.

1st. OF those who have never been brought to feel their unholy and guilty hearts. The human mind may go on long in a doctrinal belief of our original depravity, and still be wholly without just apprehensions of its own sin; never be slain by the law; never discover the true nature, and reigning power, of that sinful taste which fills the heart; never discover a real opposition to the character of GOD and the nature of holiness; never be brought feelingly to cry, on any principles whatever, help Lord or I perish. Education first fixed a doctrinal belief, and life hath gone on in assenting to the truth, without any feeling of the evil within. The security of life prevents examination. Such persons, from motives of this world, may be regular in their manners and in a visible attendance on many religious institutions. They are friends to every thing in religion but the experimental and evangelical part of it in the heart.—Having never seen their own unholy, guilty want of a supreme love of GOD, they depend for eternal safety, on their visible regularity and the general mercy of GOD through a Saviour. There is no evidence that such persons have been born of the Spirit, or that dying in their present state, they can escape the wrath to come.

2d. This subject shows the error of all who deny a change of heart to be necessary for salvation.

These persons cut themselves off from eternal life.—They deny the appropriate office-work of the Holy Spirit, in the salvation of men; which, is resisting him in a high manner. However firmly they may think the death of Christ to be necessary, they prevent their own benefit from it by rejecting the application; for they will never reason themselves into that true holiness, which is necessary for seeing God. Indeed, it is an opposition to holiness, which is their temptation to deny the need of a change; and the denial proves that sinners do not desire such a heaven as Christ died to purchase. If they did truly choose it, the need and offer of renovating aid, would instantly appear to be a desirable truth. Let all, who deny, think well on this point. Let them examine, and compare their own hearts with the nature of gospel holiness. If this be seriously done, they must be convinced, there is an opposition in the heart which divine power only can remove.

3dly. Those, who think that an alteration of the external circumstances under which the mind acts, will cause a sufficient change of heart for eternal life, are in a dangerous error. They never will find a change of external circumstances and situation, sufficient to change the moral principles or relish of the mind. Men are not sinners, because the circumstances of their existence, in this world, are a rational inducement to sin; for it is always contrary. Being in the body, and surrounded with such objects and events, as are commonly called temptations, is not the cause of a sinful heart. These, may be means of driving a heart, which was before finful, into more vifible exercife; yet are not the caufe of fin. Sin hath a deeper origin than the external circumftances under which the mind acts, and is in the heart itfelf. It is an original and governing wrong temper, which change of circumftances may varioufly difcover, but never eradicate. Therefore, death and a removal from the tempting objects of the world, will have no tendency to fit us for heaven. The foul, when ftripped of its body and removed from this world, will ftill retain the moral character or relifh with which it departed; nor will the objects of another world have a power to change the temper. If the departing foul diflikes GOD and holinefs, a clearer fight of him, will produce the moft enraged enmity. The circumftances of this worldly exiftence are, therefore, fo far from being the caufe; that it is probable they are principal means, of preventing the excefs of fin and torment, which revelation teaches us will overtake the departed impenitent. With what alarm ought all unrenewed minds to think of going into another world! They will meet a difpleafed GOD, who out of CHRIST is a confuming fire to finners; and go to a place, where there are no objects of enjoyment fuited to the relifh of their minds. They will be felfifh and proud without opportunity of gratifying the paffion, which through difappointment muft increafe to all the rage of enmity. An utter defpair, either of deliverance or change, will make the mifery dreadful. Thefe folemn confiderations, fhow the importance of teaching the doctrine of JESUS CHRIST, *Verily, verily, I fay unto thee, except a man be born of water, and of the fpirit, he cannot enter into the kingdom of heaven.* AMEN.

SERMON XI.

Receiving CHRIST by faith.

JOHN i. 11.

But as many as received him, to them gave he power to become the sons of GOD, even to them that believe on his name.

TO become the sons of GOD in the gospel meaning, is to possess and be entitled to all that a wise mind can desire. Among all the descriptions, which GOD usesto express the near relation between him and his people; that, of his being their father, and they his sons, is most expressive of an endearing union, and the great benefits which they derive from it. Between a father and his son there is a mutual love, and the father's honor is the happiness of the child. The son is the heir. The apostle saith, *of children then heirs, heirs of GOD, and joint heirs with CHRIST.*

Tho' the sovereignty and property of all things, can in no sense depart from GOD, and the christian will forever feel a state of most perfect dependance, rejoicing that he is thus, and that God is all in all; still he is graciously admitted to be heir of all things, even the whole fulness of God, in the highest sense that the nature of things permits. He hath *the promise of the life that now is, and of that which is to come.* All things here, even afflictions, shall turn more to his good, than he could possibly order, if the government of the world, were in the most absolute sense, under his own direction. The fulness of God and of his works, is the good man's portion.—Being qualified by holiness of heart, he will perfectly enjoy the eternal displays of Godhead, and feel the greatest delight, which his finite capacity admits, in beholding every divine perfection, and the opening scheme of infinite love.

This, is being an heir of God in the highest, the most glorious and desirable sense we can conceive; and this, is the portion of the sons of God. To the unholy and unbelieving, we know this must be a description which sounds great, still without any meaning which they apprehend. Placed under the light of the gospel, they have often heard it; and perhaps, have sometimes searched the scriptures to find more perfectly what this portion is. They will remain in ignorance of it, until their hearts are made right towards God; so that they may see the moral glory of the divine character and government. Those who have become the sons of God by receiving Jesus Christ, having tasted this happiness, know it to be real, most excellent in its nature, and most full and durable; because it arises from knowing an infinite and eternal God. From the foretaste, they feel assured that the perfection is fulness of bliss, and heaven a most glorious state. A right to this is derived through God's gracious promise, by receiving

Christ.—To as many as received him, to them gave he power to become the sons of God.

By a power to become the sons of God, is meant a title to all the privileges of a justified state, the pardon of sin, freedom from the penalty of the law, and a right through the promise of sovereign grace, to an eternal life of holiness and peace, in the enjoyment of God himself.

Receiving Christ, means a saving faith, which, in the text, is also called believing on his name. The scriptures represent our justification to be granted through faith in Christ, on which account, this holy exercise of the heart, is eminently distinguished by the sacred writers, as an important one, in the manner of our salvation by free grace; and with those who sincerely examine their own state, it becomes a frequent inquiry whether they have a true faith.

Though it becomes us to encourage such inquiry, it ought also to be understood, that faith is not in its nature more excellent than other christian graces; nor is a knowledge of our own faith any better evidence of final salvation, than the same knowledge of other holy exercises; for where there is faith, there is love, repentance, and submission. One of these graces certainly implies the other; and supposing the existence of one, and absolute non-existence of another, implies an impossible and contradictory character. The work of God, which is efficacious to salvation, is begun by his own power giving a new heart; and holy exercises will succeed. So far as the fountain is made sweet, all the streams will be purified. In describing a christian character, the word of God joins faith with love, repentance and a holy practice. Whatever our faith may be, if we have not also a sensible love of God, and mourning for sin, there is great reason to suspect the holy sincerity of our hearts. This will appear by a further description of the nature of saving faith.

1st. FAITH is an exercise of a renewed heart.

IN the sacred description, it is joined with other graces and fruits of the spirit. The text describes faith and its benefits; and the succeeding verse tells us, it is found in those, who are *born not of the flesh, nor of the will of man, but of* GOD. Whatever kind of faith an unrenewed person may possess, it hath no holiness and cannot plead the promise of free grace, forgiveness and eternal life. Until the soul is born of GOD, there can be no union of the will and affections to the Redeemer. If unrenewed persons attempt to go to CHRIST, and to receive him, there is no union of their hearts to him and his kingdom; and in the want of this, consists the insincerity of the attempt. Therefore there can be no saving faith, without a change, *not of the flesh, nor of the will of man, but of* GOD; which will also appear by a further description what faith is.

2d. FAITH is receiving CHRIST.

THIS is the description in the text, where it is also called, believing on his name. This receiving must mean a saving faith, because it gives a power to become the sons of GOD. The words *faith* and *belief*, are sometimes used, for a perception of the understanding, or credit yielded to certain facts or truths, supported by historical and natural evidence. In this sense, they do not imply a holy state of the soul. Sinful minds may credit gospel truth, and still be opposed to it. The devils believe and tremble; they believe and hate the truth, which they cannot deny. Thus sinful men may give credit to the holy scriptures, and to the gospel of salvation by CHRIST; and at the same time, have hearts opposed to the terms of salvation, and to the holy character and doctrines of the Redeemer. This faith or belief cannot be saving, and is not that receiving of CHRIST to which a promise is given. Religion, is receiving *truth in the love of it.* *With the heart man believeth unto righteousness.* Evangelical faith is one which *works by love. It purifies the heart,* and must therefore imply a conformity to CHRIST's character; a choice of him as a Saviour, and of such salvation as he offers; and a preference, in every particular, to the manner of deliverance, which is proposed in the gospel. This receiving of CHRIST forms a voluntary union with him and his kingdom.

FAITH, may properly be called, the first act of the soul, which covenants with GOD and CHRIST. Salvation is offered by GOD, in a covenant way through his Son. Faith, is that choice of the will, which receives the gospel, in contemplation of its author, his mediatorial offices, his personal glories and sufficiency; and which receives GOD, gloriously reconciled through him. In an unrenewed state, men may see their danger, and wish an escape from it; they may think of the gospel as a favorable institution, and tremble at the thought of loosing it; but they tremble only because personal danger follows. They remain unbelieving, through a disrelish of the holiness there is in CHRIST and the scheme of grace. The selfish may tremble. They often do this, and think they are willing to have CHRIST and try to exercise faith; but he cannot be found by them, in his saving offices, until they love him for what he is, choose him for his precious ness, and choose his gospel for its fitness to honor GOD.

In a saving faith, the soul receives him with love, embraces and becomes a joyful party to the offered covenant, and feels a moral union of affection, trust and dependence on him. Faith includes a sense of his sufficiency and the wonderful fitness of the gospel to exalt GOD, and save guilty sinners. An unholy sinner, in previous meditation on becoming a christian indeed, thinks he shall rejoice greatly in an apprehension of the safety he has obtained. It is true, that when he finds and fiducially receives CHRIST, he will rejoice greatly; but with quite another kind and ground of joy, from what he supposed. It will be the joy of beholding the glory of GOD in the face of JESUS CHRIST, and the happiness of committing himself to an all-sufficient Saviour, who is infinitely worthy in his own nature, and able to glorify GOD in redeeming men. The believer, by faith gives himself up to JESUS CHRIST, trusts in him for all he needs, and desires to be accepted, only in such a way, as sovereign wisdom sees to be best. Thus the covenant of grace, ordered sure in all things by infinite wisdom, is compleated between GOD and the believer. GOD has accepted him in sovereign mercy, and will be faithful to fulfil all his promises of grace. The believer, is united in holy affection to CHRIST and his kingdom, and will be preserved in perseverance unto eternal life, by the power of GOD.

THE first exercise of a saving faith, is not always known to be such, by those who have it. It is most common, for a peaceful hope to be gradually formed in the mind, by mature reflection on its own exercises, and a growing acquaintance with the life of evangelical holiness. All the doctrinal knowledge, which can be attained by an unsanctified person, will not give him a true apprehension of gracious feelings. The apprehensions of speculation, will forever be different from those of experience; nor can spiritual blindness be removed by rational inquiry, or by any means of informing the mind. The sinner, in previous speculation, may suppose the change to be great and wonderful, and it is great beyond his expectation; but the greatness and wonder is of a kind he had not conceived. The feelings of the heart are sweet and placid—joy unspeakable and full of glory—a joy in GOD—a sight of glory, solemnizing but sweet, full of majesty but divested of pomp and glare. It is the glory of infinite love, and the sight of it is transforming, *Changing the soul into the same image, from glory to glory, even as by the spirit of the Lord.*

3dly. A FAITH which is saving gives new evidence of the reality of things invisible; of divine glory; of the divine government, its excellence and stability; of all gospel truth and the rewards of another world.

AN unholy mind never can have that strong and sure belief of these things, which is felt by the people of GOD. Therefore, a saving faith is sometimes described by a firm persuasion and knowledge of the truth, of the invisible things of GOD, and the realities of the world to come.

MOSES *by faith endured as seeing him who is invisible.* His persuasion of GOD's being, perfections and government was altogether greater, than the most learned unbeliever can possess. The same also happened in the list of eminent saints recorded in Heb. xi. They had a persuasion

Z

and knowledge of GOD's being and government, which is never attained by unholy perfons. Through this perfuafion, they could act and fuffer in the caufe of GOD, beyond other men. It is for this reafon, that the apoftle, in the beginning of the chapter, defines faith, to be *the evidence of things not feen.* An evidence different from the moft learned fpeculation.

THE fame apoftle faith, *If our gofpel be hid, it is hid to them that are loft.*—*In whom the GOD of this world hath blinded the minds of them that believe not, left the light of the glorious gofpel of CHRIST, who is the image of GOD, should shine unto them.*

THE hiding of the gofpel here fpoken of, is common to all the loft ; whether they be heathen, or chriftians only by doctrinal knowledge. It is the want of that perfuafion and knowledge of the truth, which is peculiar to a faving faith.

WHOEVER *believeth that JESUS is the CHRIST, is born of GOD.*—This means a believing to falvation, and contains that certainty of unfeen things, which is peculiar to the people of GOD, and is the evidence of things not feen. The unbeliever, even when his reafon and confcience are entirely convinced, fo that his mouth is fhut before GOD, hath not that kind of certainty concerning the invifible things of GOD and another world, which is felt by the believing difciple.

THERE is one branch of evidence for the truth, which an unholy mind never can receive ; and to thofe who have received it, this is the higheft of all evidence. It is a fight or feeling of the glory of truth—its fitnefs—its perfect excellence—its fuitablenefs to the glory of GOD and the beft interefts of being, whereby, the great whole is the moft bleffed it can be. There muft be a good heart to fee this glory.

When the sacred writings mention believing that Jesus is the Christ, as evidence of final salvation, they always mean believing the truth on christian evidence; and christian evidence, is a sight of the moral glory of truth. A saving faith is *believing with the heart*. Faith of the understanding flows from rational evidence; faith or believing of the heart from a sight of moral excellence in the object or truth believed. Faith of the understanding, is common to wicked angels and to men both good and bad; faith of the heart is peculiar to the saints of God, and flows from that evidence, which is distinguishingly christian, a sight of moral glory.

Take an unbelieving sinner, in whom conscience is alive, and set before him the doctrinal evidence of God's character, and of Christ's divinity and mediation.—Describe to him the divine miracles, the fulfilment of prophecy, the providence of God, owning and preserving his own cause, together, with all external evidence of the christian scheme.—In this case he is rationally convinced, his conscience testifies to the truth, and he is a speculative christian.—His conviction and belief are of that kind, which makes his guilt compleat, and exposes him to eternal punishment; but with all this, he hath not attained that peculiar evidence, by which the true believer knows that Jesus is the Christ. He hath not seen the moral glory of Christ, the glory of the Father in the face of Christ, the glory of the gospel scheme, nor the true glory of that heavenly state revealed in the christian scriptures.

A sight of moral glory, is the high and all-conquering evidence, which gives to the mind a sense of reality, and raises it above all doubting. This sight of glory, is the compleating evidence of things not seen, and gives a kind of certainty similar, in many respects, to the certainty that is felt in the vision of heaven.

Let there be all possible rational evidence, without this, the mind turns on itself, and asks the perplexing question, Where is the real excellence of this scheme? It appears to be compleat, its parts are well adjusted and meet each other, there is no want of testimony, for nature, providence, miracles and prophecy conspire to confirm it.—Conscience assents, and there is a sense of guilt in resisting, and a fear of coming before the God who hath published it. Still where is the excellence, and loveliness of the scheme? If I could see this I should not doubt. The unholy in heart never can see this glory. The sight is confined to those who are born of the spirit, and it is the peculiar evidence which experimental christians have, making them sure and certain that Jesus is the Christ of God, and his words eternal truth. Therefore, it is said that faith is the evidence of things not seen; that he who believeth Jesus to be the Christ, that is, believeth on the true christian evidence, is born of God. A saving faith is, in the holy scriptures, often described by this certainty of the invisible things of God and eternity.

To those who have faith, it is a piece of spiritual armour, whereby they are enabled to resist the doubts suggested by Satan. It is hard to make the believer, who is a christian indeed, call in question the oracles of his God.—His faith is a shield, whereby he resists the fiery darts of Satan, of wicked men, and an alluring world. Let his powers of intellect and reason be weak, and his doctrinal knowledge small; still, he resists all the arguments of evil men and stands unshaken in the midst of a wicked and adulterous generation, and hath courage, though alone, to be on the side of God. To such a believer, his faith is the evidence of things not seen; God is present with him; the gospel is the power of God to salvation.—An approaching judgment and eternity with its rewards, are as much substantiated to him, as the daily events of sense with which he is surrounded; therefore, this faith is also called the substance of things hoped for.

4th. From the description that has been given, it doth not appear, that the first act of saving faith, is precisely the same in all christians.

Tho' it be of the same holy nature, and implies all other holy exercises, it is not in all cases, precisely the same truth, which the heart first receives in believing. Men are under a necessity, by a limitation of their understanding, to view a scheme of truth by its parts. These parts are all congenial in their nature. The temper which honestly receives one, will receive all; on their being presented, in succession, before the understanding. The gospel scheme contains many such truths, which are so connected, that one of them implies the others; still, they must be viewed in succession, by the finite minds of men. Such is, the glory of God and of all his perfections, in the manner of redeeming sinners through Christ; the sufficiency of the Redeemer to save to the uttermost, those who come to God in this way; the fulness of the gospel salvation to relieve all the miseries of sinners, who are by nature unholy, guilty, and justly condemned; the excellency of that kingdom which is formed by the mediation and atonement.—These, with several other truths, are essential parts of the gospel scheme. Doubtless an infinite understanding may view them simply as the same truth; but a finite mind, must view the parts in succession, and which ever of them the heart firſt receives, it is ſaving faith. Every chriſtian in the progreſs of a life of faith, will ſee, receive and rejoice in all theſe truths ; but they may not be preſented, in the ſame order of ſucceſſion, to all holy minds. Therefore, the firſt act of ſaving faith, may not be preciſely the ſame, in all who are brought to ſalvation through JESUS CHRIST.

THIS, in part, accounts for the various deſcriptions, of this moſt eſſential grace, which are found in the ſcriptures of truth.

THE goſpel ſcheme is preſented to the underſtanding of men, in the form of a covenant between GOD and the ſoul. This covenant embraces many evangelical truths, and receiving any one of them with love, is a ſaving faith. It is meeting the terms of the covenant, and proves that holy ſtate of the heart, which will rejoice in GOD's character, and the whole ſcheme of his government.

FROM the nature of a ſaving faith, the following things appear.

1ſt. THAT believers are united to GOD thro' JESUS CHRIST, in the moſt glorious and bleſſed manner.

IT is a union of moral character, of will, of affection, and of eternal bleſſedneſs. This was the object of JESUS CHRIST in laying down his life, therefore, he prayed to the Father, *Sanctify them through thy truth. That they all may be one ; as thou, Father, art in me, and I in thee, that they alſo may be one in us.* This oneneſs of moral character and affection, makes the ſaints of GOD the moſt glorious and bleſſed they can be. A conformity to the infinite holineſs of GOD, is the greateſt perſonal glory they can receive. The manner of their union, through the mediation of the Son of God, is in the highest degree glorious for a creature, and so wonderful that we may cry out, *O the depth of the riches both of the wisdom and knowledge of God.* How broad the base for blessedness to the redeemed? They stand by the mighty power of God, are one with Christ, and joint heirs of the fulness of the Lord. They may suffer affliction for the short season of this life; but when possessed of their Lord's temper, can glory in tribulation. Even when they kneel to pray for deliverance from the trials of the world, they can check the desire by submission, saying, it was one reason of our existence in this state, that we might glorify God by patience; therefore, Father, do thine own will. Whatever promotes the glory and blessedness of God's kingdom, will be their peace. God will always reign, and his will be their choice; so that nothing can happen contrary to their good. The government of the universe, through eternity, will be as they wish, verifying the sacred word, *All things are yours, and ye are Christ's, and Christ is God's.* Herein, is the manifold wisdom of God, that he can give all things to his redeemed, in such a manner, as will forever display his own absolute sovereignty. By renouncing self and choosing God and his kingdom, for their portion, they gain all things; and all things work together to promote the prosperity of that cause, which is their supreme delight. United to God in moral affection, they will enjoy him in all his fulness forever and ever. United in love to all holy intelligencies, the growing blessedness of the eternal state, will perpetually augment their delight. These are the fruits of a saving union with God, by faith in Jesus Christ.

2dly. Having contemplated the nature of faith, it becomes us to inquire, whether we have thus received Christ?

It is only thofe, who have thus received him, that obtain power to become the fons of God. All others are, in his fight, enemies to his kingdom; and though life is fet before them by the gofpel, the offer will eventually prove, *a favor of death unto death.* There is much room to be deluded concerning our own faith; and perhaps multitudes are in this ftate.—There is the faith of education, the faith of rational conviction, the faith of felf-love, the faith of fear, for the devils through one kind of faith tremble before God; and all thefe, not working by love, have an effential defect.

There is, in chriftian lands, a general affent to the gofpel, arifing from education or fome other caufes, on which men are prone to rely, thinking it is a faith which will fave them. They believe in Christ doctrinally, becaufe he was the Saviour of their fathers; or becaufe they have heard it faid, God is merciful in this way. They have never felt the exceeding finfulnefs of their own hearts, and the need of a purifying faith. On this general belief, joined with fuch vifible morality as may flow from felfifh motives and a civilized ftate of fociety, they think themfelves good chriftians. Such perfons, may occafionally become zealous and contend for the faith, in which they fuppofe themfelves to ftand, while wholly deftitute of evangelical holinefs. It is a faith which may be reconciled to living without God in the world, and requires little denial of human pride. A true faith always works by love; it beholds the moral glory of God in the face of Jesus Christ; it makes Christ very precious to the heart; it purifies the foul from all sin; it forms a union of the will and affections to the divine character, counsels and government; it makes the invisible things of God and eternity both real and influential on the mind; it shows the vanity of self and all the creatures; and produces a most holy walk with God in obedience to all his commandments. By perusing the life of those saints recorded in scripture, who were eminent in faith; we may learn the nature of this grace, which is uniform in all who have it. By faith they endured affliction joyfully; were diligent in duty; could deny themselves and suffer for the cause of Christ; set little by the riches and honors of the world, seeking the city of God, a habitation not made with hands, eternal in the heavens. What zeal for God's kingdom, and weanedness from the world! What lives of prayer and devotion! What a love of souls, and holy aspirations to be with Christ, were manifest in those saints, who are recorded to animate our zeal, and instruct us in the nature of christian grace. The faith of every true christian is of the same nature, and wrought by the same spirit. It is a view of heaven and heavenly things, and a union of heart to them, which irresistibly draws the believer to the glorious object of contemplation. Unless, we can find something of this nature in our own supposed faith, we are still without Christ in the world and aliens from the communion of saints.

3dly. Our meditation, on receiving Christ by faith, leads us to see the nature and guilt of unbelief.

The disbelief of heathen, finds an excuse, in having never heard of Christ and his doctrines; but the unbelief of instructed people is without excuse. That unbelief, which lives in a neglect of CHRIST, is the fountain of all sin; and it is the very unholiness which subjects sinners, under gospel light, to eternal misery.

It is a mark of very dangerous security, not to feel the guilt of unbelief. The want of faith in CHRIST is the highest evidence of a wicked and rebellious heart. Particular sins are but streams, of which unbelief is the fountain. GOD comes to sinful men in the gospel of his Son, displaying himself in all his holiness and grace, in his scheme of counsel and government, calling on them to be partakers of his holiness and the blessedness of his kingdom. Unbelief is that state of the heart, which rejects the whole, and refuses the union of holiness and love. CHRIST says, *he that receiveth me, receiveth him that sent me;* so that a neglect of JESUS CHRIST must be a rejection of GOD. The only reason, sinners do not feel the guilt of unbelief, is an ignorance of their own temper; and if they ever come to themselves, so as to return to their Father, they will know this hardness of their hearts, to be worthy of GOD's everlasting displeasure. That state of the heart must be a very criminal one, which sees no beauty, no preciousness in the character of CHRIST; no glory in a holy GOD and his method of grace; no loveliness in the law and gospel; and no obligation on men to seek the glory of GOD in all they do. This is the state of all those persons, who do not live by faith in JESUS CHRIST the Son of GOD. They mean to be secure and at ease concerning religion and another world. They excusingly say, we injure no man, neither do we dishonor GOD by any open sin. But consider, O sinner, who art at ease in Zion, whether this be true. Is not unbelief a dishonor to GOD? Is it not dishonoring GOD, to live in such a manner, as shows a neglect of his Son, of his gospel, of his infinite wisdom and goodness in redemption? Does not a thoughtless life, both deny and disapprove all the counsels of his word and providence? An unbelieving heart, is a rejection of the divine government in the work of redemption, which is to the Lord the most precious of all his works. Whoever intends to abstain from aggravated immorality, and in some future time, become more thorough in religion, thinking he shall grow no worse in the sight of GOD, is under a great delusion. He is becoming worse, and treasuring up wrath against the day of wrath, by neglecting the glorious Redeemer, who is worthy of eternal love and praise. Thus, a secure life is a great increase of guilt; and the security, which is thought to be so harmless, because free perhaps from visible crimes, is adding to the weight of guilt and shutting the thoughtless soul out of heaven. May all, who are now secure, think of this, and awake from the sleep of death, before they are fixed in a state, where the offers of assistance are heard no more. AMEN.

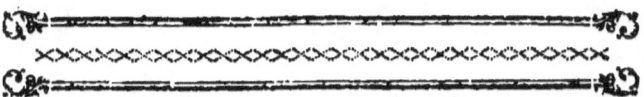

SERMON XII.

The life of faith.

HEBREWS x. 38.

Now the juſt ſhall live by faith—.

THIS epiſtle was written, at a time, when chriſtians were expoſed to great perſecution. The ruling powers of the world, were bitter enemies to the doctrines of CHRIST, and the purity of chriſtian practice. This accounts for many things, in the ſacred epiſtles, deſigned to ſupport believers under outward trials and the loſs of worldly good. The apoſtles endeavoured to animate them, by the conſideration that they were ſuffering for GOD's cauſe. Alſo, by the promiſe of a peaceful enjoyment and communion with their Lord, in the world to which all are going; and by the example of eminent ſaints, who, before their time, had been called to ſuffer for GOD. Theſe, through the efficacy of faith, had acted boldly, ſuffered patiently, and given evidence of a ſtrength derived from heaven. The life of faith, in holy diligence and patience, when exemplified by the conduct of GOD's people, is a high evidence of the reality of religion, and that GOD assists those who trust in him.

A CHRISTIAN life, especially if it be attended with worldly difficulties, carries conviction to the conscience of unbelievers. They are convinced of a principle in the heart, which they never felt; and that, in their own case, there is a want of something, which it would be desirable to have.

A REVIEW of the faith in ancient christians, and the effects it wrought in them, is also animating to us their weaker brethren. It shows the divinity, and sufficiency of our religion; and that the weakness of our own faith, is the only cause we ever shrink back from duty, and despair of the divine care. In the verses before our text, the apostle exhorts christians, to patience and fortitude, under the trials they were called to endure. He tells them *The just shall live by faith.* Faith gives the christian his strength, his diligence, his boldness in the cause of GOD, his patience and firmness under bitter trials, his inflowing of support from CHRIST, his consciousness of a GOD present and cloathed with all perfection, his certainty of a speedy triumph, and an end of his conflict by being received to the presence of CHRIST. Considering these things, as effects which flow from the very nature of faith; and also considering, the darkness, sin and trials of the world in which we live, it may fitly be said *The just shall live by faith.*

ALTHO' the pardon of sin and our acceptance by GOD, is graciously promised to the first exercise of faith; it never becomes unnecessary for the christian. It is as useful in his succeeding life, as it was necessary for his first acceptance. The very same faith, which is required for justification; preserves the union with GOD through

CHRIST, and receives and exerts the strength derived from him. Faith, being continued by the quickening of the Holy Spirit, and exercised in daily trust and obedience, is *the life of faith*, which we are now to consider. By it the ancients obtained a good report; and by it we are to serve GOD in our generation, until he shall take us to himself.

THROUGH the xi. chapter, the power and effects of faith, in a number of glorious examples, are described. In other places, especially in his epistle to the Romans, the apostle Paul described faith as justifying and uniting the soul to GOD; in this place, he describes it as a persevering principle of holy life. This principle was made apparent, by the exercise of spiritual strength, derived from GOD, in suffering for him and acting boldly in his cause. They were enabled to bear and do things impossible to depraved humanity, without such assistance. In the instances recorded, the saints were enabled to trust in the divine word against all natural appearances; to despise the honors and pleasures of the world, when brought in competition with their duty; expose themselves to the greatest danger in honoring GOD and doing good; and endure the most exquisite tortures under the saw and at the stake.

IN a former discourse, we have considered faith, as evidence of things not seen, by discovering to the mind the glory of GOD and his scheme of government. It is in this way, that it gives strength both to do and to suffer. When a christian sees GOD present with him; when eternity is made real to him; when the connection between time and eternity is opened before him; when a divine action in all things is realized and felt; when there is a consciousness of union with Almighty love and wisdom, the weak creature *can do all things, through* CHRIST *who strengtheneth him.* The Lord gives strength to his people, by bringing himself in his glory, his agency and government into their view; and enabling them to feel their own union to the source of holy action.

THE following particulars will illustrate the power of faith, in the christians life.

1st. BY faith he derives constant spiritual life and strength from JESUS CHRIST.

THERE must be a daily receiving, and continued communion with the Saviour to preserve the christian temper, practice and joy. The first coming to CHRIST, begins an intercourse between him and the soul, which will be eternal. He meets the believer, when coming by faith to receive; and from his own fulness, bestows all spiritual graces, with a sense of his own glory, and the joy unspeakable which follows.

As GOD grants his blessing only through CHRIST, and it is faith alone which receives him; it must of course be by faith, that spiritual mercies are received. If the christian backslides and ceases to go and receive; there is an immediate interruption of holy exercise; the sight of GOD's glory is departed; the sense of his gracious presence is lost; and the heart, being left alone, is weak, comfortless, and wretched by the temptations of the world. All this happens from an interruption of faith, which receives spiritual life and strength from GOD. When the channel of receiving is stopped, the sanctifying, enlightening and comforting power of GOD ceases to flow into the soul.

CHRIST plainly told this truth to his disciples. *Abide in me, and I in you. As the branch cannot bear fruit of itself, except it abide in the vine: No more can ye, except ye abide in me. I am the vine, ye are the branches: He that abideth in me, and I in him, the same bringeth forth much fruit: for without me ye can do nothing. If a man abide not in me, he is cast forth as a branch, and is withered: and men gather them, and cast them into the fire, and they are burned.* This passage, forcibly describes, the daily use of faith. The life of a christian is derived. It flows forth from his Saviour GOD, and his faith receives the gracious assistance. His faith is that seeking which finds; that knocking to which entrance is given.

EXPERIENCE witnesses the truth of this description, for while a believer feels his dependance, and goes to GOD for life and strength; while he is willing that GOD should have the glory of giving, he feels grace by a divine energy flow into his soul. He can say, GOD is my helper and my strength. Unworthy as I am, I feel a divine breathing into this polluted temple, and my soul ascends in adoration and praise. Perhaps, faith never applies in this way, without some sensible return, of communicated grace from the Redeemer, who is the way and the life of his people.

BY this communion from above, a general sanctification is promoted; all holy exercises increase in strength; and the conversation is in heaven.

2dly. BY faith, the christian has an habitual apprehension of a present GOD, and is familiarised in his meditations, to the things of the world to come. It has already been described, how his faith becomes evidence of things not seen, by discovering the glory of moral objects, which may be called the peculiar and irresistible christian evidence. This evidence, presented to the mind, produces an habitual apprehension of a present JEHOVAH. As GOD appears to come near, eternity with every thing great and glorious, which is revealed concerning it, approaches with him. As the natural sun arising, spreads glory over the face of creation; so, the rising of the sun of righteousness, in an apprehension of his near presence, discovers the reality of the moral system; that these moments of time, are surrounded with an eternity past and future; and the glory of omnipotence, becomes a reflected light from all his works of creation, providence and redemption. The soul feels the patriarchal description, " *How dreadful is this place! This is none other but the house of* GOD, *and this is the gate of heaven.* GOD, and the things of GOD, become exceeding real.

IT was from this sight of GOD by faith, that David said, " *Thou knowest my down-sitting, and mine up-rising, thou understandest my thoughts afar off. Thou compassest my path and my lying down, and art acquainted with all my ways. There is not a word in my tongue, but lo, O Lord, thou knowest it altogether. Thou hast beset me behind and before, and laid thine hand upon me.—If I ascend into heaven, thou art there: if I make my bed in hell, behold, thou art there. If I take the wings of the morning, and dwell in the uttermost parts of the sea; even there shall thy hand lead me, and thy right hand shall hold me. If I say, surely the darkness shall cover me: even the night shall be light about me.*" He concludes the description by expressing his happiness in this sense of the divine presence. " *How precious also are thy thoughts unto me, O* GOD*! How great is the sum of them! If I should count them,* they are more in number than the sand: when I wake, I am still with thee."

This sense of the divine presence, and the reality and glory of the invisible world always accompanies the life of faith. It is one principal thing which distinguishes the children of GOD from other people, and is generally proportioned to their degree of faith. When it is in low exercise, invisible things do but glimmer on them; sense prevails; temptations attack, and too often overcome; their armour is gone, and for a season they are led captive by the powers of sin. When faith is in high exercise, and open to receive from the divine fountain; all in the soul, is life and strength from GOD, and all around it is glory.

The immediate effects, in the believer, of GOD's being made thus present to him are very glorious. He hath meat to eat, of which the men of the world are ignorant. The glory of GOD, shining through every object around him, is his happiness.—All things, considered as part of the divine plan, appear to be right.—He is willing the government should be the Lord's.—His duty is, also, his pleasure.—He feels himself to be upheld by Almighty power and goodness; a power near at hand, and not afar off, in which he lives and is moved.

How different, in respect of peace, are the conditions, of those who live by faith in GOD, and of such as reject him by unbelief. One is made happy, by a sense of the divine approach; the other is filled with dread. One receives strength from GOD; the other with trembling, tries to fly, but sinks in his own weakness. One rises to meet the opening prospects of eternity, and a more near approach to the throne of GOD;

the other retires from them, as the moſt dreaded of all objects.

3dly. By faith, the chriſtian ſees and rejoices in the providence of God, which irreſiſtibly directs all events that will ever take place.

The providence of God is a glorious truth. It is a ſubject, either full of doubts and gloom to men; or of clearneſs and joy. In each caſe, it is according to the moral ſtate of their hearts. No ſubject has excited more doubts, fears, joys, and pains. While ſome conſider the doctrine, premonitory of their future wretchedneſs; others, eſteem it a truth in which heaven and earth ought to rejoice, and the ſure baſis of created bleſſedneſs. It is not ſtrange, that unholy creatures contend with the univerſal providence of a holy God, and try to diſbelieve. It is a truth oppoſed to their wiſhes; which aſſures the downfall of vice, and its votaries; and an end to the pleaſures of ſin. Theſe pleaſures are permitted for a ſeaſon, that the downfall may be more conſpicuous, and the glory of holineſs more compleat. Not only a fear of evil to come; but alſo a diſreliſh of leading principles in the ſupreme government, and an ignorance of its beauty, will make bad men oppoſed to the doctrine of an univerſal providence, by which all events are efficiently determined. They can ſee no glory in this government, and the mind will try to diſbelieve that, in which it ſees no glory.

The wiſdom of God, in his providence, is an unfathomable deep to angels and men. He does good, in a way ſo much above the higheſt created intellect, that there will be the myſteries of providence, even to the holy. They are often obliged to follow God by faith, in cloudy and dark ways; and if their faith be ſmall, it will be with them as with pious ASAPH, *their feet being almost gone, and their steps well nigh slipping*, thro' the mysteries of the divine government, and the apparent incongruity of GOD's promises and providence.

IF this be the case, in those hours when faith is weak; what cavils and doubts may we not expect in the wicked, who both fear and disrelish the providence of JEHOVAH, and see no beauty in its operations. Sometimes they will doubt; sometimes they will deny; and at all times feel opposed. Seeing no glory of GOD around them, they think he is at a distance, and are tormented between doubting, fearing, and the power of temptation acting on their inbred corruption. This life of unholiness must be a miserable one; for tho' the creature needs a GOD to uphold and a providence to keep him, he dreads to receive either as truth. If he would be honest, to observe his own feelings, he might find in them the embryo existence of that hell, which is threatened in the sure word of revelation.

How blessed! is that state of the heart which delights in the principles of divine government! How excellent the grace which sees the presence of GOD's irresistible providential power, and can rejoice in it!——Here the believer, by his life of faith, is made blessed, confirmed against doubting, and reconciled to what takes place. From an apprehension of the divine presence, he knows there is wisdom, though he cannot trace it; and that the things, which appear dark to human discernment, will be most for GOD's glory and the good of his kingdom. He has accustomed himself to consider a divine agency, in all that happens, even the falling of a hair from the head; so that every thing which he sees, hears or feels leads him up to GOD. Placed in the midst of a scene of life and action, of causes and effects; the whole appears to him the action of God, the great first cause; who is holy, in the midst of the unholiness of his creatures; pure, in permitting from the most glorious motives, that which they do from motives the most base and worthy of punishment. In sight of this providence constantly acting, and every where existent; binding all the parts of the universe into one most perfect plan, tending to the most perfect end; in sight, by faith, of the glorious and blessed kingdom, which will be formed by the energy of the power and wisdom that now worketh; in sight of the union between things in heaven, and things on earth, in Jesus Christ the Lord, by whom all things were created and are named, the holy, believing soul *rejoices with joy unspeakable and full of glory.* The faith, which can see this providence in nature and grace, will give a blessed life on earth and triumphant entrance into eternity.

4thly. By faith, the just are enabled to support an habitual apprehension, of the vanity and unsatisfying nature of all earthly things.

It has been said, that faith brings God and the things of eternity into view of the mind. In sight of these, if the heart be right, it may be expected that all present things will sink in esteem. *Vanity of vanities,* is the true description which infinite truth and wisdom hath given of the world. By this, it is not meant, that the present state of things is badly adapted to the end designed by governing wisdom. A world, better adapted to the end of its existence, infinite wisdom could not form; and thus the good man views it, therefore does not repine at what God permits, or think he could have ordered better.

Still, compared with what is to follow, the present appears vain to him, in point of inherent excellency, of duration and of power to satisfy the mind. Without undervaluing present good, or want of gratitude for what is now received, his sight of another state by faith, draws his affections hence to the pleasures in heaven. He says, with truth, this is not my home; these idols of the world, are not my GODS; I long for the full vision of what faith hath discovered, and in contemplation of that discovery, thirst to be with CHRIST which is far better. It is this prospect by faith, which weans the disciples of CHRIST from the world, making them pilgrims and strangers in the earth, seeking a habitation, a city not made with hands, eternal in the heavens. They have not lost a relish for happiness, as the unholy may suppose; but have a taste for moral glory and a society different from this world.

5thly. By faith the christian can with fortitude bear affliction; especially, if called to meet it in the service of CHRIST, and to promote his cause in the world.

AFFLICTIONS are, naturally, as terrifying to christians, as to others; and they will either repine or sink under them, if not supported by a fiducial trust in GOD. Natural evil, of every kind, is in its nature undesirable, and the mind can be reconciled to it, only by seeing moral wisdom in the appointment. It was this which enabled one saint to say, " *Though he slay me I will trust in him;*" and another, " *Although the fig-tree shall not blossom, neither shall fruit be in the vines; The labour of the olive shall fail, and the fields shall yield no meat; The flocks shall be cut off from the fold, and there be no herd in the stalls; yet will I rejoice in the Lord, I will joy in the* God *of my salvation.*" Faith beholds God in afflictions, and receives them as a Father's wisdom and goodness. Jesus set the example, who prayed, *If it be possible let this cup pass from me, nevertheless, not my will but thine be done ;* and his people, actuated by the same principles, can follow him.

There are sundry considerations which will enable the afflicted christian to acquiesce, yea, even to glory in tribulation. He feels his own desert, and can kiss the rod, as being deservedly appointed. He sees God glorify himself, and can joyfully suffer, that the Lord may be honored. He relies on the promise, that afflictions shall purify him, and with pleasure reads the covenant, "*If they break my statutes, and keep not my commandments : then will I visit their transgression with the rod, and their iniquity with stripes. Nevertheless my loving kindness will I not utterly take from him, nor suffer my faithfulness to fail. My covenant will I not break, nor alter the thing that is gone out of my lips.*" He considers the divine government as a perfect system, neither defective nor redundant in its parts, and all leading to the most glorious end, in God's display of his own nature and the creatures enjoyment of him.

Faith, places even the afflicted christian, in the mount of triumph. The place of affliction is often his Pisgah, and the time of suffering is the hour of his ascent, from whence he views the heavenly Canaan and his God. Raised to the mount by faith, with a perfect confidence in God he hears and sees the storms of time beat at its foot. Though his body is pained his mind is at ease ; though the world is his enemy, God is his friend ; though his earthly prospects are desolated, he finds a sufficient portion in this truth, that the Lord reigns. It is only by the life of faith in GOD, that this peace can be attained.

IT would surpass my present limits, even to hint all the benefits of a life of faith. It is thus that duty is made easy and pleasant.—Fear of men is removed.—The path of duty, and the performance of it, are as a shining light, shining more and more unto the perfect day.—JESUS is beheld, reigning in his own Zion, and promoting his cause, both by the obedience of friends and the opposition of enemies.—The world with its temptations, and the flesh with its lusts are conquered.—God is seen governing the nations, and pointing the wrath of men, who mean not so, to the completion of his glorious counsels.—The peaceful, humble believer, is guided through a world of turbulence and pride, until he quietly sleeps in the arms of JESUS.

THIS subject must teach the deficiency and guilt of christians, in the present day of deep declension.

THO'. GOD doth not leave any of his called to final desertion ; they are often left to great backsliding, to lose their first love, and live too much conformed to the manners and spirit of the world. What cause christians have to blush! to mourn and weep for themselves! and confess a departure from GOD.—From whence doth this come ?—Is there any defect in the gospel scheme through which they have been called ?—Is there not a fulness, in the power and grace, which first raised them into spiritual life ?—Is not GOD faithful to his promise, that those who seek shall find ?—Is not the way, in which they first went to GOD for life and holiness, still open to apply, and to receive fresh communications of such grace as will make them faithful, holy, and abounding in the joy of their Lord?—Certainly the way is open; Jesus still reigns; God still reigns, and hears every prayer that is fiducially offered to his name; there is strength enough in God, and he never denied granting to the prayer of faith. "*Draw nigh to God, and he will draw nigh to you,*" is a promise which will never be infracted. All this lowness in the duties and comforts of a christian's life, arises from the failure of faith. God is out of sight, the shining of his glory in the soul has ceased, and there is no application to receive from the fountain of spiritual life; consequently, lusts break forth afresh, and the world conquers.

The ancient cloud of witnesses, who by their patience, zeal and good works, showed a connexion with heaven and the power of God acting in them, all lived by faith. Thus they were enabled to witness in their lives and by their death. They were living evidence for the power of divine grace, and the excellence of holiness. When faith fails, and love waxes cold, it will not be thus; and the cold, formal lives of christian professors, will be a means of hardening sinners in their infidelity. Thus Christ is dishonored, his cause is weakened, christianity is ridiculed, and christians themselves become a stumbling block, over which unbelievers fall into eternal destruction. This state of christians is a wilful sin; for though they have not spiritual strength in themselves, there is a fountain, where it exists in infinite abundance, and a promised way of drawing it from the eternal source. *He that abideth not in me, is cast forth as a branch, and is withered.* The moment they leave Christ, through whom God communicates his grace; the sensible power of religion in the soul will cease, and visible duties, though retained, will be performed in a very formal manner. The scriptures call this state "*having the form without the power of Godliness,*" and to all such the admonition of CHRIST applies. *I know thy works, that thou art neither cold nor hot: I would that thou wert cold or hot. So then, because thou art lukewarm, and neither cold nor hot: I will spew thee out of my mouth.*

MULTITUDES, who think they have experienced the sanctifying grace of GOD, are in this state. If they think right, GOD will not leave them to a final falling away; for the same gracious power which called them from total sin, can reclaim from deep backsliding. But is it the comfort of a real christian to think he shall in some future time be awaked from his sleep? It was not thus with CHRIST our great example. His meat and drink was, at the present time, to do the Father's will and glorify him. The true christian comfort is to be constant in beholding and glorifying GOD. To hope without present evidence is a presumptuous thing. To hope without a present faith is hoping in the midst of misery. I am sensible, that unholy persons do not conceive the true comfort of religion, and this is one principal reason they think christians to be joyless people; but this is not the only reason. Many who think themselves to be christians are really unhappy. In a state of backsliding they halt between two opinions. They know the world will not satisfy, and are afraid to mingle unrestrainedly with its pleasures; and at the same time, are so lukewarm, so weak in faith, as cuts them off from the happiness of sensible communion with GOD.—This is indeed a joyless state, which is often discovered and improved by the ungodly, as evidence against the excellence of piety. It ought not to be thus. Christians ought to show they are happy in their Redeemer, and they never can do this without the life of faith. The declension which dishonors CHRIST, doth also wound their own souls.

SUCH backsliders ought not to expect the supporting presence of GOD in the hour of death. It has, sometimes, been thought strange, that among those who are hoped to be sincere, there are so many instances, in which their death bed is deprived of the high comforts of religion. But it must be expected that a life low in faith, will be followed by a death of the same kind. Infinite wisdom, in particular instances, may vary from his general manner of dispensing. There may be reasons for a life of eminent faith to be left in darkness at death, and for a great backslider to be filled with triumphant joy; but this is not common. The frequent imparture of high comforts in death, to those who have lived low in faith, would be too great evidence in favor of christian deficiency; and take off from natural fear, which the wisdom of GOD improves in exciting men to diligence; therefore it may not be expected.

LET the people of GOD endeavour to feel their own defects, their weakness, their need of constant communication from CHRIST who is the way and the life. Let them look immediately to GOD to increase their love and faith, and with hearts emptied of human strength and dependance, look directly to him who gives of his own fulness, knowing that it is GOD who worketh in them both to will and to do. AMEN.

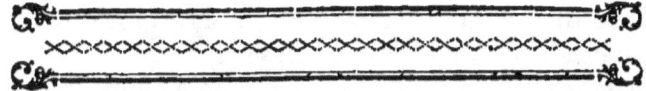

SERMON XIII.

Evangelical Repentance.

EZEKIEL xxxvi. 31.

Then shall ye remember your own evil ways, and your doings that were not good, and shall loathe yourselves in your own sight, for your iniquities, and for your abominations.

IT is known that the Jews are a people cast off by God. For their disobedience, and especially for their rejection of the Messiah, the awful denunciations in the prophecy of Moses, have been long in execution. As he foretold, they are scattered among the nations of the whole world, and have suffered incredible miseries by the hands of other men.

Tho' we hope their period of misery is drawing to a close, the curse appears to be still in force; and it is a wonderful evidence, for the truth of the christian scriptures. God hath told us, in the word of prophecy, there shall be limits to this state of punishment; when the Jews, together with the fulness of the Gentile nations, shall be united in the peaceable, holy, glorious and everlasting kingdom of CHRIST.

WHEN the conversion of that people happens, they will be as eminent in their zeal for the Redeemer, as they have been for their opposition and bitterness to his cause. Their restoration is also foretold, in such language, as implies they shall be gathered into the same land which was given to Abraham, and which their fathers, for many ages possessed.

THE particular events leading to a recovery of their former country, and its complete accomplishment; are either untold, or expressed in a prophetic manner difficult to be understood before it is unfolded by the fulfilment. The restoration of that people, with its accompanying circumstances, will be the completion of a long chain of evidence for the truth of revealed religion. This began in the calling of the patriarch Abraham, and hath been, and will continue to be carried on, in the events happening to his family, and in GOD's dealings with them; until they are brought to the lasting possession of the promised earthly inheritance. The concluding evidence will be the greatest. It will be attended with events most astonishing to mankind, and most convincing that JEHOVAH is GOD, and his scriptures the word of truth.

WE are in the begining of an eventful period, in which the scheme of divine evidence for his own truth, is rapidly disclosing by the natural events that now are, and will very soon happen, conformable to the predictions of his word; among these, the conversion and recal of the Jews to their ancient land, will be a principal event.

A PROMISE of this recal, and the temper with which they shall return to GOD is contained in the chapter, from which the text is taken. By his prophet God defcribes their difperfion; the great difhonor they fhould do to his name, by their conduct among the people where they fhould be carried; and then lets them know, that after this, for his name and mercy's fake, he would bring them to repentance and be their God. And that as the judgments they fuffered, magnified his juftice, his holinefs and hatred of fin; fo their repentance and return would honor his grace, and teach the children of men, the exceeding riches of his mercy.

He is very particular in telling them, *" Not for your fakes will I do this, O houfe of Ifrael, be it known unto you; but for my own great name's fake."* I will do it for my own honor; the honor of my grace; and that men may every where know, I am the Lord of the whole earth, and can direct national events with as much eafe, as I ordain the condition of individuals.

The honor of his fovereignty, and acting in all things for his glory and mercy's fake, is what God every where claims in his word; and in his government he is careful to maintain it. Creation flowed forth from his will, and muft forever be governed according to the fovereign counfel of uncreated wifdom.

It is required, as a condition of mercy to finners, that they be willing to depend on fovereign grace; and when brought to evangelical repentance, they rejoice to have it fo. This may be learned from the defcription of repentance found in the text. The verfe defcribes, what the penitent feelings of Ifrael will be, after they are reclaimed by the gracious power of God, and look back, in the exercife of a chriftian fpirit, on their own paft conduct.

Then shall ye remember your own evil ways, and your doings which were not good, and shall loathe yourselves in your own sight, for your iniquities, and for your abominations.

Let us improve these words for our own instruction in the nature of a gracious repentance; and then collect from the text, some marks of trial, whether we have sincerely repented before God.

I. We inquire the nature of evangelical or saving repentance.

As we are, in our own case, exposed to mistake, there being many affections of the mind, which in some respects resemble holy exercise; we should labour for distinguishing ideas of that repentance towards God, to which final salvation is promised. We may do much, which appears like the fruit of repentance to those who are observing us, and may be so esteemed by ourselves; while it doth not thus appear to God, the great and omniscient judge of hearts. We may think much about our being sinners; may take much pains to find what is called sinful by the law of God; may be afraid of sin; may with great agitation of spirit mourn that we have transgressed; may be convinced that every violation of the divine law is unreasonable, and on principles of public justice, exposes us to punishment; all this may be, without such repentance as is required by Jesus Christ.

The connexion between sin and misery is so well known, and has been felt so long; there is danger, through this association of ideas, of thinking we loathe sin, when the abhorrence arises, entirely from the misery that is expected to follow.—Through selfish prejudices, it is many times difficult, in our own case, to distinguish between the legal repentance which hates misery, and the evangelical which abhors sin. To determine this, we ought often to inquire of our hearts, why is sin so evil a thing? And why do we feel opposed to it? If the only answer we can obtain of our own hearts is this; that hereby we are personally exposed to pain, affliction, and the death of the body; and that GOD, a being of such power as we cannot overcome, denounces his anger to pursue us in time and through eternity; it is no evidence of a gracious mourning for sin.—All this may be, with hearts opposed to the divine character. All this may be, without a supreme love of GOD, and with such a relish of heart, as would commit sin with greediness, if the penalty were removed.

TRUE repentance has respect to the infinite nature and perfection of GOD, which creates an obligation on all creatures to love and serve him, and abstain from every thing, by which he is dishonored and his kingdom injured. David, in the hour of penitence, and in contemplation of a sin, which was the highest outrage upon purity and the justice due to men; still confessed to GOD, *against thee, thee only have I sinned.* A sense of violated obligation to GOD, and of the dishonor done to his name, swallowed up all other considerations of mourning. He was not insensible of the injury done his subjects, and the church; but injury done to GOD, pierced him with the deepest sorrow. Holy Job thus describes his own repentance. *I have heard of thee by the hearing of the ear, but now mine eye seeth thee; wherefore I abhor myself and repent in dust and ashes.* In this case a sight of GOD, and sense of violated obligation to him, were evidently the cause of holy sorrow. Hence it is called, *repentance to-*

wards God. A mourning for sin, as committed against the perfection, the rights, and glory of the Lord.

An evangelical penitent, rising above selfish regards, beholds an infinite God, glorious in holiness and worthy of all obedience. He beholds a scheme of creation and created good, to which all sinful principles and practice are opposed.—A law, just and good, which forbids transgression; a supreme government of the whole, conducted in infinite reason, and aiming at great and eternal good. In view of these, his sin appears great beyond description. It seems to him more base than finite conception can comprehend. As is the deepness of mourning for a first born; such is the depth of sorrow, for his own vileness and ingratitude. The affliction of his soul is of such a nature, as withdraws his thoughts from an apprehension of danger to himself, and fixes them on the odiousness of sin, and the unspeakable guilt of opposing a glorious God. When sin is thus apprehended, there is no difficulty in confessing it to be an infinite evil. The cavils of a contradicting heart are silenced. The disputatious philosophy of men, and all palliating descriptions are banished. The penitent wishes for words, of a thousand fold more descriptive energy, than human language contains, that he may use them in confessing his vileness before God.

One great difference, between legal and evangelical repentance, arises from the motive of sorrow. In both, there is a sorrow for sin; though the two states of the heart from which they proceed, are in direct moral opposition, and one dislikes, in the most essential respects, what the other loves. If it were left, to the choice and power of the two characters, to make a heaven; they would act on oppoſing principles, and the heaven of one would be a hell to the other. Place the greateſt and moſt unholy ſinner on a death bed; let him know he is going directly before a GOD, who is oppoſed to him, and will puniſh ſin in a very extreme degree; let him believe there is a place of torment, and that death will be his entrance into it; and he cannot refrain ſorrowing that he hath ſinned. In the moment of agitation, it is not probable he will diſtinguiſh between a hatred of ſin, and a hatred of miſery; and thus ſuppoſe himſelf a ſincere mourner before GOD. It is on this account, that a death-bed repentance is ſo open to be ſuſpected of inſincerity, if there hath been no previous penitence. In moſt ſuch inſtances, if the proſpect of immediate danger ceaſes, the mourning for ſin and the imagined diſlike of it are felt no more. The reſcued ſinner returns to his vice with new eagerneſs. In ſuch caſes, we have no reaſon to ſuppoſe there is repentance towards GOD. Pain and loſs are the thing lamented; and if there could be a way to avoid theſe, the mourning ſoul would mourn no longer.

IT is not thus with the gracious penitent. His heart is right—ſin is contrary to his taſte—the thing itſelf is unpalatable. There is no need of danger and pain to make him ſee its unreaſonable nature. He laments the diſhonor done to a glorious GOD, and condemns the cauſe of it, and can condemn himſelf, as readily, as he would another.

THE difference of motive, in theſe two ſtates of the heart, is eaſily conceived by all true penitents; but ſuch is the blindneſs of impenitence, that there are ſome caſes of great obduracy, in which it is hard to communicate, even a doctrinal deſcription of the ſubject.

II. I AM to confider thofe marks for trial and felf-examination, which are contained in the text.

1. IN the text it is faid " then fhall ye remember your own evil ways, and your doings that were not good." Thofe who are brought to a faving repentance, are difpofed to look back on their own ways, and hide nothing from GOD or their own fight.

A LEGAL repentance wifhes to fearch and fee no more of fin and its evil, than will barely fuffice for fafety. Fear is the principle of action, and an efcape from danger is the object fought. When there is a fuppofition of fafety, this point being gained, there is an end of the fearch; and it becomes more pleafing to forget and throw a veil of oblivion, than to fearch deep into the heart, or by remembrance look back on many doings that were not good.

IN an evangelical repentance, the heart being right, fin itfelf is feared and would be feared, though no perfonal danger attended. It is feared on account of its bad nature, and its injurioufnefs to GOD and his kingdom. To be freed from unholinefs is a reigning defire in the foul, and for this purpofe, it becomes neceffary to look deep into the heart, and examine motives, defires and ends—to look back, remembering old habits, difpofitions and actions. A defire of turning the eye from our fins, and of extenuating them, ceafes. Their number and aggravations are fought out diligently. GOD is befought, by earneft prayer, to affift in the examination; and his pure, omnifcient fpirit is invoked for aid. The prayer of David is often made, "*fearch me and try me, and fee if there be any evil way in me.*"

The spiritual mourner for sin, often compares his thoughts, words and actions with the holy law—with gospel precepts—and with the Saviour's holy life; that he may know the extent of his own sin. When by searching he sees any sin, not before discovered; though he mourns for the evil, he rejoices in the knowledge of it, that he may confess to God and purify himself. This will always take place, in that repentance, which is accompanied with a love of God and dislike of sin. Although a love of danger and misery is not natural to men, and in no case a duty; yet the escaping of danger, is but a smaller motive, with the evangelical penitent. In a legal repentance danger excited him, and he wished to know only so much, either of his past or present sin, as was absolutely necessary for an escape. When holy mourning succeeds the legal fear, danger is much less thought off, and the exceeding sinfulness of sin becomes a burden on the heart; tears of grief gush from the eye, for having been so impenitent and base.

Then, God was feared as a threatening judge; now, he is feared as a being so excellent and worthy, that it is evil beyond description to act against him. Then, the law was feared because it has a penalty annexed to it, and a terror of the penalty stung the mind; now, it is feared, on account of holy obligation, which is sacredly binding on all creatures.

It is not strange that a person, with this state of heart, should be willing to look deep—to look over a whole life—and go back far as memory can help, that all may be confessed before God. When of another temper, he feared divine omniscience, lest his sin should be known; now he rejoices in this glorious perfection, that God may see and discover to him, the extent of his corruption.

2. A HOLY repentance is attended with self-loathing. "*Ye shall loathe yourselves in your own sight, for your iniquities and your abominations.*" TRUE holiness is, in all respects, different from the sinful temper, which is natural to men.

LOATHING himself, is a paradox to the natural man, and having no experience, he thinks it must be a miserable state. Self is his lawgiver and GOD; and self-advancement the rule by which he measures right and wrong, loathsomeness and agreeableness. Let the idol of self be thrown down, and the true GOD throned in the affections, in this respect, all things become new. Reason and judgment are set at liberty, and the most GOD-exalting doctrines and duties appear most excellent to the mind.

THE mourner in Zion sees that GOD is glorious, in being opposed to his former character, and that all good creatures, by their aversion to his former temper and delights, give the highest evidence of the rectitude of their own hearts. Even, if GOD had prepared no punishment for sin; the spiritual mourner, in lively exercise of repentance, would determine it better to cease existence, than to remain forever with so base and unjustifiable a disposition.

To this description of penitential feelings it may be objected. If repentance, in its nature, implies self-loathing, the gospel penitent must always be an unhappy person.

To which I reply, this is an objection, which will never be made by those, who have experienced the grace of repentance in their own hearts.

The self-loathing mentioned, is not a loathing of their own existence, or any of the natural powers, faculties and capacities GOD hath given them. Existence, simply considered, is always desirable; and it is the perversion of it, which to holy minds becomes an object of dislike. Penitents are not made perfectly holy, and so far as they find sin reigning in them, they must be unhappy; for sin is the affliction of a christian. It is not proper to call this the unhappiness of repentance; for if the christian were made perfect by the sanctifying power of divine grace, in a loathing of his former corruptions he would be perfectly blessed. It is the remainder of sin, and not the loathing of it; which makes unhappiness, in the present state of GOD's people. Those, who have experienced this state of mind, will readily answer, our self-aversion on account of sin, is so far from making us miserable; that it is a necessary ingredient of a blessedness, the most pure and perfect we ever enjoyed. Our sin is our unhappiness; but our self-loathing is our comfort. We feel a consciousness of being right, so far as we can abhor remaining transgression.

To be a spiritual mourner, is very often an exceeding peaceful state of mind, and accompanied with that light of GOD's countenance, which gives joy unspeakable and full of glory.

THOSE, who have not true religion, often think a life of piety to be an unhappy one. To them it is inconceivable, how others can be happy in spiritual duties, in thinking so much of GOD, and in worshipping him so often. As they do not think of another world, except when driven by terrors of conscience, they are ready to think pious people must be driven by similar terrors, and therefore must be miserable; herein is a great mistake, for pious people are drawn by love, and not forced to duty by terrors of confcience. The heart of one is wholly different from the other. A love of God, will make a life of confecration to him, in the duties of religious obedience, a very pleafant one. As God is, in his nature, more excellent than the creatures ; fo the happinefs of ferving him, will be greater and far more fatisfying, than any enjoyment of the creatures.

By this fubject we ought to examine ourfelves. Truth is of little fervice to us, without an immediate application to the ftate of our own hearts. Examination difcovers us to ourfelves. Do we remember our evil ways and our doings which were not good ? Do we look deep into our own hearts, and encourage confcience to fpeak freely, that the worft of our cafe may be difcovered ? Do we loath ourfelves for our iniquities againft a holy Lord God ? Doubtlefs mifery is difguftful; but this is not enough, and is no evidence of a good eftate. May the Lord, of his infinite mercy, enlighten, fanctify and prepare us for his heavenly kingdom. Amen.

SERMON XIV.

The objects of christian love.

1 JOHN iv. 16.

—He that dwelleth in love, dwelleth in God—

IN this state of sin, our minds are not good enough to attain the most just notions of divine things. Through the darkness of sin, we are hindered from such doctrinal knowledge, as all would have, if our hearts were right. In subjects, which are really within the reach of mens finite understanding; we often remain in speculative ignorance, through the influence of a bad heart, on the faculty of understanding and judgment. There is no object, to which the sinful mind is more powerfully blinded by an evil heart of sin, than the KINGDOM OF HOLINESS. This kingdom is infinite, for GOD the head of it is so in his own nature; and the created parts, though not in their own nature infinite, are the emanation of infinite action, energy, power and wisdom from the creator. They are a finite effect, which will glorify an infinite cause.

This kingdom of holiness, containing God himself and his intelligent creation, is the object of holy love. This object, though it can never be comprehended by creatures; to those who obtain a true sight of it, exceeds in glory, and they perceive themselves filled with blessedness by the enjoyment. Even a partial sight brings conviction into the mind, that the object, though not comprehended, in its nature, is the greatest possible; and that a full enjoyment would be perfect blessedness.

It is this kingdom of holiness, united in moral character, which is held up as an object of love by the revelation which we have from heaven. Conformable to this is the command, *Thou shalt love the Lord thy God, with all thy heart, with all thy strength, and with all thy mind; and thou shalt love thy neighbour as thyself.*

God and our neighbour compose this kingdom. A love of God and our neighbour is the whole law—and a perfect compliance, is perfection in holiness.

By attending to the word LOVE, in the extensive use made of it by the sacred writers, it is apparent, they meant the whole of that, in which morality or holiness of character, temper and action consist. *God is love*, and in this is his whole worthiness. If this be his nature; his law, gospel, government, and every true expression of himself must be the same. *Love is the fulfilling of his law*, and therefore nothing more will be required from any of his creatures, be their powers of acting what they may. The perpetuity of this in angels is their standing in holiness; and the restoral of it to men, through the gospel, is their christian perfection. *He that dwelleth in love, dwelleth in God—Every one that loveth is born of God*—These passages, describe God as the source, from which holiness proceedeth into the hearts of his creatures; and the exercise of it, as a moral union with him and his kingdom. The phrase, *dwelling in GOD*, is expressive to the greatest degree, and describes the highest union that the nature of GOD and creatures can admit. One being dwelling in another, must imply every thing short of an absolute identity of existence; and such is the goodness of JEHOVAH, that he gives his holy creatures, every thing except his own unalienable nature and rights.

THE words of our text, *He that dwelleth in love, dwelleth in GOD*, may therefore be considered, as describing both the christian's character and the objects of his affection. It is to the last of these it will be applied in the following discourse. In character, he is so far conformed to DEITY himself as a creature can be to an infinite creator; and in the objects of his affection and choice there is a complete sameness. Dwelling in GOD, is choosing him in his whole GODHEAD, and in all his counsels and works. According to the degree of knowledge communicated, in the perfectly holy creature, there is as complete a union of interest and will, as there is between the Father and the Son.

THRO' the weakness of human conception, the glorious kingdom of holiness must be viewed by us in its parts, as they successively come before the understanding. The great object of holy affection, must by us be considered as a number of objects, connected in the counsel of GOD, but of the same holy nature. A union to these objects by love, is a sufficient proof we belong to GOD and his kingdom.

1. God himself is the object of supreme christian affection.

He is the fountain of excellent being, to whom all love is due, and the excellence of the streams is communicated from him. In the fervor of devotion Asaph said, *" Whom have I in heaven but thee? And there is none on earth that I desire besides thee.* In the divine character, as he hath described himself by his works and word, every thing appears amiable to a good heart. All the attributes of his glorious nature; all the counsels of his infinite wisdom; and all the energy of his action in creating, governing and redeeming, delight the soul. Divine loveliness is a center on which the affections rest, with a full satisfaction; so that nothing can be wanted nor any thing added. This is meant by the commandment, " *Thou shalt love the Lord thy* God *with all thy heart, with all thy strength, and all thy mind.*

Tho' the divine character is discovered to us by the creatures, the heart doth not rest in these; but ascends through them as a medium of discovery, up to God himself, and rejoices exceedingly in his glory. All the divine perfections, wisdom, truth, justice, mercy and forbearance are loved with the same intensity of affection. This love is of that kind which produces obedience and submission; so that when it is in exercise, trials do not cause impatience or a wish to have the divine nature and will changed. God is omnipotent and his glory fills every place, so that thus dwelling in God by love, must be a state of great peace.

2dly. The revealed law is an object of christian love. There are many expressions of this in the holy scripture. *O how I love thy law, I meditate on it day and night. The law of thy mouth is better than gold. I delight in thy law. The law of the Lord is perfect converting the soul. I behold wondrous things out of thy law.* All who are good, will unite in these descriptions, and this is a reason why the holy scriptures are read with such pleasure. They exhibit the moral commandments which are a chief object of holy love. The revealed law promotes two important purposes. It teaches our duty to God and men, and describes to us the divine character; so that the good mind will repair to the law, both to know what he ought to be, and to behold the Lord.

In this respect, there is a great difference between the sinner and the sanctified. The sinner reads the scriptures, only to know how he may escape danger; the sanctified to find, behold and adore their heavenly king.

It is difficult to suppose any person a true christian, who daily neglects the scriptures. If God be loved supremely and the heart delight in him as its chief treasure; if it be pleasant to meditate on the unsearchable riches of his glory, and conceive of him, as according to his own infinite knowledge he hath described himself, how can such an one neglect the written law? In this the Lord makes himself present to us—brings infinite wisdom down to the apprehension of feeble and blind sinners—describes his goodness, with all the diversification of moral excellence, into which it spreads—and reveals to us the great end of infinite action. Receiving the law with love, is dwelling in love, which is dwelling in God; and is evidence of holiness prepared to enter into the joys of the eternal kingdom in the presence of God forevermore.

3dly. Jesus Christ, the Son of God and son of man, in the fulness of his mediatorial character, is a chief object of christian love and adoraration.

On him, the holy mind looks with reverential delight, for he possesseth the *fulness of the* Godhead *bodily, and is the express image of* God. *Unto all who believe he is precious.*

All men who doctrinally believe there is salvation in no other name beside Christ, will see something which they call loveliness in the Mediator's character.——It is therefore fit I should mention, the different grounds of that loveliness, which is seen by a believer, and an impenitent mind.

The threatening and prospect of misery is undesirable to all. To every one, means of deliverance from misery are acceptable. After hearing a description of eternal pain, to which all are exposed, without a salvation of grace, the possibility of escape must be a pleasing truth. Thus far the mind may go without any self-denial. It may indulge in present sin—be in full opposition to the doctrines and precepts of the gospel; and still be highly pleased with the truth, that there is a way through Christ, in which eternal misery may be escaped. Christ may appear lovely as a deliverer from natural evil. This is not uncommon for those who live under gospel light. Neither is it uncommon for them, to mistake this notion of excellence in the Redeemer, for that preciousness which a true believer sees in his character. In this case, neither the real evil of sin, nor the guilty state of every unpardoned sinner, nor the true excellence of the Saviour, are seen. There is only a distant apprehension of one who will deliver from a distant danger; and it is supposed he will be very precious when the danger comes near. All this passes in the mind without any clear apprehensions of sin, of guilt, and a loveliness of character in the redeeming God. It is in this loose way that unholy men may love CHRIST; and their supposed safety makes them secure in sin. They are inattentive to their hearts, praising God with the mouth while, in practice they deny him.

THOSE who dwell in God through JESUS CHRIST, see far different and greater glories in his character, and he becomes the object of their affection for more noble causes. In him they see the glory of a divine nature and love him as they love the Father. The mediatorial excellency with which they are delighted contains many particulars, of which a principal one is, that he hath honored God—hath revealed him—displayed his perfections—glorified his truth, justice and goodness—caused the divine attributes through his own face to shine on benighted sinners, and by the same means brought the greatest honor to God, and a most rich salvation to the guilty. When divine honor is near the heart, CHRIST will be loved for having glorified the Father; and in meditating on mediatorial excellence, this is selected as a reason for admiring him.

HE loves CHRIST JESUS for having *magnified the law, and made it honourable.*

To a pure mind the law appears very excellent, and being an expression of God's most holy will is an object of ardent love. Both the precepts and penalty of the law, are made more glorious than could be without the gospel, and CHRIST is precious for having magnified the commandment. Every christian heart is united to the commandment and all the means by which it is gloriously displayed.

The Redeemer is precious to a holy mind, for the display he hath made of the nature, principles and end of divine government. It is thro' the Son, that God's infinite wisdom and goodness and the perfection of his government are brought into the fullest light. Whatever the law says, the gospel approves; whatever nature discovers, the gospel confirms; and it still goes further in displaying the glories of Godhead—the excellence of his perfections—his great design in creation—the pure maxims of his universal government—the perfect justice and mercy of that administration, which flows from his nature and partakes of his holiness—the vast amount of blessedness, which will be communicated from him to his surrounding family—and his fixed purpose, as he hath begun, so to govern forever. These are the greatest causes of christian affection to the Mediator.

While gratitude for personal favors is high in the pious heart; the honor of God, his law and his government, which is promoted through the Saviour, produces a still higher affection to the Redeemer. Thus Christ is precious and beloved by all who believe—thus he is loved for having glorified the Father—magnified the law—revealed the kingdom—and united in himself both the things in heaven and the things in earth. In admiration of this vast object, the christian forgets himself and rejoices in God alone.—How different is this delight in Christ, from the love exercised by an unsanctified mind! How different from a love of him for sake of the loaves! How different from loving him through the false notions, that he hath lowered down the requirements of the law, or repealed its penalties, or died for us in particular. All these notions may consist with the pride of human nature, and without any true apprehenſion of the moral glories in GODHEAD, which emanate from him to the knowledge of creation, through his law, goſpel, and univerſal government.

4thly. ALL the doctrines of the goſpel are delightful to a chriſtian. The divine ſcheme of grace is according to the will of GOD, according to his holy nature, and in all reſpects worthy of infinite purity. The obligation to holineſs, ſubmiſſion, renunciation of ourſelves, and a perfect obedience to the law, is greater on every creature after hearing the goſpel than it could be before. It is this which cauſes ſo many objections to the evangelical ſcheme, and divides a world profeſſedly chriſtian, in their opinion of its doctrines. All men to whom doctrinal inſtruction comes will go ſome length towards receiving it. Feeling guilt and miſery, when the news of deliverance is announced, it is acceptable. When they are told, that ſalvation is through a ſacrifice of himſelf made by the Son, and that GOD is very merciful in this way, it is ſtill acceptable. Indeed they will go every length in approbation, until called to part with ſin—give up their unholy pleaſures—humble themſelves that GOD may be all in all—and be holy as he is holy. Here is the parting point between miſerable ſinners and the goſpel of grace. Here ariſes an oppoſition to evangelical doctrines, which hath divided the profeſſing chriſtian world into parties. Theſe perſons are not chriſtians indeed. They wiſh deliverance from a law terrible to them, while they cleave to the very temper which is forbidden. They do not reject chriſtianity, but do not reliſh ſuch a ſyſtem of united grace and holineſs. They make various attempts to ſeparate from the

F f

scheme of mercy, such doctrines as are most unpallatable; and to build a superstructure of faith, which will save without humbling them so low, and without that holiness, which consecrates to God the whole being and all the service of the creatures.

It is not thus with the christian indeed. Every doctrine of revelation is an object of his affection, and he doth not wish any article of faith or practice to be changed. He sees the excellence of truth in every doctrine, and feels the whole to be worthy of God and applicable to the wretched state of fallen sinners. He believes the depravity which is charged on men—feels it in himself—and beholds it in his fellow creatures. He sees that no other gospel could glorify God, sanctify the unholy, and forgive the guilty. He wishes salvation, in a way, that will give to God all the glory both of purchasing and applying; so that the doctrines of atonement, free justification, divine sovereignty, renovation by the Spirit of the Lord, abiding in Christ by faith, and doing all for the glory of God, are the very truth which bind him fast to the scheme of grace. With great humility of heart he rejoices in this system of mercy, and knows the whole to be worthy of infinite wisdom and love.

I may, particularly, mention the christian doctrine of self-denial, as one which gives pleasure to a sanctified heart. Christ often told his followers, that unless they *denied themselves and took up the cross* they could not be his disciples. To deny a few worldly pleasures, or bear some occasional worldly evils without murmuring against God, is not the whole that is meant by these precepts. It is difficult for unholy minds to go only thus far, and further they never go. The meaning of the doctrine—the true christian self-denial is to give up ourselves; not only to bear some hard things, and deny some worldly pleasures, which may be done on lucrative principles, in expectation of a future repayment; but to give up our whole selves, and willingly become nothing that God may be all in all. This doctrine of self-denial is pleasant to all who are renewed through the gospel of our Lord Jesus Christ, and their happiness is most perfect, when all their powers, faculties, and exertions are absorbed in devotion to God, and the service of his holy and righteous kingdom.

5thly. It is the law of God, " *Thou shalt love thy neighbour as thyself*"—" *Beloved, let us love one another: for love is of God; and every one that loveth, is born of God, and knoweth God.*" Also our text saith, " *He that dwelleth in love, dwelleth in God.*"

All the holy are proper objects of a complacent love, and all our intelligent fellow creatures of a benevolent affection; both of which are found in the heart of every christian. A love of God and of our neighbour are necessarily and uniformly connected; so that the absence of one, in all cases, determines the other to be wanting. The heart, which chooses God, will love his kingdom, his rational image, and the subjects capable of happiness, who have been created by his power and goodness. Hence, it pertains to the christian temper to be kindly affectioned one to another, and to embrace every opportunity of doing whatever may be for the present or eternal benefit of others. This enlargement of heart flows from the sanctifying grace of God, and will be found in his people, in proportion as his Spirit dwelleth in them. Confined affections are a most certain evidence of our wanting the Spirit of Jesus Christ. Brotherly love is essential to the temper of a disciple, and will do good on every opportunity to every creature—the whole family of heaven and earth, which is created and preserved from the fulness of eternal love.

Hence, in the divine word, christians are described to be persons, who overcome evil with good—mourn with those who mourn and rejoice with the rejoicing—do good to all men—love and pray for their enemies—are pitiful—are courteous—who abound in good works—seek the salvation of miserable and guilty souls—and deny themselves much, that many may be profited.—This comes from the nature and objects of christian love—a heart disposed to do good in the most extensive manner, and to the greatest number of recipients. While destitute of these feelings, it is vain for any to think themselves the disciples of God's Son. Unless we have hearts which seek for subjects of happiness, and desires which spread through earth and ascend to heaven in kind affection, we are not the brethren and imitators of him who died on the cross to save his enemies.

I might proceed to many particulars, in describing the objects of christian affection and love; but enough have been mentioned, to give a general idea, of the union between all holy souls and the glorious kingdom of holiness.

In the moral conformity and exercise of love, consists the union and communion of God, of angels and the redeemed saints. The words of our text describe a wonderful truth—a wonderful kingdom—a wonderful heaven of holiness and joy, where all are united in character and affection. This union of affection is begun by

Serm. XIV. *The objects of christian love.*

the christian sanctification—it is the kingdom of heaven already commencing in the heart, which shall progressively increase until the complete union in heaven, where all shall dwell in the DIVINE LOVE, and he shall fill every soul with the eternal, the lifegiving action of his holy spirit. CHRIST often spoke of his Father and himself being one in his people, and of their being one in him ; also in the scriptures there are many descriptions of this union, all of which lead our minds to the glorious subject contained in the text, the mutual indwelling of GOD and his people by the perfection and union of holiness, thus forming the great kingdom of holiness which is the object of christian love.

THIS indwelling of love is the most correct idea of heaven which can be attained in the present state. Curiosity prompts many inquiries on the subject. What is heaven ? This question often passes both in holy and unholy minds. Presumptuous conjectures are hazarded, and false descriptions are given, most commonly according to the imperfect taste of those who indulge them. Our revelation from GOD tells us nothing on this subject, merely to gratify curiosity ; but every thing which is necessary for our preparation.

HEAVEN is a most holy state. It is the indwelling of GOD in the soul, by the sanctifying energies, and the communicated sense of his love. It is all the active and affectionate powers of the soul going forth in love to GOD himself, and to the kingdom which is according to his will. The beginning of this in the heart, is that dawning of heaven in the soul, which is permitted to the sons of GOD in the present world. It is the formation of the kingdom within them which shall grow into eternal glory. It is an all-satisfying good, therefore the disciple said, *Shew us the Father and it sufficeth us*, shew us the glory of GOD—bring us near to it by communion—bring his love down into our hearts—and draw forth our most fervent love to him, and it is all we need or ever can receive. This is the only blessed and glorious heaven a good mind can wish. The desire of christians is always for a greater fulness of what they have begun to taste, and not for any enjoyment of a new kind.

THE subject is well adapted to assist us in self-examination. In a point of so great consequence, as eternal salvation or the loss of it must be, we ought to bring our expectations to the severe correction of truth, and to do it frequently. The supposed christian, who is unwilling to examine himself, and hear rules of trial brought close to his heart and conscience, discovers his own insincerity.

WE have considered some principal objects of christian love, and thence inferred a description of the heavenly state and blessedness. If these be the objects of our own love, there is sufficient evidence of our gracious union to GOD, who is reigning in his holy kingdom, and bringing sinners to himself through his Son JESUS CHRIST. He is ever glorious in the eyes of his saints—their most revered and beloved king. The voice of their hearts is, " *Oh, that I knew where I might find him, that I might come even to his seat,*" and this desire is not confined to days of prosperity. Job expressed it in days of affliction, and so will every christian. Though bruised by the strokes of the Lord's hand, instead of contending with his righteousness, the heart is drawn to him by a confidence in his wisdom, and the excellence of his nature. None can deny the most glorious GOD himself to be the chief object of christian love. Is it not a law of human action to seek the objects we love? To be present with them, if possible, and converse with them by meditation in a necessary absence? Is it not thus with the earthly objects of our choice? We seek them to be near us, and when separated by time or distance, our thoughts still pursue, and every little circumstance around us, is eagerly caught, to make their images present with us. Do we thus seek the Lord? Is he present in our thoughts? Are we looking for him in his works of nature and providence? Do we with a daily pleasure observe the marks of his being and attributes, which are engraved on all he does; and seeing them do our affections ascend to him? Certainly, if we loved him this would be the case. *Our conversation is in heaven*, said the apostle. There our thoughts and affections ascend, seeking him who is the object of our supreme love. When he vouchsafes to meet our seeking hearts, and bring us into his banqueting house, and shine around us with the light of his glory, it seems like a heaven begun on earth. Enough of this, is perfect blessedness and glory. Those, who do not feel these effects of christian love, are in an unsafe state. They may profess—they may hope—they may do many visible duties; but the whole is defective if the heart be not joined in love to God. Where there is this union of holy affection he will be remembered by day and by night, and all his laws will be obeyed.

By the word *heaven*, men in general mean a state of perfect happiness; so that from the apprehensions of that state, which they wish to establish, the moral condition of their hearts may be very strongly conjectured. Those, who are disposed to conceive artificial arrangements and natural beauties to be the principal glory of heaven, and feclude a conftant view and enjoyment of GOD's glorious holinefs, do thereby evidence their want of union to him, and of a preparation for divine communion. To a holy mind, the conftant view of infinite rectitude, with opportunity to adore and praife, will be a moft pleafing part of the heavenly life.

FURTHER, Thofe, who drop JESUS CHRIST from their life of daily religion, cannot be chriftians indeed. Many are willing to have him for a diftant Saviour, and depend on a fcheme of grace introduced by infinite wifdom through him; who, neverthelefs, do not wifh to dwell with him, to have him reign in their hearts, and go to him conftantly for ftrength to ferve GOD and refift their own lufts. To every one who believes, he is precious—his prefence is fought—he is their fpiritual life as well as the way to the Father—and their hearts mourn his abfence. They feel their ftrength to be from him, and that when his aid is withdrawn they are cold in duty and backflide to the world. If our fuppofed religion, be of fuch a kind, as can be fupported without a daily intercourfe with JESUS CHRIST, it is not that evangelical holinefs to which the promifes are made.

UNHOLY men may love thofe, who, they fuppofe love them and promote their interefts. On this principle a multitude of infincere perfons followed CHRIST when he was on earth. They were tempted by the loaves, and not drawn by the moral glory of his character. As great a multitude have followed him profeffionally ever fince, who love him, only becaufe they think he hath loved and received them. Self-love may carry men a great length, in praifing their fupposed deliverer from eternal misery; and when they add to the account an immortal inheritance, in which they expect to receive high dignity, the selfish affections may break forth in rapturous hosannas. CHRIST may be thus received without any union of heart to him and his kingdom; and he is loved only for the gifts he hath to bestow. The glory, that is supposed to be seen, is in the gifts and not in the character of the giver. Ask the selfish believer why he loves CHRIST? His heart will reply. He hath loved me, hath died for me, hath delivered me from eternal misery, has given me eternal glory. Who can refrain praising and loving one, that offers so many benefits. Propose the same question to a sanctified christian, and his heart will reply, Behold the glory of the GOD man Mediator! See how excellent he is in himself! Of all the benefits he can bestow on a guilty creature, a permission to behold, to praise and glorify him, is the greatest. I love him for his worthiness; I receive him, being irresistibly drawn by his excellence. In self-examination, the greatest care ought to be used, to distinguish these two kinds of love. It is to be feared, that by not attending to this distinction, many are deceived, and falsely think they are united to the kingdom of CHRIST. Under this delusion, natural affection may rise to great warmth, and cry, come see my zeal for CHRIST; though the whole be no more than zeal for self-interest.

WE ought, also, to examine ourselves by our apprehensions of the divine law.—If the law appear pleasant and good, and its duties be our meat and drink, we may rejoice in hope.—If we love the kingdom of GOD and wish to serve it forever, it will be given to us.—If we love the brethren, we are born of God, and shall dwell with him and with them forever more. May we all be infpired by the chriftian profpects and promifes, to purify ourfelves and grow in love unto eternal glory. Amen.

SERMON XV.

Christian doctrines reasonable.

ROMANS xii. 1.

—*Which is your reasonable service.*

THE duty, which is here said to be a reasonable service, is to *present our bodies a living sacrifice, holy, acceptable to God.* Our bodies are particularly mentioned in the exhortation, still it doubtless extends to the whole man, for holiness is eminently a quality of the mind; and the next verse, explaining the duty, says, *Be ye transformed by the renewing of your mind.* It is a reasonable thing, that the whole man, both body and spirit, in all his faculties and powers, and the perpetual application of them, should be consecrated to his most glorious Creator and Saviour. This is required by the laws of religion, and every good man both feels and rejoices in the obligation. His heart never riseth against the duty, except in certain hours of backsliding, for which he is ashamed of himself, and feels guilty in the fight of God, when reclaimed by the power of his grace.

Altho' our text, in the apostolic exhortation, applies specially to the duty of self-consecration; I shall give a larger scope to this discourse, and endeavour to show that all the doctrines and duties of christianity are reasonable—approved by a sound judgment and honest heart—and useful for the glory of God, and the best good of his creation.

In this rebellious world, every kind of objection is made against the rights of Deity and duty of creatures. Some openly espouse the reign and the pleasures of sin; and many, under a professed friendship, either insidiously undermine the doctrines of grace and holiness unto the Lord, or by their practice deny the confession of their lips. Whatever their words may be, their practice tells us, the doctrines and duties of revelation are not reasonable. Doubtless, their practice is the most true expression of their hearts. If circumstances could be so changed as to remove a fear of God and men, by which there is a present restraint, they would openly avow religion to be unreasonable, both in its doctrines and duties.

I am sensible the pious, believing christian doth not need conviction, that the faith and practice of the gospel are reasonable. His heart is made honest, and approves whatever reason approves. It is the rational fitness of christian doctrine and duty by which he is charmed, and made fervent in spirit serving the Lord. Although such can be in no want of evidence to reconcile them to their duty; it may increase the warmth of their pure affections, and renew a pleasure which they have often felt, to review the glorious fitness of their Lord's doctrine and commandments. And as the most sincere are exposed to very painful temptations, it may fortify them against those dark hours, in which the powers of sin, are loosed against them, to try the strength of their confidence and love.

It is not expected that persons of an opposite character, whose hearts are wedded to themselves and their sins, will cordially feel that religion is a reasonable service; or its doctrines worthy of a God, who hath infinite reason. Prejudiced, by an evil heart of unbelief, they are continually combating, even the weak and partial concessions of their own reason which are favorable to the christian doctrine. Their intelligence is more than misapplied, for it directly impugns the wisdom of God, calling his doctrines foolishness, and his requirements hard sayings. How strange the appearances in a sinful world! Wicked creatures rebelling against a good God; weak creatures against a God of infinite power; unhappy creatures opposing the only means for perfect peace; and creatures who glory in their reason, often denying the reasonabless of that scheme of government and grace, by which infinite wisdom brings the greatest honor to God and makes his kingdom most happy.—These sad effects of sin ever have been, and ever will be, where there are apostate creatures. But notwithstanding this, God is glorious in all counsels. The cavils of enmity and error are unfounded. On candid examination, it will appear, that every doctrine advanced, and every duty required, in the holy oracles, are reasonable. They are approved by common sense and an honest judgment; and useful to the great interests of society.

In illustrating the subject, I shall distinguish between the doctrines and duties of christianity; and concerning each of them endeavour to show, that they are reasonable, worthy of God, and consistent with such laws of natural existence as can be determined with certainty. Also, that they all tend to happiness or natural good.

By doctrines, are meant, things to be believed; by duties, things to be done.

All the doctrines of christianity are reasonable; and those which are known only by revelation, harmonize with such laws of natural existence, as can be determined with certainty.

In this discourse, the word reasonable doth not mean pleasing to the heart. It is a well known truth, that the most reasonable duties are very disagreeable to an unholy mind. They never can be otherwise, until the heart is changed by the power of divine grace. If any, when they call the doctrines and precepts of God unreasonable, mean unpleasing to themselves; we concede it in the fullest extent. We beg them to consider their own awful situation, so long as they are displeased with the infinite reason and wisdom of God. It is a condition of heart without hope and peace. It is, further, believed that many who join with the irreligious multitude, and object against the equity of christian faith and practice, are wholly governed by the taste of their own hearts. The only argument they can bring against it, is this, we are not pleased with it, it doth not delight us, and to receive it, we must part with many things we love.

A doctrine, which men are unable to comprehend, may be very reasonble. This is proved by the different rational powers imparted to mankind. A doctrine, which is mysterious to one person, through the weakness of his reason; may, in the view of another, be intelligible and gloriously rational. If it were not thus, all those truths of infinite wisdom, which are high above the understanding of mortal men, might be impeached as folly. In showing the reasonableness of christian doctrines, we do not expect to explain them in their whole extension to the weak reason of men. It is enough to show their usefulness, and that they do not imply an impossibility, nor contradict other truths which are more plainly evidenced to our understanding; and this is the case with all christian doctrines.

Some doctrines are supported by evidence both natural and revealed; others, only by a revelation from infinite truth. It is the latter which impiety first attacks, because, it is supposed they may be most easily confuted. The existence of a holy God is the most disagreeable of all truths to an unholy mind; still some acknowledge this, who affect to deny the Trinity and an Incarnation. If there were no natural evidence of the supreme existence, depravity would make men as ready to deny his being, as they be to discredit the Trinity, that peculiar and glorious manner of existing, in which the scheme of redemption originated. All truth depends on the existence and character of God.

1. The character, which is given of God in the christian scriptures, is most reasonable and glorious.

The being of a God, is not a doctrine peculiar to christianity. The belief of it is among heathen, and over the face of the earth where christianity hath not been yet received. But when *they knew* God, they glorified him not as God, by such descriptions of his nature, character, counsels and will as are worthy of an infinite and most holy being. Things the most debasing, puerile and impure have been ascribed to the Almighty first cause, by heathen superstition and sin. This hath been the case, among highly civilized people, who were eminent in refinement and arts, as well as among barbarous tribes. It proves the usefulness of a revelation in assisting men to see the natural evidence of GOD's most holy character.

How pure! how reasonable and glorious the revealed character and will of GOD!—

A BEING eternal, infinite in power, every where present, omniscient and most wise. A being independent and self-existent, who created and preserves all things according to the counsel of his own will. A being of infinite goodness, whose name is love, and whose tender mercies are over all his works. His sovereignty is the powerful ordering of infinite righteousness; and because his motives can be drawn from no other source which is permanent and good, he draws them from within himself.

HE is raised above partiality, above temptation, above the possibility of desiring what is unwise, or doing what is evil.

HE considers his only glory to consist in being and in doing good, and is most glorified when his kingdom is most blessed. All the terrors which he hath prepared, whether they be temporal or eternal, are designed to aid the operations of love—to show its excellent and glorious nature—and make his holy kingdom the most like to himself in a pure blessedness. This is the sum of those perfections and counsels, which GOD hath ascribed to himself in his word. Can there be a more perfect, more lovely, more glorious character? The justice which unrighteous men hate, and guilty men fear, according to his own unerring description is the acting of goodness; and if it did not exist, a universe now glorious in blessedness, would be a universe of pain and hor-

Serm. XV. *Christian doctrines reasonable.*

for. Is not this revealed character of GOD most reasonable, most glorious? Compare with it the notions of divinity which have been formed by heathen sin; or by the few instances of infidel reason scattered in christian lands; how debased! how impure they appear!—And all their descriptions in contradiction to natural light, are coloured with the bitterness of their hearts. It appears most clear, that seeing the truth and righteousness of God, they were still ignorant of his loveliness—and his goodness which they knew, and daily experienced was the object of their dread, and the alarm of their consciences.

2dly. IT is reasonable that GOD should give to men a revelation of himself and his counsel.

THE notion that reason supersedes the need of revelation shows great philosophical ignorance, as well as corruption of heart. What is reason, but a power of judging and determining truth, from evidence presented before the mind? Reason cannot judge between truth and falsehood without evidence. What is revelation but evidence of truth? Revelation is none the less necessary because men are rational creatures, for without evidence reason would be a useless gift. We may as well argue against the natural evidence in creation and providence, as we may against the revealed, and say, man is a rational creature and therefore doth not need it. The objection against revealed light, because men have reason, most evidently arises from an opposition of heart to the truth, and of course, to the evidence by which it is discovered.

FURTHER, it is reasonable for GOD to give us more evidence of truth than we find in creation and his providential government. There are many ways and kinds of evidence. We find this to be the case, in present things; and why not, also, with respect to the things of an unseen God, of his government and eternity to come. Can truth be too well known, our duty too plainly marked out, or our assurance too strongly built? Can we know too much of God and his everlasting counsels in which we are interested? The objection against revelation, because some of the truths which it contains, are also evidenced to us in another way, is so contrary to common sense, and to what every honest mind would wish and call a favor, that we cannot ascribe it to any cause but enmity against God. As evidence increases, the evil heart is wounded, and denies the need of light because its deeds are evil

Further, many truths which are necessary for the glory of God and good of men, can be communicated only by a revelation. This is the case with sundry christian doctrines. The Trinity of Godhead, the Incarnation, and the manner of Redemption thro' the blood of Christ, are doctrines of importance to guilty sinners. A revelation appears to be the only possible way of communicating them to our knowledge, so that our faith may give strong consolation. It is not conceived how creation, on its present construction; or providence, on the principles of divine acting, could teach these things. And was God under obligations to use only one manner of instructing? Or hath he no truth, useful for us, and glorious for himself, but what our weak reason might learn from the works of nature? To pretend this, is trifling with Almighty power and wisdom, and treating the great Jehovah with greater indignity, than one guilty and weak creature would be willing to receive from another.

How strangely sinful pride swells itself against God's wisdom, justice and goodness! This is its nature, and it will continue to swell, until the Lord is pleased to shut its mouth.

It is a most merciful and reasonable thing in God, to give us abundant evidence of his nature and will, of his government, and of our own duty and end.

There yet remains an infinite series of truth in the divine understanding, which is unknown by creatures, and which his goodness will incline him to communicate to them, as they can receive it. Infinite wisdom will determine the progress of ways, means and times, by which it can be best done. This will be a work for eternity. Those who do not like to retain a knowledge of God in their minds, will think the new lights of the world to come, to be as unnecessary as they now think a revelation to be. Every means of bringing the divine character and will into view will meet the opposition of their hearts.

It has been inquired, why, if a revelation be necessary to answer the purposes of infinite goodness, it was not given in the beginning? The question is unwise. It betrays, both a want of confidence in divine wisdom, and ignorance of the means by which the holy creation is formed and approximates to its final perfection. The way must be prepared for the communication of truth. One kind of evidence must precede to make the admission of another possible. The history of mankind, and their sins and miseries, for four thousand years; and of God's dealings with them, was necessary to prepare the human mind, for seeing the gospel scheme and doctrines, in the clear manner revealed by Christ and his apostles. We may conclude, that truth is evidenced to creatures, by all possible means of inſtruction, and as faſt as the evidence can be formed and laid before them. This is illuſtrated by the revelation we have received. How much of it, which was obſcure at the time of giving, is now made plain by events in the divine government, which have intervened. How much ſtill remains to be obſcure, which will be clearly underſtood in the approaching ages. The expreſſion is plain as can be, but obſcure to us through the want of illuſtrating events in the providence of God. We may therefore conclude, the evidence of truth by a revelation, hath been given, in the earlieſt hour it could be received, and in a manner adapted to fill the world with the greateſt light.

3dly. The Trinity of Godhead is a pillar in the chriſtian faith.

Altho' it be a deep and myſterious doctrine, it is not, on this account, the leſs reaſonable. While the Trinity of Father, Son and Holy Ghoſt is moſt clearly revealed in the ſcriptures, there is no attempt to explain it; which ſufficiently intimates, this glorious manner of divine ſubſiſtence to be above our comprehenſion. It is not ſtrange that Godhead is incomprehenſible. Who can comprehend any one perfection of the ſupreme nature. Wiſdom, righteouſneſs, love and power, by their infinitude, become incomprehenſible or myſterious to us. Neither, are myſteries confined to God's eſſential being; for the manner of our own exiſting, and the works of nature are full of myſteries. We cannot tell how a plant grows; or the mind perceives, thro' an external action on the organ of hearing. If myſtery warrants infidelity, or renders faith unreaſonable, we muſt diſbelieve the exiſtence of God and creatures.

While the scriptural doctrine of a Trinity is mysterious, it is still so limited, as to be in no respect incredible; and the revealed advantages resulting from it, both to the everblessed God and his creation, render our belief of it reasonable. His Trinity is consistent with his unity. He is not three, in the same sense, that he is one. He is not three in any sense inconsistent with unity of counsel and action. He is not three, in such a manner, as to produce counter obligation on his creatures, division of interests, or confusion of design. He is not three, so as to imply imperfection or control, in either of the persons in his glorious Trinity.

The supreme existence is most perfect, and although his Trinity be mysterious, we may see that it adds to his perfection, and may therefore, be reasonably believed of an all perfect God.

I will instance this in two respects.

1. It shows that the divine obligation to moral rectitude, and his eternal choice of holiness, arises from the nature and manner of his own existence.

2dly. This manner of existing, admits the exercise of mercy to guilty sinners, in a way most glorious for himself.

This doctrine, shows that the divine obligation to rectitude, and his eternal choice of holiness arises from the nature and manner of his existence. His nature is social within himself. His existence hath such social relations within himself as imply moral obligation. The happiness of his own glorious society, in the connexion of Father, Son and Spirit, required him to be holy, from eternity; and he could, in no other way, be blessed in himself. This internal, social communion of Almighty God is described in his word. The adorable persons of his nature love, glorify, covenant, promise and fulfil to each other. Of this, the covenant of redemption and its execution, is an instance. Here is society in its most glorious form, with all its resulting obligations and blessedness.

Hence, we see the high source of moral obligation, in the infinite ; also, in the social nature of the everblessed God. The origin is most sacred, and the divine will is inclined to virtue as necessarily as he exists. Rejoice O ye righteous for the Lord your God must be holy. The law of holiness which you love and are commanded to obey, flows from the manner of his incomprehensible existence.

2dly. This manner of existing, admits the exercise of mercy to guilty sinners, in a way most glorious for himself.

After the law of his own nature was violated by men, and they had become guilty and miserable, his manner of existing in Trinity, admitted the gospel atonement, through which there is forgiveness of sin, and an acceptance to his blessed presence. Infinite wisdom must judge in what manner sin can be forgiven with safety. It is a question, in its nature, above human determination ; and we have no reason to think forgiveness would be right ; but through an atonement. Nor have we any reason to suppose any other than the gospel atonement, which depends wholly on God's own Trinity of nature, could be adequate to the forgiveness of sin, and purchase of eternal glory. On this wonderful manner of divine subsistence, stand both the law and the gospel. It is the high, the peculiar truth of christian revelation, and goes far to enlighten us in the nature and counsels of God !

Serm. XV. *Christian doctrines reasonable.* 255

But this manner of existing is mysterious.—We allow it. So also, is every divine attribute; so, are the works of nature around us; yea, a thousand things, which we feel in our existence; yet we do not reject them on this account. A mystery doth not imply a contradiction or impossibility. A mysterious truth must be deemed reasonable, if it be implied in the perfection, and necessary for the blessedness of an infinite nature; and also for the good of his intelligent universe. Usefulness is always a presumptive argument for reasonableness.

4thly. The incarnation of Jesus Christ, is another mysterious doctrine of the christian revelation, which its enemies wish to represent as unreasonable.

This doctrine describes the Mediator to be both God and man. The Son of God in possession of his whole divinity; uniting with himself a perfect and innocent man, formed by his wisdom, for the purpose of displaying divine holiness, atoning for sin, and fulfilling a righteousness, through which transgression may be gloriously pardoned. This union of the divine and human natures, is supposed to exist, in the highest degree, without a communication of those attributes and properties to one nature, which were originally peculiar to the other. That it is a wonder, a mystery, a mighty work of God, all christians allow; but, that the belief of it is unreasonable, doth not follow. If it be possible, and also useful; it is worthy of God's infinite reason, wisdom and goodness.

The incarnation is possible.

The man Christ Jesus, was a creature of God's own forming. The power of creating, implies the power of assuming his workmanship into any kind of union with himfelf, that is pleafing to his wifdom. The myftery of this union between infinite and finite, is no greater to us, than the union between our own fouls and bodies, which no rational man will deny becaufe he cannot explain it.

The incarnation is worthy of infinite wifdom.

This muft be determined, from the effects it is defigned to produce; which are made known by the word of God. The effects are the greateft which can be conceived, and are worthy of infinite wifdom. Is it not worthy of God, to fave an innumerable company of guilty creatures, from eternal fin and mifery and bring them to a life of glorious and endlefs peace? Is it not worthy of him to glorify himfelf and make his kingdom happy by the difplay of his perfections, and thus enjoy the goodnefs of his own nature? Thefe are the effects of Christ's incarnation. Effects fo great and good muft be glorious for God; and though, in view of our weaknefs and guilt it is infinite condefcenfion, in view of the glory which God brings to himfelf, it is a moft credible event.

The facred evidence of this fact in the divine government is very great. That Jesus Christ was man cannot be doubted. He muft alfo be God, for divine names the moft peculiar to Deity, divine perfections and works, and a perfect equality and likenefs to the Father are afcribed to him. He is called the Creator, and appointed to be the Judge. Divine glory, in the redemption of finners, made it reafonable this aftonifhing event fhould take place.

To finful mortals, who are filled with the pride of rank, it may appear degrading, for an infinite God thus to unite himfelf with a creature. But it doth not appear thus to perfect wifdom and goodnefs. The jealoufy of rank cannot belong to him. His majefty is the majefty of love; and he is fearful in the praifes that will forever be offered to his condefcending mercy.

5. THE chriftian fcriptures declare the total corruption of human nature, and the doctrine is fupported by fuch evidence, as renders our belief of it reafonable.

WE muft act directly againft reafon and common fenfe to deny this truth. There is evidence of every kind, which the nature of the cafe admits; and every thing which appears in men to be any better than total corruption, is accounted for in full confiftency with the doctrine. The hiftory of the world, both facred and profane, proves this truth. All men have in practice departed from GOD, and their actions have been fuch as evince an unholy heart. Even thofe who deny it in words, by a manifeft diftruft of their fellow creatures, give proof of their own conviction; and fhow that their denial is a prejudiced bufinefs. In the rafhnefs of inconfideration, men may do and fay any thing; but no confiderate man—no man whofe confcience appears to be in lively exercife, dare deny his being naturally inclined to do evil, evil only, and that continually. As the evidence of our total depravity, by nature, hath been given in a former difcourfe, I fhall not repeat it in this place; only obferving, that if the chriftian fcriptures declared the purity of human nature, finners themfelves, would allow this to be a fufficient reafon for rejecting them.

THE introduction of fin hath been a point of difficulty in all ages. WHENCE COMES EVIL, is a queftion which hath perplexed many, and will continue to do this, until there is more confidence in God's wifdom and more fubmiffion to his fovereignty. But this difficulty doth not difprove the ftubborn fact of its exiftence. The plain and natural account of the introduction of fin, which is given in the fcriptures, muft be allowed reafonable, until a more reafonable one is offered. It is prefumed, no one will pretend, this hath yet been done.

6thly. It is a doctrine of the chriftian fcriptures, that God hath decreed whatfoever comes to pafs.

By this is meant, that in fovereign and holy wifdom, and by motives derived from within himfelf, he hath determined the whole fcheme of created exiftence, with all its parts, agents, their moral character, their demerits, and their end in everlafting happinefs or mifery. Alfo, that this determination is fo abfolute, there cannot be the fmalleft deviation from what he hath purpofed; but the whole fhall come into exiftence, exactly according to his fupreme will, in the fucceffion and at the time he hath appointed, and by fuch means as he hath predeftinated.

I know that by afferting this I am on the forbidden ground of fome, who, without doubt, believe the chriftian fcriptures; alfo, of the whole multitude who difbelieve, and whofe hearts are ftill unhumbled by the fanctifying grace of God. But if this doctrine be moft exprefsly revealed in the chriftiain fcriptures; if it be pleafing to a holy heart; if it be neceffary to prove there is a God of infinite perfection, and for the higheft good of the rational univerfe, it is reafonable to believe it.

This doctrine is moft clearly revealed.

It is written, *He hath determined the times before appointed. Being predeftinated according to the pur-*

pose of him who worketh all things after the counsel of his own will. Therefore hath he mercy on whom he will have mercy, and whom he will he hardeneth. The counsel of the Lord standeth forever. My counsel shall stand, and I will do all my pleasure. The Lord hath made all things for himself, yea the wicked for the day of evil. I form the light, and create darkness; I make peace and create evil, I the Lord do all these things. In these, with a multitude of other places, the supreme efficience of GOD, acting according to his predeterminate counsel, is most expressly asserted.

THE divine determination of all events, is a doctrine pleasing to a holy heart.

THERE needs only a sufficient degree of love and confidence in GOD to make the doctrine agreeable. A holy mind can have no rational motive to oppose the sovereign decrees of GOD. If GOD be wise and good, and able to create and govern in the most perfect manner, certainly it is best this should be the case. We must either deny these perfections of Deity, or own the doctrine to be excellent, or that our own hearts are not willing the best should take place. Few will dare deny the first; and to own the last impeaches the judgment, and denies any credit to be due to it.

SUCH a multitude of things have been said, in this rebellious world, against the absolute decrees of GOD, that it is not strange some honest minds should be prejudiced against the doctrine. It is very possible that a good man, through education and other powerful influence, should sometimes doubt; but I am ready to appeal to the heart of the doubting good man, and inquire of him. You are willing that a government the best, even in the most minute particulars, should take place

You believe God to be most powerful, wise and good; yea, far more wise and good, than you have seen, or can conceive a creature to be. Is it not best, that he should form and execute a plan of existence from eternity to eternity? Would you not trust this with him, sooner than with yourself or any other being? Under all things that happen, is it not a ground of joy to you that God reigns; and if there were any events, which you absolutely knew to be without the system of God's decrees, would not this be sufficient cause for you to fear them? I am certain every good mind, in answer to these questions, will reply, the doctrine of God's absolute decrees is to be desired. We always find this doctrine is received with pleasure, by those who give other evidence of a holy, humble and sanctified temper.

The doctrine of absolute decrees is necessary to prove there is a God of infinite perfection; and for the greatest good of the created rational universe.

Men often doubt concerning a doctrine, without considering the consequences, which will result from a denial of it. To deny this doctrine, in its consequences, falls little short of denying the supreme existence. Let those who fear dangerous consequences, take the burden on themselves, and show us a scheme of belief, which denies the doctrine and is not followed with consequences much more to be dreaded than those which they oppose.

Let them show us an infinite, all-wise, omniscient and most perfect God, as they allow Jehovah to be, acting without a plan. Let them show how it is consistent with infinite wisdom to create a universe, without determining, in all respects, how he will govern it, to what use he will apply it, or what its ultimate condition shall be. Or if he did determine these things, and hath not all within himself to effect his purpose, or if it be possible he should be disappointed; let them show how this is consistent, with an infinity of perfection both natural and moral. Let them show how foreknowledge can exist without foredetermination. By attending to these things, we must allow the absolute decrees of GOD, by which all events from eternity to eternity, are determined, made certain, and come to pass according to his predestination; or we must doubt the infinite perfections of GODHEAD.

FURTHER, this doctrine is necessary to assure the greatest good of the created universe.

THE absolute and influential decree of infinite wisdom and goodness, is the only certain evidence we can have, that all things will be conducted and end in the best manner. Go off from this ground, and we meet a gloomy uncertainty what will take place. If there be not a divine plan most absolutely determined; or if this plan is liable to be frustrated; or if the state of creatures, in point of character, action and reward be not made unalterably certain, we can have no assurance of any future glory. No individual can have strong consolation, either for himself or the general state of the universe. Order may be turned into confusion, light into darkness, and happiness into misery; and this universal and without a remedy. The predetermining decree of GOD, founded on the infinite perfection of his nature, is our prime evidence, that all things will be best.

THIS doctrine of christian revelation must be reasonable, if every good mind, understanding the subject, will rejoice in it; if the belief of it be necessary, even to conceive a GOD of infinite perfection; and if it be required to assure us, that the universe will be ever preserved in the most glorious condition. If the doctrine could be proved untrue, it would instantly spread a gloom over the universe, which could not be dissipated. If the doctrine had been unknown and were now revealed, the humble, the holy and all who delight in the character of GOD, would rejoice in the discovery, as an æra of light, beaming thro' a whole eternity to come.

7thly. WHEN we come to consider those christian doctrines, which respect the application of redeeming grace, they all appear to be glorious for GOD—worthy of his power—agreeable to his goodness—adapted to the real wants and miseries of mankind—and sufficient to raise them from death to life, from wretchedness to peace and glory.

FORGIVENESS, and a renewal to holiness are the two great things which sinners need. Both these the christian scriptures ascribe to the power and grace of GOD, through JESUS CHRIST.

WHAT is there incredible in the doctrine of sanctification by the efficacious power of the Spirit? Do we not need to be changed? Do we not need assistance in turning from sin to holiness? Do we not find our own evil will to be very unconquerable? Is not this the very wretchedness of sinners; that they will love their sin until GOD changes their hearts? Sinners may imagine they can turn when they please, but they will never please to turn, until they are turned by Almighty power. They turn from misery; but not from sin which is its cause. Herein is their remediless situation without GOD's renewing grace. That gracious power of renewing the heart, changing the taste, bowing the will, which is contained in the gospel, is one principal thing, by which it is adapted, to the relief of miserable sinners, and makes our belief of it reasonable. A gospel without the aid of divine renovation, though it were in all other respects complete, would leave sinners in the very state it finds them, under sin and suffering,——After God hath prepared the way to give his Spirit and work gloriously for himself, is it unworthy of him to create holiness, in those hearts which are now utterly destitute of it? Is it unworthy of his goodness to help the weak, enlighten the ignorant, purify the unclean, and give joy to those who have destroyed and made themselves miserable? It cannot be. The doctrine glorifies his goodness, and is adapted to the need of miserable men, therefore, our belief of it is reasonable. To those, who have felt their spiritual impotency, the doctrine appears to be their only hope. By experience, they know the need of divine power to change the heart, and to give and sustain the exercise of grace. They know their own weakness, through remaining sin, and the power temptation hath over them; so that, if there were not a promise of gracious assistance by the Spirit of God, they would still despair of eternal life. From the conviction of experience, they are disposed to ascribe every thing, to an efficacious sanctification from above.

FURTHER, What is there unreasonable, in the doctrine of our justification, by the free grace of God, through the righteousness of JESUS CHRIST? Certainly we need this favor, for we are guilty, and ruined and miserable. There can be no objection to the doctrine, as being unnecessary for sinners. So long as their own consciences condemn them, it cannot be doubted, whether God may do it juftly. To be pardoned and accepted by him muft be a defirable thing; and who, without it, can appear happily before him? It is therefore reafonable to believe we need this mercy.

Neither is it unworthy of infinite goodnefs freely to juftify miferable finners, fince his wifdom hath concerted and effected the means, of doing it glorioufly for himfelf through the righteoufnefs of Jesus Christ. Divine mercy is not an attribute, which will do a private favor at the expence of public good, and of his own glory as moral Governor of the univerfe. Since, his wifdom hath made it honourable for himfelf and fafe for his kingdom to accept finners, it cannot be thought unworthy of his dignity. It is a work of goodnefs, and goodnefs is always honorable. Goodnefs is the glory of God, and the more undeferving the fubjects of mercy, the more he is glorified in the beftowment of his free and wonderful grace.

Or is it unreafonable that this mercy to finners, fhould be granted through the righteoufnefs of Jesus Christ?

Here human pride may have its objections, and from an unwillingnefs to be dependant on grace, fo fovereignly purchafed and applied, may fay it is an unfit thing, for a finner to be accepted and glorified, through the righteoufnefs of another. But when we confider what is meant by this, all appearance of unfitnefs and inequity vanifhes. By ftanding in the place of finners, Christ did not become a finner, nor mar his own infinite purity. He did not relinquifh any divine right, nor become ftained with moral turpitude. He voluntarily fuffered that others might be benefitted. And might he not reafonably endure pain for his own glory, the glory of his father, and the procurement of eternal glory for multitudes who must otherwise suffer an eternal hell? In this gracious and glorious transaction, there is no transferal, either of sin or holiness, which were acted by one being; so as to become the sin or holiness of another being. In the scriptural sense of this transaction, CHRIST might reasonably put himself in the sinner's place. He might suffer, to make peace on earth and bring glory to GOD in the highest.

AND may not a holy GOD, acting reasonably, accept his sufferings and obedience, so, as for the sake of them, to sanctify and forgive offending sinners? GOD takes no delight in the death of the sinner. Pain or misery, considered by itself, is not pleasing in his sight. In the penalty of the law, he appointed it, not for its own sake, but to display his holiness, and maintain his government against the rebellion of sin. Whatever answers the end, for which the sinner's punishment was ordained, may be accepted; and the transgressor may thus become a candidate for mercy. The sacred obligation of the law, and all divine perfections are displayed by the sufferings and obedience of JESUS CHRIST, so, that forgiveness may be granted in a way glorious for GOD. The fixed holiness of his nature and government, beam forth more brightly, through the life, death and obedience of his Son, than it possibly could by the eternal execution of justice, in those whom he is pleased to forgive. In this case he may reasonably forgive through the righteousness of his beloved Son. The doctrine is a wonderful display of divine love, and permits those to hope, who might justly be cast off forever.

There are several other doctrines peculiar to the christian faith, which I shall not at this time mention; for it is presumed, they necessarily follow from those which have been noticed. A single discourse, from its brevity, only admits hints on this glorious subject, which deserves a copious illustration. Christianity claims, not only to be reasonable; but to be gloriously reasonable, above every scheme of faith or practice, that hath been received in the world. Its reasonableness is its great strength. The pure, great and good character, which it ascribes to God; the wonderful union, and rich display both of justice and mercy, which is made in the way of salvation; the means it provides for making God glorious in forgiving; the ability of the Mediator to save to the uttermost them who come to God by him; its sufficiency for all the wants of guilty sinners, will forever prove it to be the scheme of God's own wisdom.

Bring a sinner to penitence; to feel his guilt, his wants and miseries; to know what he is and what he deserves; and at this moment set before him every scheme of religious faith that hath been in the world, and all the ways of rendering a holy God propitious, he will say, without hesitation, give me the christian faith, give me Christ for a Saviour. If I can obtain this faith, in its true and sanctifying exercise, God will be glorious in forgiving, and I shall be happy in receiving. This faith will give me all the benefits of a pure righteousness; and though I am a guilty creature, I may be pardoned; though I am a weak creature, I may be strengthened. It will give me a balm for every wound; and the oil of joy, for heaviness. He will rejoice in hope of the glory of God.

ALL, who reject the christian revelation, must be under two insuperable difficulties, which are sufficient to cast a gloom over their most cheerful hours. They have no expiation to offer to GOD, in their pleading for mercy, but their own sinful mortifications. They have no righteousness to urge, but their own imperfect obedience. They have no assurance from his own mouth, sin can ever be forgiven; and taking it as granted that it may be, still, the manner how is left to their own loose conjecture. After they have fixed the point, that GOD is a good being, how can they be assured, his goodness will dispose him, or make it a consistent thing for him, to forgive sinners who deserve to be rejected? This is a great difficulty which must spread a gloom over their death-bed. They must think, though we feel penitence, it is not known for certainty, that penitence will be accepted; for even goodness may require us to be eternally cast off. This is a trial which reason can never surmount. They must leave the world, either, in the security of ignorance and a hard heart; or, take eternity at forlorn venture, it may be peaceful—it may be insupportable torment. Here, the christian believer may rejoice, in hope of mercy through an all-sufficient Saviour, and relying on the promise of a most true GOD.

ANOTHER insuperable difficulty in the way of disbelievers is this. They have a rational conviction of sin. They have often resolved, and found their resolutions inefficacious. They have used means without avail. They have no promise, no encouragement of a sanctifier. They believe nothing of a purchased and efficacious influence, to aid their weakness, and fit them for near communion with a holy GOD. These are the best prospects infidelity can afford, and they are gloomy indeed ! May the Lord mercifully enlighten us, and through the gospel of his Son prepare us to dwell with him forever. AMEN.

SERMON XVI.

Chriſtian duties reaſonable.

ROMANS xii. 1.

—*Which is your reaſonable ſervice.*

THE preſent is a day of great declenſion from chriſtian faith and practice. The number of diſbelievers, compared with the whole number of men, who have a doctrinal acquaintance with the goſpel, is greater than it hath been in any paſt period of time, ſince chriſtianity was publiſhed. This is a wonderful and inſtructive event. By the fulfilment of prophecy and other means, the evidence of truth is made greater than ever before. At this moment of increaſing light, there is alſo increaſing infidelity. This ſhows the folly of men, the nature of ſin, and the weakneſs of means, when not accompanied with the efficacious ſpirit. It is a proof, that men were never ſinful through want of evidence for their duty.

Lest chriſtians ſhould be diſcouraged, this defection was foretold in the ſure word of prophecy, as a mark of the laſt days, when God will come to avenge his injured cause by heavy judgments on mankind, and prepare the way for a more pure state of his church. This abounding of corruption in faith and practice, serves, by way of contrast, to discover the excellence of the christian religion. The incredulity and impiety of some, together with the practice proceeding from their unbelief, prove christianity to be necessary for the peace of the world. It must be more necessary for peace in the world to come. This conflict will end in a full demonstration, that christian doctrines and duties are reasonable, and worthy of divine wisdom.

The reasonableness of christian doctrines or articles of belief, was considered in the last discourse. Some of the most important were mentioned, and those particularly, which are mysterious to human understanding. The more we examine them; the more clearly it will appear, their mystery doth not imply contradiction, nor a natural impossibility. They elevate our conceptions of God's natural and moral fulness, and provide a remedy for the misery of sinful men, in a way consistent with divine glory. No other scheme of belief admits a God of such transcendent excellency, and a created kingdom of such purity and peace. Therefore, a belief of christian doctrines is reasonable. This being admitted, it goes far to prove the duties of christianity to be reasonable; and to this point the present discourse will be devoted.

All the duties of christianity, whether moral or evangelical; whether arising from natural relations or positive institutions are a reasonable service.

Before these duties are mentioned, I must be permitted to address a class of persons, many in number, who suppose christianty is their religion, and intend to die in this faith, yet are entirely destitute of its practice.

Altho' such do not choose to be thought infidels, their case is dangerous, and they have no title to the benefits of that belief, in which they have been educated. Their doctrinal faith is, in a great measure useless to them. *Even so faith, if it hath not works, is dead, being alone. Yea, a man may say, thou hast faith and I have works; show me thy faith without thy works, and I will show thee my faith by my works. Thou believest that there is one God; thou doest well: the devils also believe, and tremble. But wilt thou know, O vain man, that faith without works is dead?*

The end of doctrine is to produce practice in the heart and in the life. Practical religion in the heart, is more important than any thing external. Although there cannot be practice without doctrine, it is certain, that doctrine alone will never save a man. Sinning against greater light, he may be more guilty in the sight of God with, than without it. There is no need of my attempting to prove, that many come under this description. They see the great and solemn works of providence, without any consideration. They hear the word of God, and do it not, and are *like unto a man beholding his natural face in a glass: for he beholdeth himself, and goeth his way, and straightway forgetteth what manner of man he was.* They live under the full beams of christian light, still, in all respects relating to vital religion, live as they would do, if placed among a heathen people.

Concerning such persons we may observe.

They appear to think it a matter of little consequence, what men's religious opinions are.

With them it is enough, if they profess to have some opinions. It hence appears they think all religion a civil, fashionable thing, and that a holy preparation for eternity, and a pure conformity to God is out of the question. These people are in part right, for if practical religion in heart and life must be put away, it is of little consequence what opinions are embraced. On this supposition, opinions are only a fashion for the day, will die with the person who holds them, and have no saving effect for eternity.

Further, such persons are not solemnized by the truth.

They may often come where God hath appointed social prayer to be offered, and may sit before him as his people; but their service is more fitly called the civility of a christian land where providence hath placed them, than a worship of the Father in spirit and in truth. Even in the sanctuary they do not feel a present God, nor an accountableness for the opportunity. Confession, is of the tongue only, without feeling. Decorum without piety is the most that is attempted; and having paid the service of the week, though the time be still sacred, vanity rushes into the heart, flows from the lips, and marks the actions of the concluding Sabbath. Is this religion? Is this that love and fear, which is due to a God of infinite glory and holiness? Is this a true concern, or real preparation for the immortal interests of the soul? Is this a piety, which can console the pains of a death-bed, and illumine the solemn, unexperienced path from time to eternity? No, it is not.

Where is the love, the reverence, the conformity to God? Where is the deep sense of guilt, the unfeigned humility, the despair in his own services with which a self-emptied sinner goes to CHRIST? Where is the love, with which a true disciple leans on the bosom of JESUS, and finds a beginning heaven in the company of his Saviour? The devotion, the fire of the sacrifice is wanting. How astonished with the sight, and with his own guilt, will such a soul be, if taken in a moment, from the formal and fashionable worship of this world, to behold the pure devotion of Jerusalem above!

In describing persons of this character, and setting their defect before them, I ought, again, to mention.

THEY are displeased with the spirituality of religion. Duties of the heart are as much beyond their creed, as they are wanting in their practice. They are ready to wonder, as Nicodemus did, on hearing the doctrine of the new birth, and say, How can this be, or why is this necessary? This is pushing religion to an unpleasant length. If this be true, I must be in earnest; I must think as much of GOD and another world, as I do of my farms and merchandize; I must forego my pleasures, and begin a life of prayer, in which I never delighted; I must be more anxious for my soul than for my honor; more desirous to set my house right with GOD, than to cheer it with the sound of the tabret and the pipe. To such, the life of piety, and a holy walk of communion with GOD is mysterious. They know not the thing, nor do they wish to believe it. Spiritual strength from CHRIST, and rejoicing evermore in GOD and his government, is the strange thing with which they desire no acquaintance. Such are the persons, who live at ease in Zion, in the very place where GOD hath taught the spirituality of religion. While in their own opinion chriſtians; they live without GOD in the world. There is reaſon to fear, his comforting preſence will be as far from them in their death, as they have been from him in their lives.

PRACTICE is the end for which doctrine was given, and if one be reaſonable the other is reaſonable alſo.

WHAT is the practice, which GOD requires? Can it be, that a few religious civilities will ſatisfy a holy GOD? When he tells us to love him with the whole heart, to mourn for ſin, to walk before him in deep humility, to rejoice in him evermore and pray without ceaſing, and to ſtrive that we may enter in at the ſtrait gate; by all theſe, can he mean we ſhould doctrinally believe theſe things to be right, and pretend the performance without doing them? Chriſtian duty begins in the heart, and an original defect here, muſt vitiate the whole in his ſight. GOD is not a being to be mocked, and he claims an obedience of the heart as his right. *My ſon, give me thy heart.* Our love of GOD ought to be with *all the heart.* As the abounding of infidelity, juſtifies an attempt to ſhow the reaſonableneſs of chriſtian doctrines; ſo the neglect of vital and experimental practice, requires us to ſhow the danger of a general declenſion in this reſpect, and that many, whoſe doctrines are right, are periſhing through want of obedience in heart.

1. IT is reaſonable we ſhould love GOD with the whole heart, ſtrength and mind.

NEITHER a profeſſion of duty and obligation, nor any external ſervice amounts to evangelical obedience, if this ſupreme affection doth not exiſt in the heart. Moral obligation ariſes from what GOD is; from his truth, goodneſs and righteoufnefs; from the divine love or holinefs, by which he doth good to himfelf, and is difpofed to communicate from his own fulnefs in the bleffed exiftence of creatures. His character is lovely, whether we have hearts to love him or not; or whether our own fituation be defirable or the contrary. When God claims our obedience, he appeals to his own will, and what he is in himfelf, as a reafon why we fhould obey. He never attempts any other proof of our obligation, of his right to command and our duty to obey, than the greatnefs, glory and excellence of his own nature and will. It is what he is, independent of man's difpofition, which makes our fupreme love reafonable. If it were not thus, there could be no fuch thing as obligation, holinefs, fin and guilt. Whatever a bad heart may fay, ftill common fenfe approves this truth; and whatever finners may wifh, their confciences do notwithftanding certify them, that a character and moral objects which are holy, have an inherent fitnefs for which they ought to be chofen. There is no truth more plain than this; none, which hath the more general affent of mankind; and a denial of it deftroys the exiftence of moral obligation.

The divine worthinefs of love is teftified by his works. He hath not left himfelf without a witnefs, in that he hath given us our exiftence, our capacities of knowing and enjoying, fruitful feafons, the comforts of time, a knowledge of himfelf, a perfect law for the direction of our focial intercourfe, and a glorious fcheme of grace to reclaim us from fin to our duty and to eternal bleffednefs. All thefe things witnefs the fulnefs of Godhead, and prove our fupreme love of him to be a reafonable fervice.

If there be such a thing as loveliness, its existence may be traced up to Deity, the infinite fountain; so that our supreme affections ought never to stop short of him. If the creatures have any excellence, who is the author, and by whose will is it sustained in being? As every thing, which is worthy of love, flows forth from him; so, through every thing as a medium, our supreme love ought to flow back to him again, and it is but a reasonable service. Our divine instructor calls this law of loving God, the first and great commandment. Those who live in disobedience reject their whole duty and must be altogether condemned. It becomes them to inquire what excuse they can make; for they cannot deny the duty to be reasonable, neither can they plead a want of knowledge.

After all, if any doubt whether God really requires our supreme love, and marks the daily want of it, as a great sin; let them show us the reasonableness of their prostituted affections. Let them teach what there is in their own imperfect, and sinful natures, that is worthy to be loved more than God. Let them describe to us those excellencies in the perishing creatures, which are worthy to be brought into comparison with God. Let them compare weakness with strength, ignorance with knowledge, folly with wisdom, impiety with infinite holiness, and human frailty with most glorious self-existence; and then show us that it is reasonable to love themselves and the creatures more than God. None are wise, but those, who have brought themselves to the most strict examination in this point.

2. The self-loathing and mourning for sin, which accompanies repentance towards God, is a most reasonable christian duty.

THIS is practically denied by all who do not repent; and some are so fixed in their impenitence, as to make light of the grief which every christian feels, in view of his sins committed against a holy and good GOD. Turning from sin, hating it, and self-loathing for the commission, are essential to repentance. *Now mine eye seeth thee, wherefore I abhor myself, and repent in dust and ashes. Then shall ye loathe yourselves for your iniquities. Be afflicted, and mourn, and weep; let your laughter be turned to mourning and your joy to heaviness.*

IN the same proportion as sin is wrong, we ought to mourn, and to loathe both its past dominion and present influence in us. No rational man, by self-loathing for sin, understands a hatred of his own existence; but an abhorrence of the temper, through which he hath misapplied his talents to an unworthy end. If sin be wrong we ought to loathe its dominion over us, and whatever we have done contrary to our duty. It is reasonable that the degree of self-affliction should be proportioned to our injury of GOD and men, and when this is seen justly, the grief will be great— the abasement be deep and heart-penetrating. A man cannot abstain from loathing himself for what he dislikes; and those who make light of christian mourning for sin, and think GOD doth not require us to afflict our souls deeply for transgression, show the following things. That they have never seen the glorious holiness of GOD; are unacquainted with the evil of sin; have not come to a knowledge of their deep corruption; and have parted with sin only through fear of the punishment.

To see the reasonableness of repentance and mourning for sin, we only need consider the glorious objects and ends to which it is opposed.

It is opposed to GOD himself in his whole nature and government, to his blessedness, to all his rights, to his wife laws and government, and to the good of creatures. Christian repentance is exercised in sight of this, and must therefore contain a very sensible affliction of the heart. And though a mourning for sin, will not reverse what has been committed, it is necessary evidence of a present good temper, and cannot fail to be found in a sanctified soul. If it be reasonable to love and rejoice in GOD, there are the same reasons for the mourning of repentance, and they will ever be united.

3dly. THE christian duty of dedication to GOD is a reasonable service.

THIS duty is not essentially different from loving him supremely; for we are, in fact, dedicated to the object of our chief love. Love is the consecrating, dedicating act of the mind, by which we give ourselves away to the object of affection. But although supreme love and personal consecration, may one imply the other, it is proper to distinguish them in considering this subject.—Nothing is more hard to a sinful mind, than it is to live for GOD and CHRIST, and whether we eat or drink or whatever we do, to do all for his glory. This christian requirement appears unpleasing to all who do not love GOD. They can find no happiness in it; nor do they conceive, how it can be a pleasant thing, to regard the Lord in all their thoughts, words and actions. It appears to them an obstacle in the way of all their joys, and that the happiness of living must be given up, thus to obey. The unpleasantness of this duty to every sinful mind is conceded; but this is no evidence it is not reasonable.

Serm. XVI. *Christian duties reasonable.*

GOD is the fountain of being, from whom we received our existence, and who upholds us every moment. All we are, all we possess, all our powers of acting, and capacities of receiving, are his gift; so that we are his property in the highest sense. Is it not reasonable he should have the use of his own property, and command us according to his pleasure? If there be such a thing as the right of property, it belongs to the creator; and the requirement is reasonable concerning our own personal actions and services.

ALL we possess is a divine gift, placed in our hands, under certain limitations of use.

Is it not reasonable we should devote our use of his gifts to his honor and the purposes of his infinite goodness in giving? He gives on these conditions, and we have no right to depart from the conditions of the gift.

THE Lord our GOD is most excellent, in his nature. His glory and blessedness exceed a whole creation in value, beyond any proportion, which can be described. Is it not reasonable for the finite and dependent creature, to devote himself to the great *all in all?*

THE glory of GOD and the happiness of his kingdom are inseparably united in the divine counsel and providence. What infinite wisdom hath thus joined together, no creature hath right to put asunder. Christian consecration is, therefore, to the kingdom of GOD. Every service of holy dedication, tends to promote the good of our brethren. It either glorifies GOD whom they love and delight to see honored, or is beneficial to our brethren of his family. And is it not reasonable to have our whole being devoted to the glorious kingdom of Christ—to do good—and to promote that holiness, from which the most pure happiness proceeds?

To be devoted to God, and whether we eat or drink, or whatever we do, do all for his glory, is the greatest honor, and most perfect happiness of a creature; and therefore a reasonable service. The selfishness and pride of sin are self-disappointing. With a purpose of exalting himself, the sinner falls into deep degradation and looses the perfection, of which his nature is capable. With the purpose of acquiring happiness, and under the power of an all-grasping self-love, he looses the rational bliss of intelligence and sinks into pain. Separated from God he hath nothing, but the littleness of a dependent guilty creature. He can never make himself more than he is; nor by other means be so honorable, as he may by consecrating himself, body and spirit, to the service of the Lord.

To become a living sacrifice to God is beginning the life of glory. And let the common sense, even of an unholy person answer, which is the greatest happiness; either to enjoy himself and the few things within his grasp, for a short season, or to be made of a temper, which prepares him to enjoy God and his kingdom forever and ever. By calling us to *present ourselves a living sacrifice, holy and acceptable to God*, he is calling us to the greatest dignity and peace, and therefore the duty is reasonable.

Still the refusing heart will object; to be so consecrated to God, as to seek his glory in eating and drinking, and in the common actions of life, is a thing impossible, and it is beyond the power of weak man to comply.

But let me aſk, how is it impoſſible, and why are they unable to comply? Men do now act from motives in eating, drinking, and the common actions of life. Is it not as poſſible, to do the ſame things from better motives, as from the ſinful ones by which they are now influenced? Unlawful things ought not to be done from any motive whatever; but, reſpecting all things which are right, it is as poſſible to do them from good as from evil motives. The want of a good heart is the only difficulty in complying. It is poſſible to do all things from right motives. It is poſſible to perform every action, under a ſenſe of duty and moral obligation to God and the ſyſtem of exiſtence with which we are naturally connected. This is what is meant by that conſecration to God, which doeth all things for his glory. It is feeling ourſelves to belong to God; to be his creatures; that we have duties appertaining to us, which are ſufficient to fill up the whole time of life; and actually doing them with this temper. Although, it may be impoſſible to have the glorious nature of God in actual perception, every moment of time and in every action performed; we may ſtill act, in every thing we do, under a ſenſe of moral and holy obligation. This is the duty required, and it is a reaſonable ſervice.

4thly. It is reaſonable, that the lives which we live in the fleſh, ſhould be by faith, in Jesus Christ the Son of God.

The ſupreme giver of every good and perfect gift, even in the caſe of thoſe who never ſinned, may rightfully preſcribe the manner in which he will beſtow. This is an evident right of ſovereignty; and from his infinite wifdom and goodnefs, it may be prefumed, he will appoint the beft manner. Much more may he prefcribe to guilty finners, who deferve utter rejection, how they fhall approach to afk, and how receive his undeferved favors. From his own information, we know that infinite purity forbids any other approach, than through his Son. Thus he can honourably give; and thus we may moft copioufly receive. Neither prefent nor future bleffings can be claimed as a matter of right. Faith in Jesus Christ, is going to God through him as a Mediator, to receive what we need. Is it not reafonable that creatures fhould go to God for the fupply of their needs, and that guilty creatures fhould go in the manner he directs? Do they not need a daily affiftance—the light and quickening of his holy fpirit? Looking to God through a Mediator, with a fenfe of their dependence and unworthinefs, for fuch temporal and fpiritual mercies as they need, is what chriftians mean, when they fpeak of living by faith, in Jesus Christ the Son of God. It muft be reafonable for God to beftow and for us to receive, in the manner, which is moft glorious for him, and which, at the fame time, fupplies our wants moft perfectly. It is conceived, no one can object againft the daily communion of faith in God and Christ, unlefs pride of heart forbids, and divine holinefs is diftafteful.

Every other chriftian grace is approved by reafon. Is it not reafonable for creatures, in all cafes, to fubmit to divine fovereignty; knowing that infinite wifdom and goodnefs will appoint in the beft manner? The inefficacy of a refifting will, and the ignorance of creatures what governmant of the univerfe is beft, are confiderations which teach the propriety of fubmiffion.

Patience under afflictions is a moſt excellent chriſtian virtue. The condition of human life is expoſed to innumerable evils, and no man hath a right to expect himſelf exempted from the lot of ſinful, weak humanity. A great portion of the ſacred writings is calculated to inſpire a patient ſpirit.—And is it not reaſonable? We have the example as well as the command of Christ. To ſhow the wiſdom of providence in impoſing trials, we ought to conſider our deſert at the hand of a holy God—the witneſs he ought to bear for his own rectitude, by his treatment of us—and the benefit of afflictions, to thoſe who endure them. They are a purifying furnace.— *Now no chaſtening for the preſent ſeemeth to be joyous, but grievous: nevertheleſs, it afterward yieldeth the peaceable fruit of righteouſneſs, unto them which are exerciſed thereby.* Patience is a moſt reaſonable duty.

5thly. Visible chriſtian morality, in all its branches, is a reaſonable ſervice, being neceſſary both for the glory of God and the good of ſociety.

Very few will dare to queſtion the excellence of chriſtian morals, as deſcribed in the goſpel. The moſt vicious fear the crimes of other men, ſo that there is a general conſent, even of the immoral, that viſible morality is reaſonable and to be deſired. In this reſpect, the chriſtian precepts excel all other writings. Arguments for viſible morality are drawn from the higheſt ſource, the nature and relations of God and his creatures.

Christian duties muſt proceed from an honeſt and benevolent heart. Such general rules of practice are given, as will comprehend every caſe. *Thou ſhalt love thy neighbour as thyſelf.— Therefore all things whatſoever you would that men should do to you, do ye even so to them.*—The law of the decalogue, is explained by innumerable gospel precepts, giving it the moſt extenſive application to every character, condition and circumſtance of life. Our neighbourly love muſt reach to all men. All are to be treated juſtly and honeſtly.—Their rights of perſon, property, purity and reputation are declared to be ſacred.—The higheſt good of every one, for time and eternity, is to be ſought.—We are to love and pray for enemies and do them good.—Revenge is forbidden, in every caſe; and we are to recompenſe evil for evil to no man, but to overcome evil with good. We are directed to be ſubject to government—in honor to prefer one another—to be kindly affectioned—to purſue the things which make for peace—to remember the poor, the widow and the afflicted, and to be like CHRIST who went about doing good.

FROM a multitude of ſimilar precepts, we learn the excellence of viſible chriſtian duty to men our brethren. It is alſo eaſy to ſee why the chriſtian morality, is more pure and extenſive than the heathen. The heathen morality is all drawn from ſelfiſh principles, and extends no further, than they were driven by neceſſity for their own immediate ſafety, in the civil compacts of life.—The chriſtian morality has a higher ſource in the principle of benevolence to being, and will, therefore, include every thing and extend to every caſe, where the happineſs and perfection of rational minds is affected. This law of viſible morality is good like GOD who gave it. It will make us reſemble him—make us the moſt happy we can be, and moſt inſtrumental of good to our brethren. If there were no evidence in favor of chriſtianity, but the ſuperior reaſonableneſs and excellence of ſuch moral duties, as are commanded between men; this would be enough to establish its obligations on all. In comparison with it, every other scheme of faith and practice must give way.

In christian practice, we may also include several duties, which depend on a positive institution. Of this kind are the gospel ordinances of baptism and the Lord's supper. That these are reasonable, will be contended by none, who have a previous conviction and love of the doctrines and personal consecration to God, which have been already considered.

The fitness of prayer to God, is acknowledged by those who have not the christian scheme of faith. Although prayer be much enjoined it does not wholly depend on a positive institution.— So with respect to the Sabbath, there is natural evidence that some part of time ought to be devoted to the worship of God. The positive institution, of a seventh part of time to be thus devoted, appears reasonable. If we had not this precept, through our inclination to forget God and depart from holiness, all worship of him would be soon omitted by the greatest part of men. The heathen, who have stated seasons for their idolatrous worship, appointed by their own authority, have succeeded in perpetuating their times and rites, only by making them carnivals of sin and sensuality. The sanctification of a Sabbath is, therefore, a reasonable service.

The more we examine into christian doctrines and duties, the more apparent it becomes that they are agreeable to reason and common sense; glorious for God and declarative of his perfection; and adapted to relieve sinners from their guilt. The christian may challenge mankind to search his doctrines and law of practice; and he may be assured that examination will terminate in their favor. If it be demanded why he glories in being a christian, he may appeal to his doctrines and law of holiness to answer for him. If it be objected, that many unreasonable articles of belief and wicked practices have been found among the professors of christianity, who claim high seats in the church; he must appeal from these scandalous examples, which cannot be denied, to the Holy Bible, which contains his creed and his law. He must show the objector that the most holy institutions, doctrines and laws, may be perverted, prostituted, and mingled with corruption by unholy men. He may appeal to the objector's own heart, and tell him; that the same aversion to christian holiness, through which he opposes the doctrines of revelation, hath led others, who have still called themselves christians, to misrepresent, to divide, to explain away, or to mingle human invention with the pure truth and precepts of GOD. Also, that many, retaining a true faith, have had the form without the power of godliness.

CHRISTIANITY hath a right to be judged, by its own books, and its written articles and laws; and those who dishonor it, either by wilful perversion to accommodate it to their own lusts, or by disobedience, must bear their own guilt.

SOME few, who have fallen into infidelity, have done it after much inquiry and with an actual knowledge of the evidence in favor of christianity. Such persons have followed the choice of their own hearts, and there is very little reason to expect they will ever be reclaimed. They have treated GOD and his gospel contemptuously, and *because they received not the love of the truth, that they might be saved. For this cause, GOD hath sent them strong delusion, that they should believe a lie.* It is the duty of christians, to use all means for reclaiming even such, still, there is little reason to expect success.

There is a very great number of people, in a different situation, whom I importune to consider. It is those who doubt, and have not yet come to a fixed conclusion. They are willing to reject christianity because they find no pleasure in the duties of religion.—It forbids many things, which are agreeable to their taste; it restrains their appetites; and calls them to a disagreeable self-renunciation. On these accounts, they are willing to disbelieve, if it can be done safely. Added to this natural temptation, they find a multitude of their neighbours in the same case, who are ready to make a common cause with them, in doubting the most sacred truths. They hear some, who are far advanced in the school of scepticism, ridiculing and scoffing; and others, of incurable morals, blaspheming. These greater sinners, are often found, among the affluent, the professedly wise, and the powerful ones of the world, by which means, they have a great advantage, either insidiously to seduce or haughtily to insult. Thus seduced, by their own inward corruptions, and the temptations around them, their doubts are becoming more bold. Instead of consulting the holy scripture, with a candid wish to know the truth; they rush into circles of impiety, hoping to hear some jest or argument against the religion of Christ. Instead of going to the closet, and imploring direction from the Father of light, they take counsel at the mouth of persons, who are talkative through vanity and ignorance. They are really, all this time, ignorant of christianity, and their whole attention hath been to find objections, rather than

to underſtand its doctrines or ſearch for the reaſonableneſs of its duties. They begin to conſider
reaſon and revelation, in a ſtate of natural oppoſition. They begin to eſteem their appetites, a
guide to happineſs and greatneſs.—They begin to
eſteem the piety of their Fathers to be ſuperſti-
tion, and pity the ignorance of the laſt age.
They conſider the lethargiſed ſtate of their own
conſciences to be a fortunate circumſtance, and
hope ſoon to find the liberty of ſin, in thinking
and acting as they pleaſe, without any premoni-
tion of death to come.

O UNHAPPY men! You are near the limits,
beyond which, ſovereign grace, either never or
very rarely, brings infidels back again to hope
and peace. You are not abſolutely fixed in rejecting his word, nor are your conſciences finally
ſeared. A few ſteps farther, in this courſe, will
probably place you in a ſtate, with which GOD
hath ſaid his Spirit ſhall not ſtrive. After a few
ſteps further, you will probably feel eaſy concerning another world, and there will be no bands in
your death. You have ſeen ſome of this character die without fear; but do not hope much from
this circumſtance; for the worſt of men, as often
die in ſtupidity, as the beſt do in chriſtian
triumph. Stupidity, though preſumptuous, hath
no peace in it.

IF death ſhould approach, while of the character I have ſuppoſed you to be, you will be terribly
ſurprized. You will not dare to die; you cannot
hope. You will find a GOD angry with ſin, and
feel the need of a mediator. You will find, that
ſin is miſery; that your own unholineſs is a curſe;
and that GOD need only leave you to yourſelves
to make you eternally miſerable. Conſcious of
guilt in reſiſting the light, you will groan in ſpirit, not daring to look towards an injured heaven
for needed light and grace. You probably will

say, I feel myself unable to pray, and you will beg the serious persons, whom you once ridiculed, to pray for you. Alas! Your case will pierce their hearts with sorrow, and they will try to pray, but it is uncertain whether they can; for if God hath left you, they will find their closets deprived of that divine aid, through which, on former occasions, they have often called fervently and effectually on God.

To all, who have not formed an ultimate determination to reject, let me propose the following questions; and let me beg of them to consider and give an answer to their own consciences, in some place suited for prayer and meditation on God, and with an open Bible in their hands.

Was not a distaste to the duties of religion, the true reason you began to doubt?—Do you not wish to find arguments against the law and gospel of God; and if you do, are you not prejudiced judges against the truth?—If prejudiced ought you not to suspect yourselves?—Have you ever examined the scriptures thoroughly, to know whether its doctrines and duties are reasonable?—Are not those persons who are tempting you, and on whose professed sentiments, you are building your own opinions and your ease, unworthy to be trusted in the immortal concerns of your soul?—Are not some of them very ignorant, vain, assuming, full of words without knowledge; and are not others of them immoral; and are not all of them persons in whose hands, you would not trust your worldly interest, without a check on their conduct? If so, is it not unwise in you to be influenced by their opinions, in a case of such infinite importance, as the obtainment or loss of eternal happiness? When you have thought danger approaching, did you not feel the need of a gospel and of a Saviour to make your appearance before God safe? Do you not sometimes feel guilty even for your doubts; and are not these doubts the greatest, when such indulgence of appetite, as you know to be wrong and dangerous to society, is most prevalent in your conduct?—Do you not find the duties of life, which all men allow to be fit, are most easily performed; and that temptations are most easily resisted, when the revealed commandments of God appear most real to you?—If God be our creator, he can give us the best instruction; and as he dwells in the praises of eternity, must be able to teach us the attainment of its blessedness; and have you by prayer asked his direction, that he would enlighten and fit you for the greatest good? If you have ever prayed, when were your doubts the greatest, either after you had looked to heaven for direction, or in the total neglect of duty? Have you ever found in your approaches to infidelity, such real peace of mind as you wished to obtain? If God were now to place you on the bed of death, could you say I depart peacefully? Could you forget your sins, and coming boldly into his presence, demand his mercy? Or, if you should thus do, is he under obligation to hear, and grant your request?

Before you reject the word of revelation, go into retirement, lay the holy scriptures before you, and lift your eyes for direction to him who created and now preserves you, and answer to your own conscience the questions I have proposed. Do it in solemn remembrance that God cannot be deceived, and that the consequences of your acting will be forever borne by yourself. I am certain, that, in this course, you cannot call the duties of religion unreasonable. You will find yourself to be both ignorant and guilty, and in need of the gospel salvation. May we all be enlightened unto eternal life. Amen.

SERMON XVII.

Christian resignation.

PSALM xlvi. 10.

Be still, and know that I am God.

THE text leads us to consider the nature, duty and effects of christian resignation. The whole Psalm is remarkable. It is a description of holy confidence in God; an exhortation to continue trusting in him; and a prophecy of the desolations he should make in the earth, to prepare the way for that peaceful state of the Messiah's kingdom, which will succeed the many ages of violence that have been in the world.

In the 10th verse, the prophet calls on the church, *Come, behold the works of the Lord, what desolations he hath made in the earth.* In the next verse he passes on to describe a period, which is still future. *He maketh wars to cease unto the end of the earth, he breaketh the bow and cutteth the spear in sunder, he burneth the chariot in the fire.* Then follows the text. *Be still and know that I am God;*

I will be exalted among the heathen, I will be exalted in the earth.

God ruleth in infinite and unsearchable wisdom. In the midst of darkness he is preparing for light, and in a way above the comprehension of men, is carrying on the scheme of infinite wisdom, so that all will redound to his greatest glory and the best good of his holy kingdom. It is creatures only, who are exposed to do evil; it is God alone, who brings good out of evil. This truth is believed and felt by good minds. They learn it from the word of God; from their own experience; and from the infinite glory, which they see in the God of their hope. In contemplation of this truth, the church, in the beginning of the Psalm, is represented as saying, *God is our refuge and strength, a very present help in trouble. Therefore will we not fear, though the earth be removed, and though the mountains be carried into the midst of the sea. Though the waters thereof roar and be troubled; though the mountains shake with the swelling thereof. There is a river, the streams whereof shall make glad the city of our God: the holy place of the tabernacles of the most high. God is in the midst of her; she shall not be moved: God shall help her, and that right early.* These expressions of confidence, in the goodness and safety of the divine government, are uttered by the church in view of the desolations which God maketh in the earth. They are a strong description of confidence, in all-ordering wisdom. The Lord is not to be trusted less in days of darkness and violence, than he is in days of prosperity. There is a command, *to rejoice evermore,* which is in force at all times; and though every thing may look terrifying to human wisdom, a christian faith rises from seeing the temper and actions of creatures, to a sight of divine wisdom, by which the whole is controled. In God himself we find reason to rejoice evermore, to be resigned, and still before him. This single truth, that God reigns, will in every scene, enlighten and give comfort to a pious mind.

The present is a period distinguished by calamities on mankind, through the exercise and violence of their own outraging passions. God is punishing men by their own sin, and there appears to be a preparation for much calamity to come. The word of the Lord is going through the earth, to show his truth and holiness. And though human wisdom cannot look to the end of the scene, nor see in every event what God is doing, nor determine the future times and seasons; a christian faith, directed by his word, beholds a divine hand. Faith sees the king of Zion, going forth conquering and to conquer, and preparing the way to fulfil his promise. *The kingdom and the dominion, and the greatness of the kingdom under the whole heaven, shall be given to the people of the saints of the most high, whose kingdom is an everlasting kingdom, and all dominions shall serve and obey him.* While many dark events are ushering in the desired time, faith is still, knowing that the Lord is God, and doing all things right.

The dispensations of infinite wisdom which affect great bodies of men are more conspicuous, and many suffer or rejoice together; therefore, they are more noticed in the memorials of past ages. But the same wise and holy God is acting in the daily events of time, which are confined in their influence, to the condition of families and individuals. Here also, faith and resignation are necessary for the peace of men. There are so many pains, disappointments, and overturnings, that it is scarce possible to go forward a single day with peace, unless we *know that the Lord is* GOD *and are still before him.* Resignation, flowing from a belief of GOD's infinite wisdom and holiness, is a principal ingredient of christian peace. Resignation is the fortitude of a christian, for it is that, by which he overcomes and is happy. Resignation, even if we judge on worldly principles, is the honor of a christian; for it needs more firmness and self-command to be resigned, than it does to complain. Resignation is the duty of a christian; for infinite wisdom hath a right to direct in all cases whatever. Resignation is necessary for all mankind. Many evils must be borne. Frailty is attached to our persons, our properties, and the condition of our existence, and those who are most successful in life, must endure many disagreeable things. There are pains and sorrows due to the nature of man in this world, which his power cannot overcome nor his skill evade. The christian, who hath a promise of GOD, that all things shall work for his good hath no promise to escape them; and the divine help which he is encouraged to seek, is patience and resignation to bear. He must have pain; perhaps, poverty and blasted expectation in his offspring and his interest; the calumny and persecution of enemies; an endless variety of trials from the sin of others, his own sin, and the frailty of every surrounding object; the more in number and richness his blessings are, the more capable they become of bitterly afflicting him by the loss; and he must finally part with the whole, that is desirable in this world. Through this path of life the good man must walk.

THE covenant of grace gives him no encouragement of exemption from these trials; so far from this that it saith, *I will visit their transgression with the rod, and their iniquity with stripes.* Nevertheless, *my loving kindness will I not utterly take from him, nor suffer my faithfulness to fail. If ye endure chastening, God dealeth with you as sons: For what son is he whom the Father chasteneth not?* To those who forget God, afflictions are necessary to teach them the end of sin. To those, who have an interest in the covenant of grace, they are a covenanted portion, for their purifying and the trial of their faith. In each of these dispensations God is wise and holy ; and all men, on one principle or another must expect them. Let resignation or stillness before God, be therefore sought, as a temper necessary for the happiness of man in this world.

To illustrate the nature, duty, and effects of resignation, the following things shall be considered.

I. What is designed in the text, by knowing that the Lord is God.

II. The reasons of christian resignation.

III. The blessed effects which follow a resigned temper.

IV. To describe certain kinds of resignation, which may be found in an unholy state, and mistaken for true grace.

I. What is designed in the text, by knowing that the Lord is God.

There are many truths, which men by their actions do not appear to know. They act as if ignorant, or fully determined to treat them with no regard. We often speak of persons, as being ignorant of truth and duty, when they act, in all respects, as if they did not know. Although none are absolutely ignorant of the being of a God, for all must have heard this glorious truth; there are many, who act as they would do, if they supposed there were none. The truth is disagreeable; they are willing to be ignorant; they drive the subject from their meditations; and are many times so successful as not to be molested by the remembrance. *The fool hath said in his heart there is no* GOD. This is directly opposed to knowing that the Lord is GOD, which implies,

1st. A BELIEF and practical apprehension of his being and glorious attributes; of his presence and constant efficiency; that he is near and not afar off; that in him *we live and move and have our being.* For the exercise of any christian grace we must *believe that he is, and that he is a rewarder of them that diligently seek him.* An ignorance of GOD's being and presence, is a foundation for all impiety. It is a principal cause of the crimes, with which a sinful life is filled; for if there were a just apprehension of him, they would be restrained, although the heart is not right with him. Hence, we find in the holy word, such pains taken to impress our minds with the being of GOD; that he lives, that he acts, that he is every where present, that we are in his hand, that we are ever near him, and subject to his sovereign will. A sense of this truth, is the beginning of all serious consideration in sinners; and the quickening of all gracious affection in christians. Whoever is still before GOD must know that he is, and be filled with an apprehension of the reality, the glory, fulness and eternity of his being. It may justly be feared that many good people, suffer the world so far to intrude and drive an apprehension of GOD from their minds, as to prevent resignation. They are impatient, are fretful with the things taking place around them, not recollecting that GOD is here; and thus great sin is committed. In such cases, it is not a sufficient excuse, that the impatience is not pointed immediately against GOD; for the probable reason it is not, is becauſe he is out of ſight. Impatience with a condition, though there be not a preſent recollection, that it is ordered by the Almighty; is ſtill a ſin againſt him. The creature ought to ſee and adore him in every thing.

2dly. In knowing the Lord to be GOD, is implied an apprehenſion of his all-directing providence. As he made, ſo he ſupports.

THE power which acted in creating, acts continually in a providential government. It ſeems to us, as though the ſight would be wonderful, to ſtand and ſee a world of creatures riſing into exiſtence by the creating will; but ſetting aſide the novelty of the ſcene, it is as wonderful, to behold a world of creatures continue exiſting, upheld, moved, acted upon, and deſtined to their end, by the providential efficiency of the Almighty. The exiſtence which we feel, and the things which we ſee, are effects of a power now acting. He upholds the laws of nature. All things, from the upholding of a world, to the falling of a hair, are the preſent work of GOD. This conſtant acting of Deity is what we call providence. It is univerſal, taking in the whole; and it is particular, extending to the moſt minute events. It is a divine action, here and every where preſent. There is no power or wiſdom, foreign to himſelf and the effects of his will, by which he is influenced.

THIS apprehenſion of divine providence, will make every good mind very joyful, and at the ſame time, very ſolemn. A providence of this kind is eſſential to GODHEAD, and unleſs we have ſuch apprehenſions of him, we do not know him as GOD. Doubtleſs an unholy mind will object againſt this conſtant ſenſe of providential action, and confider it as a caufe of unhappinefs; but unholy minds do not know the Lord, as God. Nothing ought to be called chriftian refignation, which doth not thus realize a fupreme and all-directing providence.

3dly. Knowing the Lord to be God, includes a full conviction of his perfect wifdom and goodnefs in governing.

Many who believe there is a God, and a fupreme providence, do not appear to have a conviction of his wifdom, in his own nature and in all his works. They do not confider perfect wifdom and goodnefs to be fo effential and neceffary to Godhead as infinite power. In this cafe, they are judging from the darknefs of depravity, and do not by their opinion honor him as God. There may be apathy; there may be the fubmiffion of neceffity; there may be the fubmiffion of a felfifh heart, willing God fhould reign for its own benefit; but there cannot be holy refignation, without a belief of infinite wifdom and goodnefs in the divine government. Chriftian refignation, is an exercife of a holy heart, directed by a rational underftanding; and reafon can never approve a fovereign action, which is not wife and good. The Gods of the heathen are vanity and a lie; fo may be the God of many in chriftian lands. Thofe who have chriftian means of information, may be refigned through falfe apprehenfions of the divine character, of his wifdom and the nature of his government, and thus their fervice be neither rational nor holy. A full conviction of divine wifdom and goodnefs in his government is neceffary for knowing the Lord to be God, and for a holy fubmiffion.

II. I am to defcribe the reafons of chriftian refignation.

Serm. XVII. *Christian resignation.*

The exhortation, be still and know that I am God, relates to the state of the heart or will, in view of divine sovereignty ordering all events which take place. Reference is particularly had, to the affliction dispensed in divine judgment; for it immediately follows a call to behold the desolations, which God makes in the earth, as a preparation for his own peaceful kingdom. Being still before God means a quiet submission to his will, and all the works of his providence. A heart acquiescing in the purposes of his government, and the means by which they are executed.

A christian is conformed to the divine character, and having the same objects of love and desire, is inclined to acquiesce by the same reasons which move God to decree and execute.

In all cases, where the reasons of infinite wisdom are known, they become reasons for resignation. The glory brought to God by a display of his holiness; the advancement of his kingdom; the suppression or punishment of sin, are, in particular cases, motives to divine action, and they are reasons for christian resignation.

Further, the infinite wisdom and holiness of Gdo, is, in all cases, a sufficient reason for men to be resigned to his government. He cannot do wrong; he cannot act unwisely; cannot desire any thing that is unfit, or choose improper means to execute a good end. Infinite wisdom and goodness, enable him to devise and execute in the best manner; so that his whole government is right and glorious. This is the great reason for christian resignation, and is sufficient at all times, and under all events.

It is desirable, if God permit, to know the reasons of his government, and we may humbly search to find them out; but if they remain hid, it is, notwithstanding, our duty to be resigned. A knowledge of his infinite and holy wisdom is sufficient cause to rejoice and be still.—This cause for resignation is as sufficient in days of trial, as it is in times of prosperity; for GOD is wise in both. In view of his infinite perfection, and in a love of his government and the kingdom he is forming by the best means, a holy mind under trials will say; though he slay me, I will trust in him and be patient; although the fig-tree shall not blossom, I will rejoice; although I am not personally benefitted, he will be glorious and his kingdom be made happy, I will therefore resignedly say, his will be done.

It is not difficult to see, that these reasons for resignation may exist and operate in times of the deepest personal trials. Indeed, it is in such times, we have the best opportunity for examining the sincerity of our submission. One end of GOD's covenant faithfulness in sending afflictions, is, thus to assist his people in examining their own sincerity, that their joy in his grace may be very great.

III. I WILL next describe some benefits of a resigned temper.

ALTHO' our resignation is due to the perfection of the Lord and of his government, and this is the great reason which influences a holy mind; we ought also to remember its benefits, which are great to the possessor.

1. RESIGNATION will make us happy in GOD himself. Our relation to GOD and dependence upon him are natural and necessary. They ever have been and must ever remain; nor can we in any situation, nor for any moment detach ourselves from the consequences of his universal action. His will which acts is uniform and un-

changeable. Whatever our belief may be of his infinite perfection, and however clear our rational conviction; unless our hearts are resigned to his character and providence we cannot be happy in him. His counteracting will and works, will soon raise in our perverse hearts, an enmity against his very existence. Every prospect of his being, will be attended with wretchedness, and the growing misery of opposition. As we are situated under the divine government, nothing but resignation can make us happy in GOD himself. If resigned, in every display of himself, he will appear to us most excellent and glorious; we shall constantly rejoice in his infinite perfection; and become more happy in our knowledge and union to him.

2dly. RESIGNATION will make us happy in the reality and truth of a divine providence. According as the state of the heart varies, the doctrine of a supreme providence is a source of the most sensible pleasure or pain. A mind in opposition to the general principles of providence, must be unhappy in a knowledge of its reality. His governing agency will be dreaded, through a suspicion that his designs are unfriendly, and will end, either in direct punishment or a denial of desired enjoyments. Holy resignation produces the reverse of this. The universal providence of GOD is a pleasing subject for meditation. Resigned to the principles and certainty of divine government, the mind can look on every scene with composure, and comfort itself by reflecting; though all things appear dark and confused, there is wisdom, power and goodness ordering the whole. All will be right. I have confidence in this direction. Though it be impossible for me to see the wisdom of many events, or how my own personal trials will turn to good; they are

the ordering of a wife God, and muft be right.—
Thus the refigned chriftian is made happy by
his certain knowledge of God's providence, for
when every event appears dark and threatening,
and his own weaknefs great ; he cafts himfelf on
the light of infinite wifdom and the ftrength of
infinite power.

3dly. Hence it appears that refignation is the
true balm for all the wounds given by an afflicting world; yea more, it is a victory over the
world. It is an exercife of the new born heart,
and a fruit of that faith, of which the apoftle
fays, *For whatfoever is born of God overcometh the
world: and this is the victory that overcometh the
world, even our faith.*—Under the reviling of enemies, it can fay ; Let them curfe, becaufe the
Lord hath bid them do it. Under actual fuffer-
ing, it can obey the command, *Love your enemies,
blefs them that curfe you, do good to them that hate
you, and pray for them which defpitefully ufe you,
and perfecute you.* It can pray under the trials of
providence. *If it be poffible, let this cup pafs from
me: neverthelefs, not as I will, but as thou wilt.*—
For the inftruments of affliction, however wicked in their conduct, it can pray. *Father forgive
them ; for they know not what they do.* Under
bereavement of friends, it can fay. *The Lord
gave, the Lord hath taken away, bleffed be the name
of the Lord.* When outward comforts of the
world fail it can rejoice. For *though there be no
herd in the ftall, I will joy in the God of my falvation.*
The mind thus fortified, is placed above the power
of man and the world. Its peace is founded on
the rock of ages. It can fee the glory of God,
when his way is in darknefs and the deep waters.
It can kifs the *rod, and the hand which appointeth
it ;* and fay, *it is good for me that I am afflicted,* and
the government which doth this is the govern-

ment of my choice. The wisdom of GOD is so perfect I can wish no change in his plan, or its execution. If I am pained, let me be pained, for the honor of GOD requires it. This resigned soul, in the closing of the earthly scene triumphs, *O death where is thy sting, O grave where is thy victory.*

Is not this a victory over the world, over sin and death? To be happy in duty is to conquer; and this is the only victory a creature can have. In these sentiments, a humble christian, tho' most sensible of his own weakness, can rejoice because the Lord reigneth. When the world of unbelieving sinners, behold a christian who feels these things; let them reverence the power of sovereign and sanctifying grace. Let them know that the effectual, fervent prayer of this disciple avails much. Let them here see the strength of GOD, made perfect in the weakness of a creature; and infinite truth fulfilling the promise, *Lo! I am with you alway, even unto the end of the world.*

4. CHRISTIAN resignation will make duty easy to the people of GOD.

THE christian law of holiness is called the *perfect law of liberty.* The most glorious and excellent of all freedom, is that which disposes us to follow truth and duty. If CHRIST shall make us free; if we be free in doing our duty; if we be delivered from the reigning power of sin, this is being free indeed. This freedom is felt in resignation and makes all duty easy, to the obedient believer. Unholy persons never obey in an evangelical sense, and their legal attempts to obey are a slavery of the mind, between a love of sin, and the terrors of the law and an accusing conscience.

CHRISTIAN resignation makes duty easy and pleasing. Experience gives conviction, that there is, in most cases, a sensible benefit in obeying. But if there be no sensible and personal benefit from obedience, resignation can take up the cross and follow the commands of CHRIST in a dark way. It can say there is comfort enough in duty, from the single consideration, that GOD hath commanded and CHRIST is honored. These are among the happy effects of that resigned temper, which CHRIST commanded his people. When they do their duty best, they are most happy; and it is not in the power of man to destroy their peace.

IV. I AM, next, to describe certain kinds of resignation, which may be found in an unholy state of the heart, and mistaken for true grace.

To all, who are deceived in their own state, this is the most interesting part of the subject; and it is probable that not a few are in this case. Resignation is so plainly a christian grace, that no person of any consideration, will dare think himself safe, without supposing he possesses it. Many, both live and die quietly, by thinking they are resigned; at the same time, there is perhaps no grace, concerning which men are more liable to be deceived. Whatever prevents a sensible resistance and enmity to the divine government, may be mistaken for resignation; and this may be prevented by the most selfish considerations, which have in them, nothing of holiness, or a love of GOD for what he is, or approbation of the principles by which he governs.

1. A WANT of feeling, a loss of all sense of moral obligation, may be mistaken for a resigned temper.

This is the case with many, who have long given themselves up to sensuality, to a careless and licentious life, and a neglect of those divine institutions, which are designed to promote seriousness. True religion increases all the sensibilities of the soul, and at the same time, makes men submissive to a law, by which they may be happily exercised. The apostle, in enumerating the effects of original depravity, adds with other things, *without natural affection*. The original corruption of human nature, makes men hard hearted, and stupid. This is first discovered in their feeling towards others, and afterwards towards themselves. Even while a sinful pride and self-love are gaining strength, there is a stupidity concerning their own future well-being. When conscience is seared, their apprehensions concerning futurity and their future appearance before God are seared also. If they can have sinful indulgencies, for the present time, they are swallowed up in these, and are ready to say, *Soul, take thine ease, eat, drink and be merry*. This apathy concerning another world, is, sometimes, strangely continued, through those scenes of pain, which commonly precede death; and the unhappy soul mistakes the bands of security, for a pious resignation. These persons are sleeping the sleep of death, for evil is near them, and they cannot be made sensible. The surprize of a change will be great, and the tormenting powers of a condemning conscience will break on them when no resistance can be made.

2dly. I must next mention the resignation of selfishness.

All errors have their day of increase and decline. Certain prevailing sentiments of the present time, expose many to be deceived by the resignation of self-love. They accede to the truth, that GOD is good; and then draw the unscriptural consequence, if GOD be good we are safe—all in the end will be best for us.—Though we now suffer pain, GOD in the end will make us more happy, and in some future time, pay to us the debt of happiness, which we are purchasing by present afflictions. Thus they are resigned to present evils on the principle; that GOD will refund to them, in some after time, for what they now endure. They overlook justice. They have no regard to their demerits. They make their own particular benefit and not the general good, a rule for determining the wisdom and equity of providence. They bear pain now, without murmuring, to be repaid hereafter. This may be the state of the mind, and there is no telling how far it may be carried, without any holiness.

MEN have a natural conviction, that they ought to be resigned. They are often told that GOD is infinitely good. If to these, they can join a belief, it will in the end be best for them to endure; they may meet the losses of a disappointing life and the common terrors of a natural death, without any great discomposure. Especially, they may do this, when they find an allcontroling necessity which cannot be overcome. In this way, the unholy may be resigned, and are often deceived. They are resigned, because they suppose GOD is on their side, and doing better for them by his wisdom, than they can do for themselves. In this resignation, there is nothing different from the labor and fatigue of an inordinate worldling, which he chooses for himself one year, that he may be more happy, through many years, which he fuppofes are to fucceed.

To try this refignation let the fcheme of infinite truth and wifdom be brought into view. Let it be allowed, that God hath infinite wifdom and goodnefs; but that thefe do not require him to make every one moſt happy in the end. Let demerit be ſtated. Let there be given a defcription of the glory and good, which will redound to God and his kingdom, by treating fome finners according to their demerits. Let God's right to feek his own glory, be eſtabliſhed as a governing maxim of the divine government, and this fubmiffion will be gone. In the place of refignation, there will be cavils againſt the divine adminiſtration, and the rebelling heart will ſhow itfelf. The divine government will be called hard and unreafonable, and the fcriptures which propound thefe doctrines will be rejected.

Of all the fources of deception, this, at the prefent time, is one of the moſt common. It hence becomes an incumbent duty, on all the friends of truth and the fouls of men, to explain and vindicate the nature of holinefs, as confiſting in a difinterefted love and obedience to God. So long as men ferve God, are obedient and refigned to him, for their own fake alone; it is not true religion, and thofe may do it, who have not a ſingle heavenly ingredient in their character.

3dly. The refignation of neceffity, is often miſtaken for efficacious and fanctifying grace in the heart.

There is in the moſt unholy men a natural conviction of their dependence. The daily pains, wants and difappointments of life force them to believe what they do not choofe. Through a long and unfuccefsful refiſtance they defpair of succeeding against God. A supposed impossibilty, destroys the vigor of desire, and makes them think they do not wish that, which they would seize with the utmost avidity, if the thing were known to be possible. Hence comes the resignation of necessity, of which many make a merit to themselves in their lives, and a hope in their death.

When their earthly prospects are blasted, either in ambition or interest, they renounce the world because they cannot have it. If those, who think they feel submission, in such cases, would faithfully examine their hearts, they would find a lurking suspicion of partiality in the divine government; or the first springing of enmity against more fortunate adventurers in the change of the world. By this they might know their own insincerity, and detect a heart, which is deceitful above all things.

When their friends are laid in darkness, the heart quarrels with God, until it is found, that a contending will cannot raise the dead. Then, some other object of idolatrous affection is found. The heart, being weaned from its old attachment by a new one, becomes calm, the pain ceases, and this is called christian resignation.

When death approaches the struggle is more severe; but even here, the delusion may prevail. All the aid of reason and philosophy is called in, and perhaps the physician's opiate gives an unnatural ease to the paroxism of pain in the dying body and an inebriated prospect of eternity, from which many quiet death-beds have come. The decay is found to be irresistible. Both art and wishes are baffled. The soul loaths its own diseased habitation, and from the inquietude natural to men, is ready to wish a change of state. The impotence of the world to help, weans the mind from it. The appetites are laid dead through the approaching death of the body. The enfeebled animal makes the mind a babe, and to the inquiry of anxious friends it is answered, *I am resigned*. But whether this be a holy resignation; whether there be a love and submission to GOD for what he is, and the wisdom of his government, is a solemn question which eternity and an appearance before his all-searching bar, will answer best.

It is hard to wound the feelings of a deathbed. Nothing, but a deep and an uncommon sense of the worth of souls, will enable any one to do it. Let not the healthy and the living defer the question of the sincerity of their own resignation, until that precarious moment. How exposed it is to a delusion! How unable the mind is, then to judge! How hard for surrounding friends, to be the messengers of alarm! How hard for the watchman in Zion, at this untimely moment, to terrify the dying, and fill the hearts of mourners, with many sorrows!

If wise, we shall often examine the state of our own hearts, previous to the approach of death. Now we have opportunity, instruction, and a judgment unimpaired by the weakness of the body. Whether we have a christian resignation, and are prepared for another world, is a question which ought to be most solemnly and rationally determined, before the hour of bidding a hasty farewel to the world. In examining the sincerity of our souls, let us be guarded against that selfishness of the human heart which is its sin. A reverence and love of divine perfection in his nature and government, is the cause of a holy resignation. May we, through the grace of GOD, experience this and be happy. AMEN.

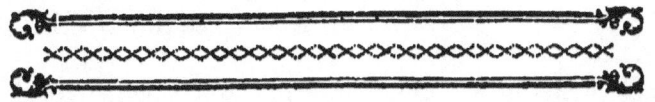

SERMON XVIII.

On the evidence of forgiveneſs.

JAMES ii. 18.

—*I will ſhow thee my faith by my works.*

THERE are two ſacred paſſages, written by the apoſtles Paul and James, which may appear contradictory, if we do not attend to the very different ſubjects they were conſidering.

PAUL ſaith, *Therefore we conclude, that a man is juſtified by faith without the deeds of the law.*

JAMES ſaith, *Ye ſee then how that by works a man is juſtified; and not by faith only.*

THE two apoſtles are explaining very different points of chriſtian doctrine. In ſeveral chapters, Paul explains and proves the doctrine of our juſtification to eternal life, by the free grace of GOD, through the righteouſneſs of JESUS CHRIST. Juſtification is an act of free and ſovereign grace, forgiving ſin and accepting the guilty to eternal life. It is a judicial act or determination of GOD, acquitting the tranſgreſſor from puniſhment, and decreeing to him the forgiveneſs of ſin and eternal bleſſedneſs. The ſuffering and obedience of CHRIST, are the righteouſneſs, on account of which, unworthy ſinners are forgiven and have a promiſe of moſt glorious redemption. This righteouſneſs is the only meritorious ground of juſtification. Sinners can do nothing to purchaſe forgiveneſs. Perfect holineſs, if it be found in a creature, is no more than his preſent duty; ſo that if there be any atonement or meritorious cauſe of forgiveneſs, it muſt be from without himſelf. One ſin, if it were to be followed by no more, would require an infinite mediator to ſave. The moſt pure and ſanctified chriſtian hath as much need of a redeemer and of ſovereign mercy, as the moſt guilty ſinner. Although there may be more ſins to forgive, in one caſe, than in the other; both need the ſovereign grace of GOD, through his Son CHRIST JESUS. The ſtated way, of receiving juſtification or the benefits of free grace through CHRIST, is by faith. It is not required that we purchaſe, for this is impoſſible. We are required to receive, as a free gift, through the righteouſneſs of CHRIST, which is of infinite value. Receiving or chooſing GOD, who offers himſelf and his grace, in this way; and receiving CHRIST and his goſpel with the law of holineſs contained in it, is a ſaving faith. It is alſo called a juſtifying faith. In this ſenſe, the apoſtle Paul ſaid, *Therefore we conclude, that a man is juſtified by faith without the deeds of the law.* Faith does not merit, but only receives a ſalvation merited by CHRIST; and in this ſenſe it is called a juſtifying faith. In this ſenſe we are juſtified by faith, and not by any deeds of obedience which we can render.

WHEN James ſays, *Ye ſee then how that by works a man is juſtified, and not by faith only,* he is explaining another doctrine. He is describing, not the manner of our justification by GOD; but the evidence that we are justified, or that our faith is a sincere one. GOD hath promised to justify all who have faith. For our comfort, it is necessary we should have evidence, that we are accepted according to promise; and our works are the only evidence, which the nature of the case admits, for the sincerity of our faith. Paul was describing the manner of our personal justification by GOD. James is describing the justification or proof that our faith is sincere, or in other words, the proper evidence to ourselves and others that we are forgiven, and have a right thro' the mercy of GOD to eternal life. That this is the meaning of James is evident by attending to the context from verse 14 to 20. *What doth it profit, my brethren, though a man say he hath faith, and have not works? Can faith save him? If a brother or sister be naked, and destitute of daily food; and one of you say unto them, depart in peace, be ye warmed and filled; notwithstanding ye give them not those things which are needful to the body; what doth it profit? Even so faith, if it hath not works, is dead, being alone. Yea, a man may say, thou hast faith, and I have works: shew me thy faith without thy works, and I will shew thee my faith by my works. Thou believest there is one GOD: thou doest well: the devils also believe, and tremble. But wilt thou know, O vain man! that faith without works is dead?*

MEN are disposed to think well of their own state, and often suppose it to be good, without any reason. They may, on false grounds, or without any grounds at all, suppose they have faith, and are forgiven. There is faith of a kind which is not justifying, as in the instance of the fallen spirits. This kind of faith, will be no more effectual in us, than it is in them. It is therefore prudent to bring our faith to a trial, and see if there be any evidence which will prove or justify its sincerity. If there be, we may hope; if there be not, it is a false and unholy faith, and of no more efficacy to salvation, than empty words are to clothe and feed the naked and the hungry.

WORKS, in the large latitude, which the word must be here understood, are the only evidence that can justify or prove the holy sincerity of our faith, to ourselves and to our brethren. It is conceived, that works, mean the whole of a holy temper and practice. The christian sanctification is a new heart, exercised in an assemblage of holy affections and graces, and terminating in a visible obedience to the whole law. Holy exercises can never be separated, in such a manner, that one may exist, where there is a total want of all others. Repentance will accompany a love of GOD. A love of GOD will be followed by a love of the brethren. If our faith be holy it will be joined with other holy exercises, and a general obedience in heart and life. Although every christian grace hath a known moral nature, by which it is essentially different from sin; yet if we suppose ourselves to possess it and it be not accompanied with other graces, there is reason to fear we are deceived. It is more probable we are deceived, than it is that one holy exercise exists alone. Also, however firmly we may believe the sincerity of our hearts, it is more probable we are deceived, than it can be that a sincere and holy heart will produce a very wicked life. In trying our faith, we must therefore, for evidence, have recourse to our whole temper and practice; to our works, in the large sense, the word has been defined.

In the judgment we make of the state of others, we must, for evidence, have recourse to every thing either in their words or actions, which explains the moral state of their hearts, and is descriptive either of their conformity or want of conformity to God and his kingdom. All who have faith are forgiven. By this train of thought we are therefore brought to the following point.

To consider the evidence of faith, or in other words, to consider the evidence of a gracious forgiveness and acceptance by God. I will divide the subject into two inquiries.

I. What is the evidence, on which we ought to judge our neighbour to be forgiven and accepted by God?

II. On what evidence may we judge ourselves to be forgiven?

I. What is the evidence, on which we ought to judge our neighbour to be accepted by God.

As God hath committed our eternal interests, specially to our own care, it is a matter of much the greatest moment, that we judge rightly of ourselves, and here our principal labor should be directed. Still, there are cases, in which we are called to judge of the spiritual state of other men. It is necessary for our christian communion with them; for determining the propriety of committing into their hands the offices in the church of Christ; and for treating them in a manner the best calculated for their salvation, for their awakening, if they be unsanctified, and for their edification and comfort in the faith, if they be the true people of God.

All, whose faith is right, *are created in Christ Jesus unto good works.* They have, from his fulness, received *grace for grace*, that is, some degree of moral virtue conformable to all the moral perfections of the divine character. There is a beginning sanctification of the whole heart, the beginning of experimental grace and the duties of a holy life. In seeking evidence of other mens sincerity, the inquiry is not to be confined to their faith or any other particular grace or action; but extended to the whole moral character, both practice and the inward state of the heart, so far as the heart can be evidenced to our understanding and entitled to the credit of others. The heart of man is expressed to others by an infinite variety of words, actions, and their whole appearance in society. Actions may so effectually contradict words, as to destroy their credit; and where some capital actions of life are irreprovable, there may be many things expressive of levity and an insincere heart. In all cases, the following things, are necessary evidence of a holy heart and true faith.

1. A professed belief of the doctrines of grace and holiness, as they are revealed to us in the word of God.

But few will deny this, who really believe the scriptures, and suppose there is any thing in religion, and any eternal consequences depending on our present conduct. There may be persons in christian lands, who really are of no religious faith. These, either for the sake of reputation or some worldly and selfish cause, may choose to be thought of the christian faith. As they wish to have their own christianity received without evidence, they may be willing to extend the same liberality to others. Travelling together in the road to infidelity, yea, even with souls under their guidance, *they may agree to disagree*, in the most holy truths of revelation. These persons betray their want of gospel sincerity, by avowing, that articles of faith and profession are of no importance ; though it be a most certain truth, that mens practice, in the sight of GOD, will be according to their faith.

ALL, who are willing to have the gospel practice ; all who love the souls of others ; all who know the pleasure of holy communion in the faith of CHRIST's gospel ; all who believe that religion is a moral principle of the heart ; all who have only the low degree of christian understanding, which perceives the connexion between doctrinal belief and practice, will see a personal profession of christian doctrines to be necessary evidence of a holy heart and of true faith.

IT is evident, by reading the scriptures of CHRIST and his apostles, that we are required to show great boldness in the faith, and even to give up our lives in defence of it. But how can this be, if a personal profession of faith be not required from us ? It would have been a strange doctrine to the apostles and primitive martyrs, to hear it said, by men who still meant to be called christians, that articles of faith were of little importance, if a man's life be civil. They did not so learn CHRIST and his gospel. On these principles, they might, have been good apostles ; and at the same time have saved their lives in the courts of heathen lawgivers and judges. The law of JESUS requires christians, not only to profess, but to abide in their faith, even to death ; and those who disobey in this requirement do not give christian evidence that they have faith unto forgiveness and eternal life.

Further, every sincere christian loves the law of God and the doctrines of the gospel. He sees in them a beauty and glory, which charm his heart. He is made happy in reading and obeying them; and it is impossible he should hide this happiness from others. So far from this, it will be his daily endeavour, in a public and humble manner to declare his faith. He will esteem it his duty, thus to honor God; and thus to call his unhappy fellowmen, to the salvation of peace and holiness. Although we have no right to prescribe the faith of others, benevolence will dispose every true disciple of Christ, to teach mankind the doctrines and duties of that gospel, by which he has found comfort, and a deliverance from the wrath, that is to come on the ungodly.

2dly. Another evidence of a true faith, which we have right to require from other men, before we receive them as our christian brethren, is a visible obedience to the moral law.

The moral law is the law of a christian temper and practice. Grace without a holy practice exists no where, except in the imagination of guilty men, and is no where described in the christian scriptures. Moses and Christ gave the same law of holiness, for the hearts and visible practice of men. Christ says of the law, *I am not come to destroy, but to fulfil.* In another place, *For had ye believed Moses, ye would have believed me.* In respect of holiness, both of heart and life, the gospel and the law command the same things. The gospel of free grace and forgiveness, saves men by creating in them a spirit of love and obedience to the law; and though this obedience hath no merit, it is the preparation for heaven, and the only evidence of a gracious forgivenefs. Faith receives the juftifying righteoufnefs of CHRIST ; and conformity to the law in heart and in vifible works of holinefs is the evidence of a right faith. Hence it appears, that vifible morality, is a neceffary evidence of true faith in JESUS CHRIST. Faith is an exercife of a holy heart ; and a holy heart will always fhow itfelf in a pure practice, in a vifible obfervance of the moral law, and of fpecial gofpel inftitutions. We therefore find, all moral duties to GOD and man commanded in the gofpel ; and all immoralities, are confidered as fufficient evidence, againft chriftian fincerity. A holy life ; a pure practice ; actions denoting reverence and a love of GOD ; juftice and mercy to men ; perfonal purity and fanctification ; and a dedication of all our active powers to the glory of GOD and the good of mankind, both for time and eternity, are enumerated as the proper life of chriftians, and the only evidence of their fincerity. There are the moft exprefs laws, enjoining chriftians to reject from their communion and the fellowfhip of their holy body, all, who by their practice, do not appear to love the holy commandments of JESUS CHRIST. The unjuft, the difhoneft, the profane, the impure of every defcription, the difturbers of fociety by their wilful injury of mens reputation and interefts, the intemperate deftroyers of their own ability to do good, the neglectors of GOD and his inftitutions, and thofe who by any wilful crime injure fociety and their neighbour, can give no evidence they are chriftians indeed. The law of CHRIST confiders all fuch, as infincere perfons, until by reformation, they give evidence of their repentance and faith.

3dly. THERE may be what is commonly called a moral life, while the heart is unholy. A conviction by experience, that there is no other way of safety in the fociety of the world, may, influence men to a moral life, in this fenfe of morality. They may be tender of other mens reputation, merely to preferve their own. They may be honeft in their dealings to engrofs a great worldly property to themfelves. They may join in the public worfhip of GOD, from a conviction that often meeting together harmonizes the paffions of men, which are naturally ferocious, and tends to preferve a civil government that protects their honor and their properties. All this is often done, where there is no love of GOD's holinefs—no fenfe of moral obligation.

THE queftion arifes, is that, which is commonly called a moral life, fufficient evidence of forgivenefs and of being a chriftian indeed?

CHRIST tells us, *Wherefore by their fruits ye fhall know them*. The fruits of a good and holy heart are proper evidence of fincerity and forgivenefs. And what are thefe fruits? The defcription, *a moral life*, may be extended to include every thing expreffive of the heart; but it is not commonly thus ufed. A fupreme love of GOD and all holy objects is the chriftian fincerity to which forgivenefs is promifed, and this will always exprefs itfelf, in ways beyond what is commonly meant by a moral life. A man may treat his neighbour morally, while it is very apparent that he does not love him, and delight in his profperity. All mankind fee the difference between formal complaifance, and the refpect of fervent love; between formal obedience, and a fincere one; between an action delightful in itfelf, and one that is done to ferve another purpofe and in which the heart takes no pleafure. There are innumerable cafes in which the heart is moft perfectly expreffed, by things which cannot be defcribed, and duties which can never be reduced to a written rule. The sensibilities of the heart appear in ways which words cannot picture. They are conceived, they are felt, but never described in language. We always expect to find this evidence of sincerity, in forming the friendships of the world; and a want of it at once excites our distrust.

CHRISTIAN sincerity requires an evidence which rises above formality. If men feel a supreme love of GOD, of his character and government, of his law and doctrines; there will be a natural expression of this love. They will be ready to express, in language which will be intelligible to all who have felt the same, their happiness in beholding and serving GOD. Their communion will be sweet in frequent conversation, instruction, advice and prayer to the glorious object of their common adoration; and the whole scene of their christian connection and obedience will be raised above formality. By a mutual engagedness to glorify GOD, to advance the kingdom of CHRIST, and save the souls of others, they will give evidence of their own sincerity and faith—that the glory of GOD is near their hearts —and that they think and act to promote it. Their thoughts will appear to be on the things of GOD and another world. This will banish that frivolous discourse and those foolish actions, in which many are constantly engaged, thereby proving that they never think of their own solemn destination, and the account they have to give before GOD. On the evidence which hath been mentioned, the communion of CHRIST's people in this world ought to be founded; and no part of it can be omitted, without substituting the form without the power of godliness. True obedience is of the heart. Whatever expresses this, describes the man as he will be finally judged by the christian law. Those who are afraid to have the heart searched, think differently from JESUS CHRIST. They discover insincerity, a want of conformity to GOD, and of preparation for *the day when he shall judge the secrets of men by JESUS CHRIST.*

. WHAT is the benefit of formality? Hath it any benefits in the earthly church? Is there any advantage in allowing, that formal persons are sincere. To them, it can be of no eventual advantage, for it only tends to continue them in a most dangerous slumber, from which they will suddenly awake in an awful eternity. Humanity and christian love forbid this. To the cause of CHRIST in the world, it can certainly be of no advantage. For hereby enemies of the truth gain an advantage, to corrupt both the doctrines and practice of the gospel; and the secure, seeing the formality of their appearance, are led to conclude there is no sincerity in religion, and that all believers are deceitful persons.

II. I AM to consider, on what evidence we may judge ourselves to be forgiven?

THIS is a most solemn point of inquiry; and who that realizes what it is to be happy or miserable forever, will not feel the weight of the question. If we misjudge concerning the sincerity of our brethren, though they may suffer some present disadvantages thereby, their eternal state is not endangered; through our misjudgment they will not suffer; and omniscience, which cannot err, will determine right. If we misjudge, in our own case, the loss is infinite. There is not another life of trial to correct the mistake. A false opinion cannot be pleaded in its own excuse. The lot for eternity is cast.

The sincerity of our own faith, or evidence of our forgiveness must be derived from our works, in the large sense the word is understood in this discourse. Although faith hath a determinate moral nature of its own, it is not safe to conclude we have it; unless we feel other gracious exercises of a holy heart. It is always to be presumed, that faith will be accompanied with a sensible love of holy objects, repentance, resignation, patience, and evangelical affections. It must, likewise be presumed, that a true faith will make all who possess it, conformed in their practice to the laws of CHRIST. They cannot believe without loving; nor can they love without observing his known commands. Sundry remarks will be made to assist in this examination.

1. To prove the sincerity of our faith, and that we are forgiven by GOD we must find in our hearts other gracious affections, which always accompany an evangelical faith. It is not credible, that we have received GOD and CHRIST by faith, if we do not love the essential and unchangeable perfections of the divine nature; such as his truth, justice, sovereignty and infinite holiness. It is not credible that we have faith, without a delight in the doctrines of CHRIST.— Whoever receives CHRIST will receive his commandments and all those truths, which he came into the world to teach and died to magnify.— All the works of providence are conformable to divine rectitude, and harmonious both with the gospel scheme and the designs of a most holy wisdom in redeeming; if therefore, we have not resignation to the general scheme of divine government, and patience under particular allot-

ments, it is evident that we have not the exercife of a faving faith. The habitual exercife of impatience proves the habitual want of faith.

It would be eafy to exemplify the harmonious nature of a juftifying faith with all holy obedience of heart and vifible practice. Receiving GOD, is receiving him in his whole nature, law and government. Receiving CHRIST, is receiving him in all his mediatorial offices and requirements. All this is included in thofe chriftian works, by which we are to judge ourfelves accepted and forgiven of GOD.

FINDING the promife, *He that believeth and is baptized, fhall be faved ; but he that believeth not fhall be damned,* men are very folicitous to eftablifh the validity of their own belief or faith. They fingle out this grace, and try to find evidence and convince themfelves that they have it. Having attained a perfuafion of their faith, they are at eafe concerning their eternal well being. If they looked further into this all-concerning fubject, they would find that other graces and a holy practice are as neceffary in the chriftian as his faith ; alfo, that faith cannot be found alone. The heart which can believe ; can alfo repent, mourn for fin, forfake fin, love the divine law and government, be refigned and patient, be devoted to the glory of GOD, have a moft benevolent love of men and of fouls, and live in all holy converfation, godlinefs, temperance, weanednefs from the world, prayerful, and in the practice of a heavenly converfation. *Wilt thou know O vain man, that faith without works is dead. The devils believe and tremble ;* but they are not holy.—They believe only doctrinally—their faith is their torment, and there is not in it any obedience.

ONE good way of detecting an infincere faith is by looking much on the law, and confidering its requirements. Although the christian finds himself condemned and slain by the law, his faith approves every one of its commandments as holy, just and good. When he receives CHRIST, he receives the law to be the rule of his future temper and actions. So far is he from animosity against the law, on account of its condemning sentence; that he sees this to be a mark of its excellence, and adores the divine government for being guided by so good a commandment, which requires men to love the Lord with, *all their heart, and all their strength and all their mind.*

2. VISIBLE morality or a holy practice is required in christians; and without it we cannot have evidence of our own forgiveness.

MEN may fall into great and strange delusions. There have been many persons of a most immoral life, who appeared to think their salvation secure, from an apprehension of inward illumination and the grace of GOD reigning in their hearts. This is a most dangerous delusion, and is turning the grace of GOD into licentiousness. There can be no forgiveness without a good heart. There may be a moral practice where the heart is not sanctified, for a practice visibly right may arise from unholy motives; but an immoral practice never can come from a good heart. It is impossible there should be a holy motive to a bad deed. Men may think their motives to be holy, and thence form a false opinion of their bad actions; but in all such cases, the judgment is vitiated through a depravity of heart. An habitual bad practice proves a bad heart.

THOUGH the people of GOD are sanctified but in part and may do many bad actions; we have no reason to think that he ever leaves them to an open, long continued and habitual departure from a good practice. They are overcome by temptation; they are sometimes left by God to great and scandalous transgression, that he may hereby show them their dependance; but if they are his forgiven ones, on consideration, they see and mourn for their iniquity, and are the first to condemn themselves. It was thus with David, with Peter and all those saints whose fall is recorded in the word of God. An habitual bad practice wilfully continued, is, therefore most sure evidence of an unforgiven state. Those, who live habitually in a bad practice, however strongly they may hope, and however firmly they may suppose themselves to be the favorites of sovereign grace, are still under the bonds of iniquity.

3. In judging of our forgiveness, we ought to consider the motives, by which we are inclined to actions visibly good. Herod heared gladly, and the action was visibly good; but we know that his motive, like his character, was bad. Jehu cried, *come see my zeal for the Lord;* but his motive condemned him. It may be so with us, and before we determine ourselves to be accepted by God, we ought to search what our hearts mean by the visibly good actions, which proceed from them. Do we pray to God from a love of him; or from fear and the formality of education? Do we worship in the temple to glorify his great name; or to be seen of men, and be called civil, well-conducted persons? Are we just, right, pure, and kind in our connections with men because it is right thus to be, and a compliance with obligation to them and the great creator; or is all this done to invite their favor and make them the same to us? In the latter case, there is no evidence we are forgiven.

It is not proper to approve ourselves, without greater evidence than we possibly can have concerning other persons. We know their hearts by their actions; we know our own by consciousness. However regular, pure, and visibly obedient our lives may be; however punctual we are in the services of religion; however liberal to others, or severe in bodily mortifications; all this can be no evidence of sincerity, when we feel a conscious opposition of heart to the holy character, law and government of God.

4. Living in the practice of any sin against the dictates of conscience; or in the omission of any known duty, is a great evidence against the sincerity of our faith.

It is not said, that christians do never live in the neglect of known duty. They have much imperfection, and may sin against conscience; but it is not supposed they will do it habitually, and for a great length of time together. The question is not, how far one who hath been forgiven may backslide and, for a season, sin against his known duty; but it is concerning the present evidence of forgiveness. Certainly there can be no present evidence of forgiveness, while living in known sin or omitting known duty. Christ says, *No man can serve two masters; for either he will hate the one, and love the other; or else he will hold to the one, and despise the other. Ye cannot serve God and mammon.* Living in the omission of known duty, or the practice of known sin, is serving sin. It is serving a master, which is directly opposed to God; and at the time, God is not received. There can be no present evidence that the Lord is our reconciled God, when we are not serving him. In such a state all the evidence is against us.

There is a very dubious condition, in which many of mankind who have christian knowledge and means are found. It is the following. They believe doctrinally in the christian scheme of faith, and in the need of a gracious renovation by the Spirit of God. They look back on some former time, in which they were anxiously concerned for salvation, and obtained a hope that God had forgiven and accepted them. They have much relapsed from their former punctuality in religious duties, from their sense of divine and eternal things, and from watchfulness over themselves and against temptation. They are become greater conformists to the world; although their lives may be free from visible immoralities. Still they have a hope, built on a remembrance of their supposed, ancient, christian experience. These persons live in the omission of known duty, for according to their own idea of themselves, the fervor of piety is gone from their hearts. They are living and hoping, on ancient and not on present experience. I have called this a dubious condition; but perhaps I have called it by too mild a name, for nothing appears to show it is not a fatal one.

Why should men have a present hope, without present evidence? Can there be a rational comfort in it? Must not all men, looking back by memory on past experience of which present feeling is gone, say, we may have been mistaken. And if we may have been mistaken, in all that is past, and have no present exercise of grace—no present evidence, why do we hope? Why do we suspend an eternity, on the supposed possession of a temper, from which we find no present exercise? This is not hoping from evidence; but from a memory, that we once supposed we had evidence.

FURTHER, is there any thing in the word of GOD which thus defcribes religion? Do not all the defcriptions of grace in the heart, reprefent it, as a prefent temper and exercife—a living principle—a prefent love of GOD, and prefent obedience to his commands, in the moft fpiritual part of them? Ought we to be eafy with our ftate, on any evidence, which would not give us fortitude and peace in death; and will any thing which is fhort of prefent love, faith and repentance give this?

BUT it may be inquired, are we to derive no comfort from paft experience, and is there in it no evidence of our forgivenefs? To which I anfwer.

WITH refpect to comfort, it cannot be found in paft experience, without a prefent enjoyment of GOD. A moft unholy hypocrite may have the comfort of thinking, that he is fafe from future punifhment. The fecure finner and infidel, may have the comfort of fuppofing there is no punifhment prepared for the wicked; but this is not chriftian happinefs. It is a peace common to backfliding chriftians, to hypocrites, and to openly defying finners. The true chriftian comfort, is a prefent delight in GOD and in duty, and cannot be had by a memory of any thing that is paft.

WITH refpect to evidence of forgivenefs from paft experience; it may be of great ufe in union with the prefent exercife of holy affections. From what is paft, the chriftian judges better of what he now feels; and by a remembrance of GOD's paft kindnefs, which he knows to be fimilar to what he now feels, he is affured of divine love and rejoices with joy unfpeakable and full of glory. But to derive this benefit of paft experience, it feems there muft be alfo the prefent exercife of faith, love and repentance. A bare recollection of fomething, that is at prefent wholly unknown by the heart, muſt be a weak ground of hope. There is no preſent teſt for diſtinguiſhing between deluſion and reality. The mind can only ſay to itſelf, I once felt ſomething that I ſuppoſed to be ſatisfying, and which I then thought ſo excellent in its nature and its attending comfort, that it muſt be from God. I know that I was relieved and delighted, but I now feel nothing of the ſame bleſſedneſs ; and therefore, it might all be a deluſion, which is now leading me to eternal ruin. It is only by a renewal of ſimilar affections and views in the mind, that paſt experience becomes preſent evidence. Infinite wiſdom hath ordered, that there is no good evidence of our forgiveneſs, but by preſent evangelical obedience; and it is the ordering of goodneſs to his imperfect children. If it were otherwiſe, and there could be evidence of our forgiveneſs without the preſent exerciſe of a holy temper, it would tend greatly, to prolong ſeaſons of backſliding from him. Being left without evidence, his people are now as liable to be warned by the terrors of a condemning law, as they were before they ever fled to him for refuge. It is not reaſonable to wiſh for evidence of a divine reconcilement to us, any further than we find a preſent conformity to the God and law of infinite holineſs. We are ready to tell the unholy and profane, that they are unreaſonable in deſiring God to be reconciled to them, while of their preſent wrong temper. For the ſame reaſon, no man ought to wiſh for evidence of God's gracious acceptance, further than he feels himſelf to be returned to his duty. A wiſh contradictory to this, is ſymptomatic of ſome hidden inſincerity in the heart, which will prove fatal in the end.

There is a very falſe idea, entertained by ſome of being cloathed with Christ's righteouſneſs, and depending on this as evidence of their forgivenefs. The apoftle fpeaks of not having his own righteoufnefs, which is of the law, but that which is through the faith of CHRIST. So we are faid to be juftified by the righteoufnefs of faith; and exhorted to put on CHRIST. From fuch defcriptions as thefe, hath arifen the expreffion of being cloathed with CHRIST's righteoufnefs. They mean that we are juftified, by the grace of GOD, through and for the fake of CHRIST's righteoufnefs. Being cloathed with CHRIST's righteoufnefs, is being forgiven and accepted by GOD, for the fake of what he hath done and fuffered. But it does not mean, that the perfonal righteoufnefs of CHRIST, is made our perfonal righteoufnefs. Although our own perfonal righteoufnefs or fanctification cannot purchafe any favor at the hand of a holy GOD; it is neceffary to prepare us for the enjoyment of GOD; it is neceffary to receive the benefits of fovereign mercy; and it is alfo neceffary as evidence that the fruits of CHRIST's righteoufnefs are imparted to us. Our own perfonal holinefs is the only evidence that we are forgiven through the righteoufnefs of CHRIST. Being cloathed with humility and other graces of the chriftian temper, is the proper evidence, that we are cloathed with forgivenefs and the promifes of eternal glory.

5. A DELIGHT in the duties of worfhip, efpecially in prayer, is an infeparable attendant of the faith to which forgivenefs is promifed.

IF *any of you lack wifdom, let him afk of* GOD, *that giveth to all men liberally, and upbraideth not: and it fhall be given him. But let him afk in faith.* Prayer is the mouth by which faith offers its defires to GOD through JESUS CHRIST. When we confider the word of GOD, that none are forgiven but thofe who believe; when we further confider the office and ufe of faith, it feems impoffible that a true believer ſhould live in the habitual neglect of prayer. Of all divine worſhip, this is moſt agreeable to him. It is by prayer, that we place ourſelves moſt ſenſibly in the divine preſence; and if we love GOD, the means of approaching him and quickening our apprehenſions of his infinite glory cannot be neglected. It is by prayer that faith aſks; and if we feel our needs we ſhall make them known. It is to prayer the promiſe is made; and if we believe the word of GOD, we ſhall obey in our manner of application. The uſefulneſs of this duty is ſufficiently teſtified in the word of GOD. If infinite wiſdom had not known it to be neceſſary for a godly life in CHRIST JESUS, we ſhould not have had the commands, *Pray without ceaſing.—Praying always with all prayer and ſupplication in the ſpirit, and watching thereunto with all perſeverance.—Continuing inſtant in prayer.—Night and day praying exceedingly. —Exhort therefore, that firſt of all, ſupplications, prayers, interceſſions, and giving of thanks, be made for all men.* Theſe precepts with many other, expreſſed in the ſtrongeſt language, clearly prove the uſefulneſs and neceſſity of prayer in the chriſtian life.

THE ſame is known by the concurrent teſtimony of chriſtian experience. The people of GOD have ever borne witneſs, for the benefit, and comfort, and quickening efficacy of prayer in proſperity, in adverſity, in reſiſting the temptations of ſenſe, in mortifying their remaining ſin, in quickening all the gracious affections, and in giving a lively ſenſe of preſent duty. This is ſo uniformly true, that chriſtians may always judge themſelves in a backſliding ſtate, when their pleaſure, fervency and frequency in prayer abates.

THE ſame truth may be learned from the nature of religion. True religion is a love of GOD. Prayer is converſing with him, in ſuch a way as becomes creatures to fpeak to an infinite Creator. This Creator is always and every where prefent to hear the fupplication. He permits us to fpeak to him through the Mediator, whenever we feel a heart difpofed to praife, or any wants which need to be fupplied, or any dangers we wifh to avoid. If God be the object of our fupreme love, it is impoffible to refrain from fpeaking to him in the holy and humble manner which is permitted. Stated feafons of prayer will be pleafing, and in the midft of daily and neceffary occupations the heart will afcend to the giver of every good gift, and praife the fulnefs from which all our mercies proceed. Our hearts naturally feek the objects of our fupreme love, and it is as difficult to keep the true difciple of Christ from praying, as it is to divert thofe who are devoted to the world, from their farms, their merchandize, and their amufements.

If this be truth, we have no right to depend on our own forgivenefs, unlefs the worfhip of God, and efpecially prayer be a moft pleafing and conftant duty of our lives. It is probable, that many even among the believers of chriftian revelation, think themfelves to be religious and gracioufly forgiven, although they find none of this delight in worfhipping God. Some may think thus, who are wholly unacquainted with the clofet ; who never kneeled with their families before the God of all grace, to praife his goodnefs and afk his daily prefervation and the forgivenefs of their fins ; and who rarely look within the fanctuary of God. All fuch, will probably think this reprefentation drawn too high. They cannot accord with it, without condemning themfelves, and fruftrating the loofe hope, by which they fpend their time of trial in this world—the only trial they will have for eternity. Let fuch perfons fearch the fcriptures of Jesus Christ and of the apostles who were inspired by his Spirit, and if they can there point out a scheme of religion which will save the souls of men, different from what has been represented, their safety and their right to hope shall be allowed. If they can show the consistency of loving God supremely, and still neglecting to obey, to think of him, and converse with him ; it shall be allowed they are fair candidates for heaven.

Over the whole world there is a natural conscience in men, which disposes them to seek safety, in the present and coming world. They are generally ready to hear every scheme, which is proposed for that end. Hence it happens that innovators in religion find an easy access to mankind. They are heard with avidity, and the guilty, unholy multitude, hope they have found a way of eternal bliss, less condemning to their appetites and crimes, and requiring less holiness than they have been used to hear. There would be no difficulty in christianizing the world if the doctrines of Christ might be accommodated to a sinful heart and practice. Men will consent, for the sake of pacifying conscience, to own they belong to God, if they are not indeed obliged to serve him. They will probably go further, and consent to serve him in some visible things, if they may be excused from serving him with the heart. There is no evidence that our faith is sincere, and we are forgiven ; but a dedication of ourselves, both body and spirit to the Lord. We must be wholly his or we do not belong to him, for we cannot serve two masters. The works which will justify and prove our faith to be good, include the temper—the moral state of the heart—and all the actions of living in the world. This is glorifying him in our body and in our spirit, which are his, and the only evidence of our eternal redemption. Amen.

SERMON XIX.

On working out our own salvation.

PHILIPPIANS ii. 12, 13.

—*Work out your own salvation with fear and trembling. For it is God which worketh in you, both to will and to do of his good pleasure.*

THIS exhortation, is founded upon a previous description, of the glorious and exalted state of Jesus Christ. *Wherefore God also hath highly exalted him, and given him a name which is above every name: that at the name of Jesus every knee should bow, of things in heaven, and things in earth, and things under the earth; and that every tongue should confess, that Jesus Christ is Lord, to the glory of God the Father.* From this high description of his dignity as God, Redeemer and Judge, the writer exhorts, *work out your own salvation with fear and trembling.* The greatness of the Judge, to whom every knee shall bow, and by whom every one shall be sentenced; the greatness and eternity of the good sought and the evil to be avoided; together with the divine action of God, on the minds of all who work successfully, are considerations why it should be with fear and trembling.

The following things will be considered.

I. What is included in salvation.

II. What is meant, in the text, by working out our salvation.

I. What is included in salvation.

It is supposed there can be no dispute what is meant by the word salvation in this passage, and I describe it, not to settle a difficult point; but as preparatory to the succeeding part of my discourse. The natural and scriptural meaning of the word salvation, is deliverance from some evil, either natural or moral. Personal and national deliverances, from particular judgments, are called salvations. A subject of discourse, often limits the meaning to particular escapes and blessings, some of which are of short, and others of longer continuance.

In the word of God, salvation commonly means, that forgiveness and sanctification through Jesus Christ, by which unholy and guilty sinners, are prepared and shall be finally received, to the eternal glory and peace of heaven. This is the great salvation, ultimately including all blessings, all holiness, happiness and glory which redeemed men can receive. This is always meant by the word salvation, in the gospel writings; unless, when the nature of the subject limits it, to some particular favor. This is the salvation, which the text exhorts us to work out with fear and trembling, because it is God who worketh in us both to will and to do, of his good pleasure.

It may be useful for us particularly to consider what it contains.

Holiness is the principal thing. It is a deliverance from sin, a moral conformity to God and his law, and evangelical union to him through his Son Jesus Christ. Hence Christ was promised to *save his people from their sins.*—*Who gave himself for us, that he might redeem us from all iniquity, and purify us to himself a peculiar people, zealous of good works.*—*According to his mercy he saved us, by the washing of regeneration, and renewing of the Holy Ghost.* Salvation begins in holiness and ends in glory. It is begun in this world and grows with the personal holiness of God's people. This was meant by Christ when he said, *For behold, the kingdom of God is within you.* The sanctification of God's people, with the happiness rising out of it, is the beginning of their glory. It is the spiritual water given by Christ, *which shall be in them a well of water, springing up into eternal life.* There is no room to question, that holiness is the most essential thing in this salvation. We may hear and have the offer, but without holiness have not the thing itself.

Happiness is also included in this salvation. Infinite wisdom hath so formed the universe, and the mind of man; that happiness the most pure, the greatest and most perpetual, arises from a holy temper and practice. This is the happiness of God himself, and he communicates it to his people according to their measure of acting and receiving. When they become perfect in holiness, their happiness will be the greatest possible.

While we consider happiness as part of the gospel salvation, it must be remembered, that it is confined to such happiness as arises from a holy temper and practice. Sinners find pleasure in their vices, yet none will pretend this to be part of the chriftian falvation. The greater their pleafure is, the further they are from being faved, and the more difficult it becomes for them to enter into the kingdom of glorious peace. The ungodly relifh of their hearts is gaining ftrength, and they become more difqualified for tafting the pleafures of religion. This defcription ought not to be confined to the unhappy perfons, who are plunging deep into the pleafures of grofs fenfuality. It applies, with propriety, to the pride of felf-righteoufnefs, which, by every moment of its continuance, is fhutting the heart againft the true pleafure of chriftian humility.

II. WHAT is meant, in the text, by working out our own falvation.

To fix the meaning of a writer, it is often neceffary, we fhould know the character of the perfons addreffed. Efpecially, it is proper to confider this, when their character is ftrongly marked in the accompanying parts of difcourfe, which is the cafe with refpect to this exhortation. It is an exhortation to chriftians, whofe hearts were already fanctified in part, and in whom that work of grace was begun, which would certainly end in the falvation of final glory.—This may be known from the preceding words—*Wherefore, my beloved, as ye have always obeyed, not as in my prefence only, but now much more in my abfence ; work out your own falvation with fear and trembling.* He calls them beloved brethren, an appellation applied by the facred writers, peculiarly to the people of GOD. The exhortation is to thofe, who had already obeyed, not only while he was with them ; but alfo, in his abfence from them. They had given evidence of fincerity by a feafon of perseverance, in an age, when every professing christian was assailed by the most trying evils, which heathen and jewish enmity could inflict.

Having ascertained the character of the persons, to whom the writer addressed himself, the meaning of the exhortation becomes apparent, and is conceived to be as follows.

" I address you, as persons who are chris-
" tians, by the washing of regeneration, and re-
" newing of the Spirit. You are my beloved
" brethren, by profession and a visible obedience.
" My hope concerning you is strong; for the
" obedience which I beheld, has been continued
" in my absence. Go on, seeking perfection in
" holiness, until the day of perfect glory. Be
" diligent, finish, and make full proof of the
" salvation, which is already begun in you; al-
" ready given to you by the riches of mercy in
" Christ Jesus."

The latter part of the verse confirms this explanation. *For it is God which worketh in you both to will and to do of his good pleasure.* Real christians know the difficulties of obedience. *They wrestle against principalities, against powers, against the rulers of the darkness of this world, against spiritual wickedness in high places.* They are surrounded with temptations, the allurements of sense, the seducing influence of bad example and the company of evil men, with whom they must be connected, in many things, until God calls them from the world. The objects of their natural affection, and of family endearment, who must be their daily companions, are often the enemies of the gospel, and opposed to that holy life which they know to be their duty. They feel a remainder of sin in their own hearts, by which they are laid open to the power of external temptations. Of this, the apostle hath given us a most excellent description, in his own experience. *For I know that in me (that is, in my flesh) dwelleth no good thing: for to will is present with me, but how to perform that which is good, I find not. For the good that I would, I do not: but the evil which I would not, that I do. I find then a law, that when I would do good, evil is present with me. For I delight in the law of* GOD *after the inward man. But I see another law in my members warring against the law of my mind, and bringing me into captivity to the law of sin, which is in my members. O wretched man that I am, who shall deliver me from the body of this death!*

IN view of these obstacles, it appears to the christian, a difficult thing, to work out or effect that perfection in holiness, which is his salvation. On this account when his faith is weak, he is often ready to despond; and it seems, as though he must be destroyed by his spiritual enemies, and the treachery of his own heart. Knowing this, the apostle adds to his exhortation, the supporting truth; *for it is* GOD *which worketh in you both to will and to do of his good pleasure.*

THO' your remaining sin be great, and your temptations many, GOD is with you. You are not working alone. In this case, you ought to look back to your former unholy, unpardoned state. You now know, that if GOD had not wrought in you, by his renewing spirit, you would have been in the gall of bitterness and under the bonds of iniquity. Now you know, that it was GOD who first wrought in you to repent and believe, and that you was made obedient by a divine efficiency. You have no reason to despond; for GOD, who hath begun his own work, can finish it, and overcome all your spiritual enemies. You have the promise of his spirit, to enlighten and fanctify, to remove your remaining fin, and fit you for his own prefence. Under a fenfe of weaknefs you may plead the covenant, and afk his grace to control your wills and direct your practice.

This is all the encouragement to diligence which a weak chriftian can need, and it was proper to be added with the exhortation, *work out your own falvation*. It has the nature of a promife, to thofe who have become evangelically obedient, that God will in future be with them. To the unbelieving and impenitent, to thofe who have never obeyed, there are no promifes made ; nor is it fit there fhould be any. If God hath not begun to influence their wills, that is, work in them to will ; there is no certainty from any thing he hath faid in the fcriptures, that he ever will thus work. As they are now in a ftate of unpardoned oppofition to divine holinefs, and have never, in any refpect, complied with the condition to which final falvation is promifed, they may always remain as ignorant and obdurate as they be at prefent. Thofe who have become obedient, in their future exertions muft depend on the aid of promifed grace. This dependance, is ufing means in the exercife of faith, which to thofe who do it is never in vain. Whoever, prays, hears and meditates, looking to God for the fanctifying efficacy of his holy fpirit, will by experience find him working in them to will and to do ; and they will be fenfible no greater encouragement is needed.

To the exhortation, there is another direction added. Work out your own falvation, *with fear and trembling*. Be diligent, be ftrenuous, be reverent in all your endeavours.

Be diligent, for there is much to be done in refifting fin—and feeking holinefs, and the consequences are great and eternal. Be strenuous; for weak and intermitting efforts, are not adequate to the difficulties which you will meet. Be reverent ;. for success depends wholly on a divine co-operation, and none have right to expect his spirit, unless they have a most reverent sense of his being, action and purity. In working out his own salvation, the christian ought to have a deep sense of the danger of sin. Known and wilful sin will always prevent the sensible communication of strength from GOD. His children may be permitted to fall into wilful rebellion; but when this is the case, they must be brought into a state of trembling concern, before they will experience again a sanctifying efficacy with the means which are used.

EXPERIENCE in the christian life, will show the admirable fitness and truth of the exhortation in the text. It will convince of the need of working. That no one can grow in faith and holiness, without a most diligent attention to the means, which infinite wisdom hath appointed. Whenever, reading the word of GOD, prayer, meditation, self-examination, and a most watchful care over the heart and practice are omitted ; spiritual affection will cease to be sensible, and both the power and comforts of religion will be gone. Although means cannot sanctify, GOD never gives his influence to purify his people without them; and to hope for this, in the omission of means, is high presumption.

CHRISTIAN experience will give conviction of its being necessary for GOD to work in them. After the longest and most successful use of means, a use so successful that they dare not omit them ; there is still the most thorough conviction, that all is in vain, if the spirit of GOD be denied. When they are most vigorous in the use of appointed means ; they are always moſt importunate for a divine influence to accompany. The neceſſity of uſing means, and the aſcription of all holineſs to the immediate action of GOD, are truths which ſome pretend to conſider as contradictory. It is not ſeen, in what ſenſe, they are ſo, any more in moral than in natural events. But whatever objections there be, in this matter, chriſtian experience will ſoon remove them. All the holy, will bear a joint teſtimony, that it is of the Lord's working they are ſanctified ; alſo, they will aſſure us GOD did this, when they were moſt diligent and perſevering in the means of religion.

FURTHER, chriſtian experience will produce a deep concern, leſt we endeavour and exert ourſelves, in ſuch a way, as will grieve the holy ſpirit to deny his aid. GOD is as jealous of his own honor and of the reſpect due to his directions, in the diſpenſation of ſovereign grace ; as he is in judging and rewarding by the law. Thoſe things, which men think to be ſmall deviations from the preſcribed rule, are often a ſufficient reaſon, for the moſt holy ſpirit to deny his quickening influence. If we work in a way not commanded ; if we add human invention to commanded ſervices ; if we divide the means, which GOD hath joined ; if we uſe means, while living in any known and wilful tranſgreſſion ; or if we depend on the means, and think to obtain by our own ſtrength through their efficacy, forgetting to look to GOD, the uſe will be without a bleſſing. Infinite wiſdom and goodneſs is very particular in the ſovereign beſtowment of his aid, in order to keep us watchful againſt ſin, and preſerve in us a ſenſe of our dependence. Theſe things are taught to a chriſtian, by his experience in the life of faith and godlineſs ; therefore he works with fear and trembling, left he should grieve away the spirit of life.

In explaining this text, it has been applied to christians, who have obeyed and become sanctified in part. I here feel myself brought near to a subject of great importance, which, though plain to the experienced christian, is very liable to misrepresentation and imprudent expression. It is concerning such use of means, as may be found in persons, who are not sanctified, and forgiven through faith and repentance. Inquiring minds will come to this subject, and find difficulties in it; also, they are in danger of embracing some wrong conclusions, unless they have been experimentally taught, or instruction is given them, in the most guarded manner.

There are two errors of a fatal tendency, into which we may fall. Either, that there is nothing to be done by unsanctified men; or, that the external services to which they are excited by fear and self-love alone, are the begining of real holiness and preparation for heaven. It is dangerous to believe either of these. There is no real preparation for heaven, without some degree of moral conformity to God and his kingdom, and the unsanctified sinner hath no begining of such conformity. All his external works in praying, hearing and seeking are for himself and not for God. If a terrible law were repealed, and a way prepared for sin to triumph, he would seek no longer, and hear and pray no more. Therefore, there is no preparation for heaven, nor any salvation actually begun in his soul, by all his assiduous services. We cannot tell him that God is working in him. The design of infinite wisdom, in awakening and setting the terrors of the law before his mind, is to make him acquainted with his own heart, and convince him of a hardnefs and enmity againſt divine holinefs and fovereignty. In this cafe, to tell him that his concern and performance of external fervice, on legal motives, is fanctification begun, would be counteracting the work of God, on his underſtanding and confcience.

On the other hand, to give any reprefentation which will make him conclude he may ceafe the form of prayer, and exchange thefe fervices, for the profane and thoughtlefs circle of men, is directing him to fure deftruction. We never fee God fanctifying the thoughtlefs and fecure. It is the manner of infinite wifdom, to open mens underſtanding on their peril and guilt, before he fanctifies them. It is alfo his manner to ufe their own legal obfervances, as means of teaching them the fin of their hearts, and their abfolute dependence on fovereign, renewing grace. Tho' renewing grace doth not always follow fuch conviction, we do not fee it given in another way; and by looking through this fubject we may fee the propriety of this divine difpenfation. The whole experience of the church, can give no reafon to fuppofe God will fanctify fecure finners, who live in open neglect of a Sabbath, of prayer, of meditation on their own ftate, and of anxious concern for efcape. Thefe thoughtlefs fouls are in the broad way without knowing it.

To illuftrate this fubject, I will propofe and anfwer feveral queftions.

QUESTION I. THE text has been explained, as an exhortation to chriftians, who have already experienced fanctifying grace; may not unholy men, be exhorted to work out their falvation with fear and trembling?

ANSWER. All unholy men ought to be directed, to work out their own salvation, with fear and trembling; but we cannot give them the same encouragement, which may be given, to such as have become evangelically obedient. We cannot, in truth, tell them, that God now doth or ever hath, wrought in them both to will and to do.—The preceptive part of the exhortation belongs to all men; the encouraging and promissory part, only to the obedient.

There is but one law, one kind of obedience, one set of promises, one scheme of duty and practice placed before mankind. The command and exhortation are to all. The promise is to all, who comply with the conditions on which it is given. The threatening is against all, who remain of the temper and heart against which it is denounced. There are two characters among men; the holy and unholy. One of them is entitled to a promise; the other, only to such threatenings as are merited by disobedience. But there are not two schemes of duty to be placed in their view; one for sinners, and the other for saints. Unholy men are proper subjects of the same exhortations as are given to the obedient. In describing duty, and directing the way of salvation, we do not find the word of God makes any difference; but all are commanded to repent and believe, and live in all holy conversation. The different address of God to saints and sinners takes place in describing their character, and the way in which he will treat them; and not in describing obligation and duty, for this is the same on all. And sinners ought to be reminded of their indispensible obligation to perform all the duties of christian obedience.

Q. 2. Do unsanctified persons ever begin to work out their own salvation?

A. They never do begin.—Of the many things which they do, some from fear, some from self-righteousness, and some from false expectations; none amount to a beginning of real salvation. A consenting, willing heart is the first thing in salvation, and all they have done comes no nearer to this, than their first excitement to seriousness. Although sin hath changed its form and manner of acting, it still reigns. Visible seriousness and inquiry come from the same heart, as was before acted out, in vanity and a contempt of moral obligation. It is fear and not love which hath made the change of conversation. The character and law of God are no more amiable in their sight, and are no more loved for their own excellence, than they ever were. The sinner is not weaned from himself, and every thing is done from a principle of supreme self-regard. There is no regard to the honor of God. Therefore, salvation, which consists in holiness of the heart, is not begun.

The seeking sinner, in the situation I am considering, hath not wrought out his salvation in part. Some things, which may be matter of command, are of such a nature by the very laws of action, that they may be part done and part not done. A command to go to a distant place, requires beginning, and progress approaching towards the end of the command, and may be in part effected. It is not thus in loving and choosing God, in which beginning salvation consists. The will or choice of the heart is for him or against him; he is chosen or rejected; and no part of salvation is wrought out until he is chosen. After a sinner is sanctified and hath repented and believed in Christ, it will be proper to say his salvation is wrought out in part; but before this, he is in total disobedience. In all he does, unholy motives are apparent, and his resolutions and inquiring what he shall do to be saved, arise from a heart which doth not wish God to reign.

Q. 3. Is the awakened sinner better or worse than he would have been in a state of security and forgetfulness of God?

A. It is conceived this question tends only to useless speculation, and that it was first originated, with an unfriendly design, to discredit, either seriousness or those doctrines of revelation, which represent men utterly sinful by nature, and dependent on the sovereign action of God for their deliverance. There is no difficulty in giving this general answer to the question, that men are becoming worse, until they repent; whether they be in an anxious or a secure state. They are adding to an immense amount of past sin and guilt. The habit or strength of unholy affections is increasing. They are going further from God and duty, and becoming exposed to a more heavy doom. Continued unbelief, or living without faith in Christ and repentance towards God, always implies a state growing worse and worse. If there be any who know they are destitute of real religion, and yet think they are not daily becoming more sinful and guilty, they contradict the truth of the apostle. *But evil men and seducers shall wax worse and worse, deceiving, and being deceived.* But if the question be, whether inquiring sinners, who still remain in unbelief, wax worse either less or more, than they would, in a state of security; it is not wise. It is impossible for men to form a scale of increasing sin and apply it with any certainty to the conditions of the human heart. It is enough for us to know that without holiness, no man pleaseth God.—It is doubtless true, that the inquiring sinner acts against an increase of light, which is a circumstance enhancing guilt. It may alſo be true, that many affections of his heart, which are completely ſinful, by the terrors of the law, are laid under ſome reſtraint, and are not pointed with ſuch energy of oppoſition againſt God, as they would be if the law were out of ſight. It was before ſaid the queſtion is uſeleſs, and it was introduced in this place only to guard againſt a miſrepreſentation of ſome other ſentiments, which are freely expreſſed in this diſcourſe.

Q. 4. Is the ſecure ſinner, who thinks nothing of his unhappy caſe, and lives in neglect of the viſible ſervices of religion, as probable a ſubject of ſanctifying and forgiving grace, as others are, who attend to them?

A. 1ſt. With reſpect to the ſecure, there is no preſent reaſon to hope for them in particular, that they will ever come to repentance. We know there is a God of infinite power and goodneſs. He is able, and it is poſſible he may turn them; but as we know from his expreſs information many will be left, nothing appears why they will not be of the wretched number. Infinite wiſdom gives us 'no evidence to conclude they will be reclaimed, and every thing looks contrary to it. They have not a ſolemn ſenſe of God, his law, their guilt and danger. They neither wiſh to turn, nor ſee the danger of not turning. They are not in the way of obtaining certain points of doctrinal knowledge, which ſovereign wiſdom uſually gives to ſinners, and gives through the medium of their endeavours, before he ſanctifies and forgives. They do not feel ſlain by the law, and it is probable they never will, until they have attempted to live by it; and they will not attempt to live by it, until they are, by its terrors, awakened from security and driven to seek life in their own strength.

2dly. WITH respect to inquiring sinners, who are anxious and say what shall we do to be saved —who are performing many of the visible services of religion, and take great pains to escape the wrath to come, there is much more room to hope GOD will be merciful to them. It is the usual method of divine sovereignty, to teach men they have a disease, before he heals; to wound, before he applies the balm; to slay by the law, before he makes alive by the gospel. Knowing this to be the method of infinite wisdom, when we see their consciences alive, their fear very sensible, their apprehensions of GOD and of their own danger so real as makes them endeavour to escape punishment; though it be not evangelical obedience, we hope that free grace yet designs their good. Though they are under the bonds of sin, and have hearts as much as ever opposed to gospel holiness; though they are attempting salvation in a way which will never give it, and are thus adding sin to sin; though they are dishonoring the infinite grace of the gospel, and by every trembling service, which they offer from their present motives, are denying evangelical humility and the loveliness of CHRIST; though they appear to have no experimental ideas of evangelical obedience, we still hope that sovereign mercy designs them eternal good.

AND why do we hope this? Not because they are becoming worthy or better, or are in a gospel sense becoming obedient; for there is no gospel obedience short of faith and repentance. Not because their reigning temper would not make them eternally miserable if left under its power. Not because there is any promise of GOD to persons in this situation; for many are brought thus far, and then grieving the holy spirit by their long resistance, he leaves them to security, and they become, apparently, more hardened in sin, than ever before.

We hope, because God hath not wholly denied his convincing influence. He is acting on their minds, in a way naturally calculated, to give that experimental knowledge of sin, guilt and spiritual impotency, which is usually wrought in sinners before their change through grace. He is preparing them, through the medium of their own sinful endeavours, and their stubborn resistance to gospel submission; to receive salvation, when imparted, as a sovereign gift. They are also by this, in many respects which might be mentioned, prepared to receive and use the grace of God without abusing it. When salvation is begun, they will know it is the Lord who hath done it. They will be sensible, that all they have done, and the services by which they thought themselves to be making their calling and election sure, were wholly sinful, and the motives from which they acted were all unholy. They will ascribe to sovereign grace the glory of rescuing them, at a moment, in which they were most unworthy to be spared.

From what has been said on this subject, it appears that great prudence and faithfulness are necessary, in those who teach inquiring sinners. It is one of the most solemn situations in which a religious instructor can be placed.

The sinful person takes no pleasure in the visible services of religion for their own sake. He is impelled by danger to think. He wishes he could easily forget his own case. The services to which he resorts have nothing in them pleasing, and are only chosen in preference to a true obedience of the heart. If, in this moment, the instructor says, any thing which can be caught hold of, as an excuse for returning to former security and negligence, it will be received, and the laſt ſtate is worſe than the firſt. Or if the inſtructor leads him to ſuppoſe he is faſt growing better; that a holy God is in ſome degree ſatiſfied with his external reformation, his meditation, prayers, and zeal in a good cauſe; that if he will go on in this way, there is no doubt of his ſafety; this inſtruction will quiet conſcience, and build up a ſelf-righteouſneſs, which is directly oppoſed to goſpel holineſs.

Integrity is wiſdom. The ſinner, in this caſe hath a right to the truth; for his ſoul, his eternity is at riſque. He ſhould be led to a ſight of his heart; ſhould be told that all theſe ſervices are not the true goſpel duty required from him; that he muſt deſpair of help and ſafety by all he does, and bow before a ſovereign God, who may deliver or reject as he pleaſeth. The nature of unbelief, with all that variety of forms, which it aſſumes for ſelf-juſtification and eaſe of conſcience, ſhould be explained with moſt diligent care. He ſhould be told that all he does is evil only continually. That while he is endeavouring to make himſelf better, on his preſent motives, he is becoming more worthy of the end which he fears. At the ſame time he ſhould be cautioned againſt relapſing into ſecurity, and exhorted to uſe all means, for keeping alive a ſenſe of his miſerable ſtate. He ſhould be told, God is not obliged in juſtice ever to forgive; ſtill, that there is more hope, in his preſent caſe, than if he were in deep ſecurity. It ſhows God hath not yet ſaid, my ſpirit ſhall ſtrive no more. For perſons on whom this ſentence is paſſed there is no hope. After all, let every one remember, there is no obedience, without *repentance toward God, and faith toward our Lord Jesus Chirst.* Amen.

SERMON XX.

Sanctification of the Sabbath.

EXODUS xx. 8.

Remember the Sabbath day to keep it holy.

THE meaning of the word SABBATH, is a day of rest and holy delight in GOD and in his works. Creation and providence are natural evidence of the being of a Creator. Human reason joins with revelation, in dictating, that some part of our time should be specially dedicated to worship the Creator and giver of our existence and all we enjoy.

A SABBATH was instituted in the beginning. After the creation was completed in six days, it is said, *GOD ended his works which he had made: and rested the seventh day from all his works which he had made. And GOD blessed the seventh day and sanctified it.*

HE sanctified it. By his special command it was set apart to a holy use; to holy services, and meditation on most holy objects and truths.

This doth not imply that it is lawful to be unholy on other days. Every mind is able to make the diftinction between facred and fecular employments, both of which are fit in their proper feafon. The Sabbath is to be wholly devoted to the facred employments of worfhip and religious inftruction, and to our preparation for another world; which is defcribed as an eternal Sabbath of praife and holinefs to God.

From this early appointment of a Sabbath, together with the reafonablenefs of the inftitution, it hath been found that all people, whether chriftians or heathen, have had appointed feafons of homage to the Gods whom they adored. Tho' fanctifying a feventh part of time, has been forgotten by multitudes of men; it does not appear, that a fenfe of propriety in appointing certain feafons for religious worfhip, has been obliterated by the total depravity of human nature, even from heathen minds. Although apoftates from chriftianity travelling into the fhades of heathenifm, may have given this reprefentation of fome tribes of men; the fact doth not appear to be well authenticated. The reporters were prejudiced by their own wifh to find fuch a fact. Alfo they have been generally of fuch a character, that even heathen would early difcover their impiety, and hide from them their facred myfteries. The greateft number, of thofe who have denied the fitnefs of appropriate feafons for divine worfhip, will be found among apoftates from chriftianity. Thefe perfons, having long finned againft great light, in many inftances, appear to be given up to ftrong delufion. Their refiftance to revealed light, has ended in the ftupefaction of natural confcience, fo that reafon remonftrates no longer againft the rebellion of a wicked heart. This is the natural confequence of long continued fin against clear light. Those, who are conscious, they have been thus doing, ought to suspect their own judgment; for they are making their minds dark, and it is not improbable that God may give them up to believe a lie.

The account of the patriarchal ages, given by Moses, is concise, and only such events are recorded, as were absolutely necessary to teach the human character, and justify the succeeding events of divine government. It appears that divine knowledge, was given occasionally by special revelations, to particular persons and families, who did not wish to forget God and plunge into deep idolatry. Whatever, of those early ages, was necessary for our present instruction, may doubtless be found recorded in the scriptures. We find there hath been a church from the beginning, in which the true God hath been worshipped. We have reason to suppose, that in the church a seventh part of time was acknowledged and observed as sacred; and that there hath always been a remnant, who rested and sanctified the Sabbath of the Lord according to his own example.

When the Mosaic dispensation was given the law of the Sabbath was renewed. It was introduced as one of the ten commandments, which are a summary of the duties due to God and man. In the Mosaic revelation, we find the most positive laws appointing the day, the manner of observation, the duties of a religious worship to be performed, and penalties on the disobedient. God calls the Sabbath his covenant with the people of Israel. *Wherefore the children of Israel shall keep the Sabbath, to observe the Sabbath throughout their generations, for a perpetual covenant. It is a sign between me and the children of Israel forever.* Of such importance did God esteem the keeping of a Sabbath, that his visible appearance for them, as their covenant God, depended upon their obedience to this institution.

In all the succeeding prophets, profaning the Sabbath is mentioned as a sin, which directly exposed them to the most desolating judgments of heaven; and when they kept the Sabbath of the Lord, we find him remarkably appearing for them in the hour of peril. In the sequel of this discourse, we shall see the connexion between a holy keeping of the Sabbath, and a performance of other religious duty; so that a people or person profaning this institution, against their own knowledge, cannot be supposed holy. This accounts for the strict guard God hath placed over the Sabbath; for his promises to a faithful performance of it; and his threatened judgments against its profanation. From thoroughly examining this subject, we shall find a connexion between a holy keeping of God's day, and all the blessings men need. The blessings of this world, as well as of another.—The blessings of order—civil regularity and good government—family subordination—diffusion of knowledge among the people—personal piety—and eternal life. None of these can be had, but through an observance of God's holy day. The loss of civil and social good and of the kingdom of heaven is the penalty for disobedience. If men forget their everlasting good, they ought not to deny and neglect the Sabbath, so long as they wish for social peace and justice in this world. This view of the subject, justifies the wisdom and goodness of God, in the multitude of injunctions, reproofs, threatenings, and promises recorded in his word. It also justifies his punishment of his church by enemies and other external judgments for their neglect of the Sabbath. It was better for his people, they should be brought back to consideration by an external scourge; than suffered to go on in a neglect of divine worship, which must end in the utter extinction of that moral sentiment, by which alone there can be peace in families and justice in civil society.

UNDER the christian dispensation, the law of a Sabbath is continued in its full force. Although there be a change of time, from the seventh to the first day of the week, in commemoration of CHRIST's resurrection; a seventh part of time is reserved as sacred to the worship of GOD. The same general reasons for keeping a Sabbath, which have been from the beginniug do ,still continue. There is not an intimation of the law or duty being repealed. It was a precept of the moral law, which is of everlasting obligation. We have the example of CHRIST and his apostles for keeping holy time. And there are a multitude of precepts, enjoining holiness, christian duty, the worship of GOD, the rights and manner of instruction and worship, which teach christians the observance of a Sabbath, plainly as could be expressed by a repetition of the original institution.

ALTHO' reason can determine the propriety of worshipping GOD on stated seasons ; it doth not appear that the exact proportion of time to be thus consecrated could be known by us without a revelation. If this were left to human decision, there would be great diversity of sentiment, among those, who are well affected to divine honor ; and those who dislike his service, would soon fall into a total neglect of the duty. Infinite wisdom, looking on the natural and moral state, condition and wants of men, is able to point out the proportion of time, that ought to be consecrated as a Sabbath. Experience has confirmed the wisdom of the proportion, and shows that it does not interfere with a provision for the wants of the body, and is also sufficient for a most happy effect in present society and in preparing our minds for the world to come.

As it is proper, that the proportion of Sabbatical time should be determined by God; so it is, also, that the particular day or time should be appointed by his high authority. If the particular time were not appointed ungrateful men would defraud God of his right; and by endeavouring to accommodate sacred time to their secular purposes, all social union in the worship of God would be frustrated.

One of the great benefits of an instituted Sabbath is, that it secures social worship. The nature of men is social. Moral obligation and the laws of religion are social. The human mind is powerfully affected by a social union, in adoring and praising God—in seeking instruction of our duty—and offering up our prayers. Both social and solitary worship, are in their place absolutely necessary for a life of religion; and it may justly be questioned, whether any person who entirely neglects one, ever performs the other with any considerable propriety. If the sanctuary be deserted; there will be a loss of those holy social affections in the soul, which give warmth and fervency in the closet. If the closet be deserted, social worship will degenerate into formality or pageantry, and there will not be that solemn sense of God and our own wants, which is best gained in retirement, where external enticements are removed, and we feel ourselves alone with a great and holy God. There is a wonderful harmony between divine institutions, and the natural principles on which the human mind is constructed, feels and acts. This consideration alone, if it were thoroughly searched might go far to convince an infidel. The harmony of natural and moral law, fhows the divine author and proves moral obligation on men. There cannot be in our minds, a due feeling of the holy and focial obligations of religion, without focial worfhip ; and there cannot be any ftated focial worfhip without a Sabbath.

A MULTITUDE of perfons, in the chriftian world, who neglect public focial worfhip of GOD, do hereby fully prove themfelves to be deftitute of piety. Want of health and opportunity may be accepted as an excufe ; but after thefe, there remains no excufe. If they fay, they can worfhip alone—that they are the beft judges of their own wants—can beft call on GOD for themfelves; all thefe are no excufe. Even allowing all this, ftill they ought not to neglect focial worfhip. GOD is the beft judge, and can tell what he will accept, and how and where he will give the aid of his Spirit. If religion confifts in focial affections, it is impoffible that worfhip fhould be always beft performed alone. It is obftinacy againft infinite wifdom to contend in this point, and prefumption to think we are the beft judges after GOD hath expreffed his precept. If men neglect apparent commands, although they may think themfelves fcrupuloufly attentive to duty in many other things ; they have ftill no reafon to expect a divine bleffing on the things which they are attentive to do.

AFTER all, there is from experience, little reafon to credit the fincerity of thofe, who fay they are the beft judges of their own wants, and of the manner and time of worfhipping GOD. There is great reafon to fear it is merely an excufe for neglecting a known duty ; and that they have become fo hardened, as to pretend a ferious defence for the neglect of GOD's command. We do not find thofe who neglect public focial worfhip, attentive to duty either in the family or clofet. They do not appear to have that folemnity, that fenfe of a prefent God and of their own wants, which accompany much private devotion. Either ftupidity and thoughtleffnefs of God, or great impiety are marked in their whole appearance. If God were to fet eternity before fuch minds, in the manner it may appear to them at death, and will certainly open to them when they enter it ; it would entirely filence the excufe that they beft knew their own wants, and the proper manner and time of worfhipping God.

After thefe general remarks on the fubject, I fhall attempt the following things.

I. Inquire how the Sabbath is to be fanctified.

II. To defcribe the worldly benefits, which refult from a faithful obfervance of the inftitution.

III. To defcribe its happy influence in preparing us for the world to come.

I. I am to inquire how the Sabbath is to be fanctified.

The words *holy* and *holinefs*, when applied to minds, mean a conformity to God and his law. It is the temper, affections and practice which conftitute moral and evangelical obedience. Holinefs is our whole duty, refulting from the character of all the moral agents with whom we are connected, and from our relation to them. It is our preparation for heavenly bleffednefs, and the evidence of our forgivenefs by the free grace of God through Jesus Christ. The holinefs of intelligent minds, muſt therefore confiſt in voluntary exerciſe of the heart, and a correſpondent practice in our treatment of GOD, and our brethren of every degree in the rational univerſe.

HOLINESS is alſo aſcribed to objects inanimate—to times—to places—to offices—and to many things which can neither exerciſe volition nor underſtand. Thus the houſe of GOD, his Sabbath, and all the things employed in his worſhip are called holy. Whatever is ſpecially devoted to a ſacred uſe, is in this ſenſe holy unto the Lord, and a miſapplication is conſidered by GOD as a grievous ſin.

REMEMBER *the Sabbath day to keep it holy.* In this precept the word *holy* is to be underſtood in both the aforementioned ſenſes. The time of the whole day is to be made ſacred to the ſervice of GOD in worſhipping him. No other uſe of it, either in labor, or amuſement, or the promotion of ſecular concerns, or in thinking of the intereſts and pleaſures of the world, is to be admitted. This is making the day holy, in ſuch a ſenſe, as inanimate things admit the application of the word.

To keep it holy.—This dedication of the day is to be done with a holy heart. We are to make a holy uſe of it, from holy motives. *The Lord looketh on the heart*—he ſees our motives and intentions in all our viſible ſervice, and if it come from an evil motive, it is not accepted by him as true worſhip.—In the firſt chapter of Iſaiah's prophecy, there is a very ſolemn expoſtulation with his people, on this ſubject, which all ought to read with deep ſelf-examination. *To what pur-*

pose is the multitude of your sacrifices unto me? saith the Lord. I am full of the burnt-offering of rams, and the fat of fed beasts, and I delight not in the blood of bullocks, or of lambs, or of he goats. When ye come to appear before me, who hath required this at your hands, to tread my courts. That is, with the temper and the heart from which you perform your services.—*The calling of your assemblies I cannot away with; it is iniquity even the solemn meeting. Your new moons, and your appointed feasts my soul hateth: they are a trouble unto me: I am weary to bear them. And when you spread forth your hands, I will hide mine eyes from you; when ye make many prayers I will not hear: your hands are full of blood. Wash ye, make you clean, put away the evil of your doings from before mine eyes, cease to do evil, learn to do well.*—Here was an instance, in which the day of GOD was visibly made sacred to religious uses, but they did not keep it in a holy manner. Although the external service was according to prescription, it was vitiated by a formal, thoughtless and unholy heart. The prophet Ezekiel describes the same character. *They come unto thee as the people cometh, and they sit before thee as my people, and they hear thy words but will not do them; for with their mouth they shew much love, but their heart goeth after their covetousness.*—The proper services, by which the time is made sacred, will be presently considered; but whatever they be, omniscient holiness seeth guilt in the whole, unless it be done with a pure heart. A holy dedication of external objects and of times can never come in the place of an honest, a worshipping heart. The holiness of times and places is made to aid the holiness of our hearts; and our hearts were not made, merely to say these external things are holy, and to go no further. *The Sabbath was made for man, and not man for the Sabbath.* The great use of the day is to praise and love GOD, with the whole heart.—To understand his will and our own duty most spiritually—to search out his law—to seek a conformity to his infinite holiness—to grow in faith and repentance—and to prepare ourselves for an eternal Sabbath of holy delight in beholding him. An inward sanctification in all manner of godliness is, therefore, remembering the Sabbath day to keep it holy. On this day we are to converse directly with GOD and our own hearts, and desire those communications of the blessed Spirit, by which he cometh down into the hearts of his people, communing with them and setting them apart for himself. We should seek for such an apprehension of GOD, present at all times, but especially present through his world on that day; as will make all surrounding objects appear to us as solemn as they be peaceful and still through a cessation of earthly labors. If our hearts be right this will be the solemnity of joy, and not of dread; and we shall feel a holy rest in admiring and serving the Creator.

INDOLENCE is not the rest proposed for the Sabbath.—Heaven is a state of rest, but not of indolence.—So ought the Sabbath to be a rest, from those slavish labors of human life to which we are condemned in justice, and which are also necessary to preserve us from the tyranny of our own appetites, that lead to sin.—It is a rest from concerning ourselves about worldly plans of ambition and gain—a rest from thinking of such enticing objects as have gained an undue ascendency over our hearts through our past converse with them. If heaven is to be a state of rest, the time preparatory to it, may eminently be called the rest of good men on earth. The man who calls himself a christian, and can loiter and sleep away the

Sabbath of the Lord, when there are so many duties to be done which must be pleasing to a good heart, is indeed in the sleep of death eternal.

If there be not a solemn sense of eternal things in the mind, there is no reason to expect the Sabbath will be observed, in the manner which God requires; and so as to secure final salvation. Among those who profess to keep the Sabbath, do not many loose all spiritual advantage from it? A worldly ease is the thing they seek. The concerns of a never dying soul are forgotten. They do not reflect that they are sinners, and need sanctification and forgiveness; nor that rest from worldly concerns, implies the need of industry in the spiritual. They divide the day between an accommodation to ease and to fashion. A partial attendance in the sanctuary is the religion of the day, and when this is finished, conversation on the most vain and uninteresting subjects finishes the decorum. A week begun in such conversation, will probably be ended with very few thoughts of God. His providence will be forgotten, and daily piety will be unknown. In a Sabbath thus spent there is no advance towards heaven.

He that hath an ear let him hear. The Sabbath was given to us as a season of preparation for another state of being. Although infinite wisdom saw it best to subject us to the labors of the world, by which the greatest part of our time must be consumed, he hath so constructed things, that every seventh day may be wholly devoted to the interests of another world, without exposing ourselves to want in this.' We are therefore accountable to God for this time. We shall all be called to account for the season—to show what instruction we have gained—and what advance we have made in conformity to God.

Serm. XX. *the Sabbath.*

Having mentioned the purity and holiness of heart, which is neceffary for *remembering the Sabbath day to keep it holy;* I will, secondly, defcribe the fervices by which the day is to be confecrated to God and religion.

1. The public worfhip of God in his fanctuary.

Public focial worfhip is as exprefsly commanded by God, as the obfervance of a Sabbath. The meaning of the word convocation is, a coming together of the people. Concerning the Sabbath Mofes commanded. *Six days fhall work be done but the feventh day is the Sabbath of reft, an holy convocation: ye fhall do no work therein: it is the Sabbath of the Lord, in all your dwellings.* The Sabbath worfhip of the temple and fynagogue was exprefsly apponted, and many promifes given to the right performance, and many reproofs of neglect. Jesus Christ taught publicly on the Sabbath. *And as his cuftom was, he went into the fynagogue on the Sabbath day, and ftood up for to read. And he came down to Capernaum, a city of Gallilee, and taught them on the Sabbath days.* We find the apoftles, and the church where they were, always affembled on the firft day of the week or chriftian Sabbath. Chriftians are exhorted. *Not forfaking the affembling of yourfelves together as the manner of fome is. But exhorting one another, and fo much the more, as ye fee the day approaching.* Thefe injunctions are repeated, not to convince ferious people, who already know and are difpofed to comply with their duty; but to warm fuch as wifh to think, that it is a matter left for every man's difcretionary determination, whether he will neglect or join in the public worfhip of God. The command is pofitive and without any exception. It is fit that thofe, who receive mercies and meet afflictions in common; who fin together;

who need an assistance in duties which they must perform together, to unite in worship, in prayer, in praise, in meditating and confessing their sin, in searching the word of GOD, and seeking the spirit and practice of brotherly love, which is the evidence they belong to CHRIST.

ALTHO' the manner, the hour, and the order of particular services, are left to the prudent determination of the church, and may be varied to accommodate them to the special events of providence and the circumstances of particular people; yet the general parts of public worship are fixed by scriptural precept and example. Prayer for temporal and spiritual blessings—praise for mercies received—and instruction concerning GOD and our own duty, are services proper for all people, and have the authority of divine appointment.

THE social nature of man is strongly impressed by the services of the sanctuary. The affections of the heart become communional. Brotherly love, which if true is the spirit of heaven, is insensibly diffused through the christian assembly. Here the pious mind, solemnized by the presence of the great king of the church, and the reverence of his brethren, learns to adore, to obey, to praise, to feel a universal providence, to realize the vanities of a sinful world and the glorious communion of saints in the world to come. Here piety towards GOD is quickened, and kind affections to men are strengthened. Here we rejoice with those who rejoice, and mourn with those who mourn. Many of the duties of religion are social and our fellowmen are the objects of them, and it is impossible we should be quickened to the performance so powerfully, in any other way, as by uniting in the worship of our GOD and Redeemer.

We have the example of eminent saints on sacred record, and the testimony of christians in all ages, that the public worship of God was to them a season of great spiritual improvement and delight. David saith, *Blessed is the man whom thou choosest and causest to approach unto thee: that he may dwell in thy courts: we shall be satisfied with the goodness of thy house, even of thy holy temple. How amiable are thy tabernacles, O Lord of hosts! My soul longeth, yea, even fainteth for the courts of the Lord: my heart and my flesh crieth out for the living God. Blessed are they that dwell in thy house: they will be still praising thee.* The ardent love, and that spiritual improvement in the sanctuary, which the Psalmist expressed in these and in many other places, has been felt and testified by the people of God in all ages of the church. Although the social worship of this world is full of imperfection, through the remaining sin of those who are most sanctified; it must still be a pleasure to those, who are prepared by the beginning of a holy temper, for the social and perfect worship of the heavenly world.

2. The Sabbath is a most favorable opportunity for family worship and instruction.

Every house ought to be a temple sacred to God and the duties of religion; and every family a little congregation for prayer and praise. It is impossible that the great body of mankind, considered either as a civil or religious community, should be well regulated, when families are a nursery of disorder and impiety. All order begins in household government, instruction and religion. It is the nature of sin to break society in pieces. No wisdom below infinite, could arrange a state in which sinners may have any degree of order and peace. The infinite wifdom of God is' difplayed in preferving fo much order and peace, as is experienced in this world, where all come into exiftence under the power of finful principles. The natural formation of families is a principal circumftance in this arrangement of infinite wifdom. It is in thefe, that order and diforder, virtue and vice, happinefs and mifery begin. After we know the order, the government, the principles and practice of families, we may from this determine the character and practice of the civil ftate and of the church compofed out of them. When all reftraint and all religious inftruction are neglected in families, the next generation will come on the ftage prepared to rufh into all manner of licentioufnefs. There will be no well regulated civil government; and either the rod of defpotifm muft govern, or the more dreadful horrors of anarchy, in which every man is a tyrant to his neighbours, muft be endured. There will be no chriftian order—no brotherly love—no kind affection—none of the temper and practice by which the people of God are prepared for their everlafting reft.

The importance of family government and religion, as it relates to civil well-being, hath never been fufficiently confidered and enforced. Men may in vain feek for a union of government and freedom, when families are a nurfery for immorality. But I am at prefent called to confider families, and family religion, in another point of view, and as they ftand related to the church of Christ and the practice of undefiled religion.

Parents and governors of families are minifters of God, who have the firft opportunity of acting on human minds. By the law of nature he places the young in their hands; and by the laws of religion he gives them authority to govern and inſtruct. Thoſe who come vicious from the ſchool of education, have little proſpect of being amended. The inſtances which we ſee of reclaimed ſenſualiſts and infidels, are generally from among thoſe, who have become debauched in principles and practice, after another education had been given them. And in ſuch caſes, the early care of pious parents was doubtleſs remembered by a gracious GOD. It is hard deſtroying that tender conſcience which is formed by the aſſiduous care of a religious education. The apoſtate from firſt impreſſions, feels that they have a power over him through his whole life. He often reflects, I was not ſo taught—I am now ſinning againſt the precepts of my pious inſtructors; and it ſometimes ſeems, as though I heard them ſpeak back from that awful world to which they are gone. Family religion is of infinite importance to the young. It is thus, conſcience receives a quickneſs it rarely looſes. A habit of reverence for divine things is formed, which can never be forgotten.

THESE remarks ſhow the importance of a religious obſervation of the Sabbath in families. It is a moſt ſeaſonable time for family worſhip, and inſtruction in the principles of religion and morality. The family are convened—they are reſtrained from amuſement and labor—they can have no other lawful employment, but to ſerve GOD and ſeek their own duty—the world around them is ſtill, and every circumſtance favorable to devotion. There needs only the pious diligence of a father, a maſter, a leader in the family to guide their devotions, to impreſs ſentiments of morality, to ſhow them the connexion between their preſent obedience to GOD and their eternal bleſſedneſs—to explain and enforce the doctrines of christianity—and to instamp conviction on the impressible young mind, against the destructive allurements and temptations of a sinful world.

But this is the business of the sanctuary, saith the indolent and irreligious parent.

It is allowed that all this ought to be attempted in the sanctuary, and where it is not done the minister of the sanctuary is in fault. But can it be expected the instructions of the sanctuary will be of much avail, when they are not enforced in the family? It certainly cannot. The master of the family, ought to be a minister of religion in his own house, and add his own instruction and the weight of his authority to public institutions. He ought to address the feelings of his charge, and show them that he believes in the reality and importance of religion. He should advise, instruct, reprove, pray, and apply truth to the varying conditions of those under his care. It is his business to awaken the secure, to reclaim the wrong, to lead the inquiring, and guide the whole into paths of duty and peace. Unless he doth this, he hath no right to esteem himself a servant of the Lord in his house.

It is often a matter of complaint, that so little benefit comes from the public instruction of religion. The ministers of the sanctuary, if they have christian humility, will own their imperfection. They must own, that they have great reason to be humbled before God, for not urging family religion and the duty of christian parents with more energy than they do; but let parents and the masters of families seriously consider, whether the fault is not partly at their door. Can public instruction be of much avail, when not enforced by household instruction? Did not God design, the instruction of the temple and of the family to go together? Is it not the business of parental authority to enforce sacerdotal exhortation? Is it to be expected the prayer of the church will reach the houshold, which are never called to pray for themselves. The design of infinite wisdom, in his natural and preceptive institution of families, was to make them subservient to his church and the salvation of souls. If they neglect his Sabbath, they become nurseries of impiety and destroy the souls of the young.

3dly. In sanctifying the Sabbath and keeping it holy, the duties of self-examination and secret prayer ought not to be omitted.

These duties are required of christians on every day, and a pious life cannot be maintained without them. None, who neglect secret prayer, may expect the aids of the holy Spirit. None, who neglect daily examination, will be preserved in the holiness, purity, humility and obedience of the gospel. Daily communion with God, and increase of faith and holiness, must be preserved by the daily means, of prayer and examination. The Sabbath is eminently adapted to these duties. No good man, who delights in knowing and conversing with God, and is honestly disposed to know his defects in duty, and his transgressions of God's law, will omit these means. There is always employment enough for the closet. To examine the sincerity of our family and public duties—to lay open our hearts, our aims and motives before God—to confess our sins which are hidden from all the world, our coldness in duty, our want of love, and imperfection in every duty—to pray for the influence of his holy Spirit; these are sufficient employment for the Sabbath, in all the hours which can be redeemed from the family and public services of religion. In this union of holy duties the christian ought to spend the day of the Lord. Between his public, his family and his secret devotion, he will find time little enough to devote to the service of God.

Against this sanctification of the Sabbath a multitude of objections may be raised; for objections are never wanting when the heart is dissatisfied.

It will be said, this is a servile and fatiguing employment for the day. Whether it be so or not, depends on the state of our hearts. If it be disagreeable to think of God and of our duty, and if we be moved to it only by a fear of punishment, the employment marked out will be a weariness. The day consecrated to God and our duty, must hang heavily on a mind which can delight in nothing but worldliness and sensuality. There is no remedy for this disagreement between holiness and unholiness—between serving God and forgetting him—between coming nigh to him and going far from him. The same objection may be made against the whole scheme and practice of religion; yea, even against the rewards of blessedness prepared for the people of God. This ought to convince all unholy persons, that there is a great defect in the state of their hearts, and that they need to be made anew, before they can serve the Lord acceptably either in this or the world to come.

It is allowed, that through weakness of the human frame, the mind may be fatigued, by too long application to a particular truth or service. But even here, the infinite goodness of God hath provided against the weakness of our frame and of our minds, in that variety of services, by which we are to sanctify and keep his day holy.

In the duties of the sanctuary, the family and the closet there is a grateful variety. Every social principle, every natural affection, and every lawful self-regard are called in to make our duty light and easy, and to sustain our minds under pious thoughtfulness. The same variety which hath been pointed out in this discourse, would sustain the mind in any other kind of application. While in the house of God we are with the multitude of our neighbours, friends and brethren. The thought of preparing and going together to an everlasting heaven of social joys is enough to fill the soul with a divine transport.

And is the scene less endearing, less interesting in the family? With whom is the father of the house communing in the worship of his Saviour? With the partner of his years and of his earthly portion—with his offspring, for whom he would willingly spend and be spent in all other things—with the domestics who are committed to his care by the alwise providence of God. These souls are to exist forever. He is their guide to eternity. Must not the thought of this be interesting to him and to every one? How pleasing to think, that the endearments now formed, if on right principles, will be eternal. To complete this animating solemnity, all may unite and call on their Lord—may retire to the place where an infinite God condescends to meet every humble soul, and communicates by his Spirit, the joy which is unspeakable and full of glory.

If, after viewing these circumstances, any complain that this sanctification of the Sabbath, is a servile and fatiguing employment, what can we think of their hearts? What can we think of their christian profession, if they ever have made one? It would be hard to think all such wilful deceivers; but they are in a state worse than this, for they are self-deceivers. How solemn will the time be, when all such self-deceivers, will have their eyes opened! May the Lord open them while it is a time accepted and a day of salvation. AMEN.

SERMON XXI.

Benefits of the Sabbath.

EXODUS xx. 8.

Remember the Sabbath day to keep it holy.

IN a former discourse from these words the following things were proposed.

I. An inquiry how the Sabbath is to be sanctified.

II. To describe the worldly benefits, which result from a faithful observance of the institution.

III. To describe its happy influence in preparing us for the world to come.

The first of these has been largely considered.
I am next to describe the worldly benefits, which result from a faithful observance of the Sabbath.
Many appear to have an apprehension, that religion is something designed only for the benefit

of another world. That if we can have it at the time of death, the whole which religion can give will be attained. Such an idea arises from an utter experimental ignorance what religion is. True religion is the most perfect blessedness of rational beings, in every possible state of existence; in this world, at death and through eternity. By the present comforts of religion, a pious mind obtains the highest conviction, that it is impossible there should be a state of perfect blessedness, without a holy temper and practice. Take a person who hath experienced both the pleasures of sinning and the happiness and benefits of religion—tell him that the heavenly state is perfectly happy; and without any other description he will know that it is a state of perfect holiness. Having experienced both kinds of happiness, he will have an unshaken conviction which is the perfect one—which raises our minds to the greatest dignity they can ever possess—and crowns the weak creature with an enduring glory. If this be the fruit of a holy heart; it must be, also, of those institutions, which are designed to promote holiness and a sense of moral obligation. If there were no eternity of conscious existence to succeed the present life, the Sabbath would be a most excellent institution to promote happiness in the family, in the neighbourhood, and in the civil state. Although it cannot be supposed, that those who keep the Sabbath, only for worldly purposes, are pious people and obey the command, *to remember the Sabbath day to keep it holy*, in its high intention; there are advantages from their doing thus, which ought not to be lost. It preserves present society in a state most favorable to human happiness, and it keeps sinners from being so hardened in the ways of an unholy heart and life as they appear to become by a neglect.

A wise policy for the family and for the civil ſtate, will anxiouſly preſerve the Sabbath. The ſame reaſons which make family ſubordination and civil government neceſſary in the world, do alſo juſtify a Sabbath and call on every friend of civil and family order to maintain it by his whole influence. We hence find that infidels, diſorganizers of the civil and religious ſtate, the enemies of government in its ſubſtantial forms, and thoſe who wiſh to triumph over humanity and juſtice in their actions, have in every age gathered in array againſt the chriſtian Sabbath, and endeavoured to change it from a ſeaſon holy unto the Lord, into a carnival of licentiouſneſs and ſenſuality. This is manifeſt from that awful league againſt chriſtianity, which has been formed in the preſent century, and has by ſecret art and the practice of intrigue been carried to a more dangerous length, than any thing of the kind ſince the chriſtian æra. Theſe men, ſpread clandeſtinely through the limits of Chriſtendom, have made their grand aſſault againſt the chriſtian Sabbath and the purity of family obligation. By the means uſed to effectuate the deep malignity of their hearts againſt religion, they have diſcovered a great knowledge of corrupt human nature, how it is reſtrained and how it is let looſe to all manner of crimes. Hell itſelf deſpairs of making the world an Aceldama, of breaking down all order and juſtice, and baniſhing the religion of Christ, while the family is preſerved pure, and the Sabbath holy unto the Lord.

If there be any who wiſh to reject vital religion, yet ſtill mean to be on the ſide of worldly order; let theſe perſons know that they cannot have the worldly order they wiſh without recurring for aid to the inſtitutions of the goſpel. Let them fee the weaknefs of their own fcheme of order and happinefs. Let them behold and tremble before the dignity of chriftian inftitutions. Let them at length be fenfible, that by their diftafte to the fpirituality of gofpel doctrines and practice; they have been aiding an enemy, which attempts to deftroy the family and civil order they wifh to preferve. Let them join in fanctifying thofe inftitutions of heaven, by which alone, the focial ftate of man can be preferved and made ftrong againft the raging lufts of an apoftate world.——Some of the many benefits which accrue to fociety from the obfervance of a Sabbath I will mention.

It humanizes the paffions of men, and learns them to refpect the rights and the happinefs of others.

A TRANSIENT acquaintance, with thofe diftricts in chriftian lands, where the public worfhip of God is neglected, will give full conviction of this truth. Even a traveller cannot pafs them without obferving an unfocial fpirit. The manners are rough—the words and actions of the people difcover, either a jealous diftance or a barbarous infolence—they are lefs pitiful and courteous—lefs feeling to the rights of humanity —and much lefs fenfible of that moral obligation, which unites men as brethren and children of the great, the divine family.

There is a refpect due to the rational nature of man, whether he be high or low, rich or poor, in power or in weaknefs. There is an evident want of this, where God is not worfhipped by a public affembling of the people. Our diftinct interefts, employments, offices and fituations in the life of this world, are operating caufes of oppofition and jealoufy; which, without a check, will come to a great height. This takes place between men of different profeſſions—of different ſtate in point of opulence—and among thoſe in the ſame walk of life, where little oppoſing intereſts happen to ariſe. By ſuch means the neighbourhood which ought to be like a family a little more extended, is often divided in enmity, and their very proximity becomes a curſe.

Prodigious is the influence of a public Sabbath to leſſen or extinguiſh theſe evils. The whole people of every claſs, rank and condition in life, are ſolemnly called together. Their paſſions are huſhed by the ſacredneſs of the day.— Their enmities, unleſs exceedingly bitter, are for a moment abated.—They come together in a confiderate frame, and there is an opportunity given for reaſon to ſpeak and conſcience to teſtify. They are called to believe that God, their great, good and venerable Creator is with them. By prayer and meditation they feel themſelves tranſported before him.—Eternity with its never ending rewards is opened to their ſight. They have a new view of time, the world and their own condition in it. They perceive a moral obligation ſuperior to their own little enmities and dividing intereſts.—On the common floor of humble worſhip, and in the preſence of a God whoſe glory darkens human diſtinctions of great and little, rich and poor, they feel themſelves accountable to a holy law, and that they muſt be judged and rewarded for all the actions done in the body. Thoſe who govern remember that they are in the place of God, to execute right in the world, and that there is a court of review where their adminiſtration will be judged by the Lord. Thoſe, who are under government, remember the powers which be, are ordained of God; and that obedience to their lawful authority is obedience to him. The rich are reminded they shall fade in their ways, and that their earthly diftinctions cannot fanctify pride or crimes. The poor are taught to be patient, refigned to the providence of God, to fee the wifdom of his different difpenfation, and exhorted to lay up for themfelves treafures in heaven. All are called to brotherly love, condefcenfion, humility, and obedience to the faith of Christ. All are called to think of death, judgment and eternity. The exhibition is inftructive; it is impreffive. It humbles pride—it leffens the objects of the world, thus deftroying the caufes of enmity and jealoufy—it confoles the weak, the defponding, and the oppreffed—it makes all confiderate in the fear of God—and while every one in a confcioufnefs of his own fin feels humbled before God and man, his fenfe of a moral obligation to the duties of a holy and chriftian life, and to treat others as he can reafonably defire to be treated by them, is greatly increafed.

It muft betray great ignorance of human nature, to deny that this humanizes the paffions of men, and learns them to refpect the rights and happinefs of others. If the public worfhip of God, brings into their fight, his character and their relation to him; dependence on him; and accountablenefs to his judgment, it muft produce the happy effects which have been mentioned. Mens bad treatment of each other, is carried to the greateft height, when the glory of their common Creator and Judge is forgotten. They cannot fee him and his relation to the human ftate, without fome feeling of an obligation to juftice and benevolence towards the members of his family. The impreffion on the public mind and on public manners, by the weekly celebration of a Sabbath, according to the chriftian inſtitution, is greater than would be conceived, if not taught by experience. Its effects ſpread through human life—they are ſeen in all orders and conditions of men—in all inſtitutions, relations, and duties of human life. It is thus the public opinion of right is formed—it is thus that civilization and humanity are brought to the higheſt pitch in all chriſtianized ſtates. The moſt bitter enemies of the doctrines of CHRIST have allowed the fact. They have allowed the chriſtian morality to be the moſt excellent in the world, and the beſt adapted to make ſociety happy; and after granting this, if they were wiſe, they would allow the doctrines and inſtitutions which preſerve this morality and actually impreſs it on the mind, to be alſo moſt excellent.

HAVING remarked on the influence of a Sabbath to humanize the paſſions and prepare men for ſociety generally, in whatever lawful form it exiſts; I will exemplify this in two inſtances, the family and the civil ſtate.

THE advantages of a Sabbath for family religion, and the opportunity it gives to the father and maſter of the family to do his duty, as the miniſter of GOD in his own houſe, have been already mentioned; to which I may add, that public worſhip gives great aſſiſtance in family government. As there cannot, in any place, be public order without family government; ſo neither is it probable their will be a pious family government, without attendance on the public worſhip of GOD. This is a great means of keeping alive in the maſter of the houſehold, a ſenſe of his own obligation. By his public worſhip he is prepared for his family duty—feels an obligation from GOD upon him—and comes from the ſanctuary warmed with a ſpirit of devotion, which will enliven the endearing ſcene of family inſtruction and worship. Thus also, those under his care are prepared to profit by his instruction. They are taught the duty of family obedience and reverence, and their minds are prepared to receive more minute instruction and a personal application of the truths, which have been taught more generally in the sanctuary. Experience, which cannot be contradicted, proves the powerful efficacy of sanctifying the Sabbath, to preserve order, justice, love and government in the family and neighbourhood. Although there may be civility and polite attention, between families where God is not worshipped and his Sabbath kept, it is not difficult, through the outward show, to discover a very doubtful sincerity and a want of deep, heart-governing sensibility. It is the latter which abides in the heart under trials and crosses, and makes men friends when we need a friend. How strongly this is illustrated in scenes of family trial, sickness and death which are constantly happening. Let one be laid on the bed of danger, from among the fashionable despisers of religion and of God's Sabbath. Where are the irreligious friends, whose amity was so tender in the day of ease—who fawned around each other with professions of infinite friendship and most exquisite sensibilities of heart? They are all fled—their friendship is forgotten. The fashionable, irreligious sick one must look another way for help. Another kind of people are around the bed of groans and death. The plain, the serious, the praying people who kept the Sabbath of the Lord in his sanctuary and in their families, are now the only ones who appear to have sensibility, and who dare expose themselves to aid a dying fellow mortal. They have sought the Lord to give them such a temper, and they now find it. They can spend their sleepless nights in kind attendance and prayer around the death bed of thofe, who lately reviled them for their religious fear of God. They can pain themfelves to be like their divine mafter. O religion of Jesus, how great is thy triumph in fuch a fcene as this!

A GOOD civil government is one of the greateft benefits of human life. To this chriftianity is favorable ; and among all chriftian inftitutions, the Sabbath is moft favorable. Defpotic tyranny and the anarchy of a democratic mob are two extremes, placed at an equal diftance from good government and civil freedom. And hath the Sabbath any connexion with thefe fubjects? Yes, very much.

SUCH is its connexion, that it is impoffible in a great community, to have rational government and a true freedom reaching to the great body of a people, without a Sabbath, regarded in the ordinances of public piety. General freedom muft be founded in a general virtue of the people, and a pervading fenfe of moral obligation. Thefe cannot be without religion, and religion cannot be without a Sabbath. Heathen experience hath been a thoufand times convinced, that men muft regard another world or they cannot be held together in this, by free civil ties. Heathen ftates, from political motives, uphold a falfe religion, which they know to be of their own invention ; while many in chriftian ftates, are fo blind both politically and religioufly, as to deny their aid to a religion which is divinely true.

THERE are, in this world of paffion and fin, but two ways of maintaining government : By defpotic power, and by moral information diffufed among the great body of people. Defpotic government is one of the plagues inflicted by an angry God on guilty men. Moral information, on which freedom and order depend, cannot be diffused among a people without a Sabbath. Even under the rod of despotism, if the tyrant can be brought to keep and maintain a Sabbath among his people, it is an alleviation of their wretchedness. It so stings the conscience of oppressors and reminds them of their own accountability, that they sometimes think what they do. Though all single tyrants hate a Sabbath, they sometimes maintain it to deceive men through an appearance of piety. The tyranny of the democratic multitude always endeavours wholly to expunge the Sabbath of God. It can answer no desired end in that most awful state of society.

In a government of order, of justice, and of freedom the christian Sabbath is a most essential pillar. By meditating on the adorable rights of Jehovah, and the sacred obligations of moral love and justice, they learn their own rights in relation to each other—they become acquainted with the first principles of happiness—they learn subordination to God which makes other subordination easy—they are quickened in the social virtues which sweeten the connections of civil intercourse—they are taught obligation and brotherhood, rights to be granted to others and to be enjoyed by themselves. In effecting this, the observation of a Sabbath hath great power. Further, the observation of a Sabbath hath great influence, in promoting that spirit of inquiry, which ends in the attainment of all useful knowledge. Whatever dissipates and repels ignorance is favorable to the best interests of society. Give knowledge to the great body of any people, they will in the end gain possession of the greatest worldly blessings. The Sabbath begets inquiry concerning moral and religious subjects, and from these it is extended to every other. This folves the obfervation, which is often made, that the beft inftitutions, for the inftruction of youth, are always found, where the Sabbath is moft regularly obferved. Enough hath been faid to fhow the beneficial influence of a Sabbath upon the fociety of this world. All, who endeavour to fubvert the inftitution, are acting a part unfriendly to human peace. If their defign could be effected, the civilization on which they depend would foon become retrograde—crimes would abound—confidence would be loft—and men would gradually fink back into that brutality, from which the world is in part emerged through the influence of chriftianity.

Hitherto I have confidered the worldly benefits which refult from the inftitution and obfervance of the chriftian Sabbath.—I now come as was propofed,

III. To defcribe its happy influence in our preparation for the world to come.

If it be wife to feek the happinefs of time, and if thofe who do any thing effentially to promote it are juftly efteemed benefactors of mankind ; how much more wife it is to feek the good of an eternal exiftence. Men place a high value upon fuch good inftitutions, as in their effects, terminate upon the prefent ftate of our exiftence. Laws are made to preferve and protect them, and the public will rife, as one animated body, to repel the means of their destruction. How much more ought they to be agreed, in maintaining the facrednefs of inftitutions, which are, if poffible, more neceffary for eternal than they be for temporal happinefs. The Sabbath is one of thefe inftitutions. It was received from the command of heaven. It is neceſſary for the happineſs of earth, and more neceſſary for bringing us to the happineſs of heaven. Although God may preſerve ſome individuals in the ſpirit and practice of chriſtian piety, in places where the public inſtitutions of religion fall into diſuſe, this will not be a general thing. The general manner in which infinite wiſdom acts is by means publicly diffuſed.

1. The Sabbath is neceſſary, to preſerve in the world, a knowledge of the true God.

Altho' there be much natural evidence, and a fulneſs of revealed evidence for the being and perfections of God; there muſt be ſtated times for men to attend to this evidence, to examine and meditate upon it, or they will remain ignorant of this glorious truth. The heart of man naturally goes from God. It does not ſeek to find him, unleſs called by the diſpenſations of providence or by inſtitutions appropriated to the obtainment of ſacred knowledge. The world pleaſes a ſinful heart. Its objects, its amuſements, its cares, its occupying events are many, and follow each other in inceſſant ſucceſſion.— The more they have engroſſed any one, the more blind his mind becomes to all ſpiritual conſiderations—to the evidence of Godhead, of his holy character, and the need of a holy conſecration to his glory. As there is a prediſpoſition to ſeek the creatures, God will not be ſought without inſtituted times, in which men are debarred from other employments, and have means calculated to aſſiſt them in this. For theſe reaſons a Sabbath becomes neceſſary to preſerve in the world a knowledge of the true God. It is moſt fitly called the Lord's-day and the Sabbath of the

Lord, for without this means, it would soon come, that he would not be publicly diftinguifhed from the idols of the heathen, nor known as the Jehovah of the whole earth. This is an appointed opportunity for confidering the evidence of his being, his rectitude and wifdom, his providence, and our dependance on his will. It is poffible, that without this public call, a few individuals might devote themfelves to fuch inquiries, but it would not be done by the body of the people; whereby they would become inftantly expofed to the lufts of a defigning few. So far as they did or believed any thing, they would implicitly follow the idolatry, which has always been found to grow up in fuch a ftate of things. It is a hard thing to retain a true knowledge of the true God, in the world, where all come into exiftence with unholy hearts. There muft be natural evidence —there muft be revealed evidence—there muft be public and family inftruction—there muft be a providence perpetually inftructing men—and there muft be fixed and facred feafons devoted to feeking the character and the prefence of God. A want of one, in thefe many means, breaks the divine fyftem of inftruction concerning him, and may make all the others without avail. If men confidered the labor of infinite wifdom to bring himfelf into the knowledge of mankind, and how perfect the fyftem of inftruction is, which he hath appointed, they would not dare omit a fingle part of it.

Those, who have chriftian knowledge from the joint influence of all appointed means, not confidering the greatnefs of their advantages, are ready to be furprized at heathen idolatry; and fometimes are ready to think their hearts to be naturally more wicked than their own, or they

could not remain in fo barbarous and ftupid a
ftate. Before any come to fuch a conclufion let
them confider the multitude of their own means;
and efpecially their Sabbaths, without which they
would probably relapfe into a gradual idolatry,
which in feveral ages would become of the deep-
eft kind. This fhows the powerful influence of
a Sabbath, in our preparation for the world to
come.

2dly. For the reafons which have juft been
mentioned, it appears that a Sabbath is neceffary
to attain, preferve and imprefs on the mind a
knowledge of the holy fcriptures.

God hath gracioufly taught us by his word.
This word contains doctrines neceffary for falvation, which could be known in no other way;
even the whole fcheme of forgivenefs and fanctification through the blood of Christ. It is a fuppofition humiliating to men, but evidenced by a
natural inattention to their eternal concerns;
that if they had been left without a Sabbath, few
indeed would have been inftructed by a revelation.
The opportunity afforded by a Sabbath, for public inftruction and for private reading and examination of their doctrines, is the principal means of
teaching men their facred and all concerning con-
tents. Let the Sabbath fall into difufe, and a
knowledge of the chriftian revelation will fall
with it. Being immerfed in labor and in pleafure, if men were without a day which demands of
them to inquire at the mouth of the Lord, his
word would fall into total difufe.

3dly. Public inftruction in religion, in the
duties we owe to God, and the way of our ac-

ceptance with him, depends entirely on the obfervance of a Sabbath.

ATTACHED as men are to their worldly interefts and pleafures, it muft be conceded by every one, there would be no general attendance on public inftruction, if labor and amufement were not forbidden on the Sabbath.—Public inftruction is an appointment of GOD. The inftitution is moft wife, though it muft be executed by very finful and imperfect men. It is allowed, that thofe who are called to this duty, have reafon to lament their infufficiency, and their great defects; and own that they are often guilty of unfaithfulnefs. Still GOD is pleafed *by the foolifhnefs of preaching to fave fome.* Although there be great deficiency in the inftructors, and many times, fuch inattention in the hearers, as feems on firft thinking of the fubject, to preclude all benefit; notwithftanding this, there is a great effect. Even the moft inattentive, who regularly meet in the houfe of GOD, obtain a general knowledge of chriftian doctrines and duties. They are led to fome inquiry and examination for themfelves. If thefe perfons, with fuch means of inftruction have great remaining ignorance, what would their ftate be without them? They would doubtlefs fink into a ftate of heathenifm. If a knowledge of the true GOD, if an acquaintance with his word and the doctrines of grace and falvation, are of any advantage in preparing for another world; of the fame advantage let us efteem the holy Sabbath by which the inftruction is communicated.

4thly. A SABBATH is neceffary to teach us our own fpiritual wants. It is a feafon for felfexamination, and applying truth to our own ftate and cafe. All honeft minds will own it is a difficult thing to apply truth to their own condition, and that they feel a propenfity to delay. This propenfity is common to human nature, and when Felix faid, *Go thy way for this time ; when I have a convenient feafon I will call for thee*, he gave a true picture of the feelings and conduct of mankind. While fo many cares of the world are around us, are calling us, and we efteem it lawful to attend to them ; through a diftafte of our duty and an unwillingnefs to think our ftate to be bad, we fhall delay a thorough application of truth to our own cafe. Men fuppofe the common labors of life to be lawful, and that time thus fpent is lawfully employed ; and if they can find any employment, which is efteemed lawful, they will poftpone the humbling, and difagreeable bufinefs of fearching out their own fpiritual needs and guilt. A perfon muft be very wilful in fin, wholly to neglect this duty on the Sabbath ; efpecially if he receive a public monition and call to do it, in the plain and folemn manner it ought to be given.

Our Sabbaths were appointed by God both to obtain religious knowledge, and apply it to our own cafe ; and without them, we fhould fink into a deep ftupidity, becoming ignorant of our hearts and our need of a gracious cleanfing. Mens ignorance of their fpiritual condition is one of the ftrange effects of natural degeneracy. They often have a doctrinal conviction of truth, and know that it relates to themfelves and is of the greateft importance ; ftill remaining, as far from any perfonal application, as if the truth were entirely unknown. All this may continue to be the cafe, for a long time, without any confcioufnefs of guilt or fenfe of danger. They appear to feel as if every thing were right, their cafe fafe and their eternal bleffednefs fecured. This fhows the need of fpecial means to call our attention to a prefent fenfe of truth and our duty. We firft need means to inftruct us; and then to refrefh our memories and imprefs the things which are known, on our hearts and confciences. If a man be certain his doctrinal knowledge will not be increafed by the duties of the Sabbath; this is not a reafon for him to neglect them. The inftitution is of the Lord, and there is reafon to hope he will blefs his own appointment; and the day was alfo given to affift us, in the improvement of truth which was before known—to fearch our hearts—to underftand our errors—to confefs our fins—and to apply all divine truth to our own cafe.

5thly. By fanctifying the LORD'S-DAY to keep it holy, all chriftian graces are enlivened, and the people of GOD grow in preparation for their eternal Sabbath of holinefs and glory.

THE work of divine grace and holinefs in the heart is progreffive. It hath pleafed infinite wifdom gradually to bring his children, as they are paffing through time, towards the perfection of their chriftian character and reward. All the reafons of this difpenfation cannot now be known; but in the end it will doubtlefs appear to be as worthy of GOD, as all his other works are. In this progreffive advance to the pure holinefs of eternal life, there is a great ufe of means, among which the Sabbath is a principal one. By this day and its duties, the influences of the world, which have been encroaching on the affections through the whole week, are fhaken off—divine truth is received—the prefence of GOD is made fenfible—the glories of his holinefs are feen by a new ftrength of faith—the invifible things of another world become real to the foul—the holy graces of the heart become alive and fervent—the fpirit of prayer is increafed—and communion with God becomes moft delightful. Thefe, to the chriftian indeed, are the confequences of faithfully keeping the Sabbath. It is not ftrange that he loves the day of the Lord, for he finds a divine energy from on high accompanying the inftitution, and perceives himfelf drawing near, though in a flow and imperfect manner, to the perfection of a holy character, and the full bleffednefs of feeing as he is feen and knowing as he is known.

HEAVEN is a ftate of perfect holinefs—an eternal Sabbath of conformity to God and enjoyment of his glory, by fuch means of feeing, knowing and approaching him, as infinite wifdom knows to be the moft perfect. While this holy day gives a moft excellent advantage to the worldly and unfanctified, of learning their danger and their remedy; to the fincere and holy it is a preparative, a foretafte of their everlafting reward. If our hearts be right, our weekly Sabbaths will be a foretafte of heaven—they will be a quickening of the heavenly temper—and a practical anticipation of heavenly peace. The afcended Saviour, remembering the earthly members of his kingdom, and his own promife to be with them, will give thofe influences of his holy fpirit, by which they will find it a day of reft indeed, and of preparation for their glorious and eternal reft.

WE have proceeded far enough on this fubject, to fee the happy and powerful influence of a Sabbath, in our preparation for the world to come. It is a neceffary means of retaining in the world, a knowledge of the true God, whom we are to ferve forever. It keeps in our knowledge the revelation of his will. It is neceffary to give efficacy to the means of inftruction. It teaches us our fin and our fpiritual wants, and thus prepares us for the bleffings of the gofpel. It matures that preparation for heaven, which is begun in the people of GOD by their fpiritual fanctification. And it is the neareft refemblance to the heavenly life, which is admitted in this ftate of trial.

THOSE who diflike the fpirituality of religion, cannot be pleafed with the manner in which this fubject hath been treated. Though they may be contented with a Sabbath of fome kind ; a pure, a fpiritual fanctification of it, in the duties of the fanctuary, the family and the clofet will be diftafteful. Let all fuch perfons know, that if the Sabbath thus fanctified, is diftafteful, heaven would be the fame, if they could be admitted to it with their prefent temper. Let it teach them the radical evil of their own hearts, and that with all their advantages and hopes, they are really in a ftate of mind unprepared for the joys of the chriftian falvation. And when they find this, let them remember it will be of no avail to quarrel with a human expofition of this fubject. GOD who fet the example when he finifhed the work of creation, and hath repeated his command to men, ftill reigns and will be the judge. When he judges men will be in his hand—he will vindicate his law—and he will pafs his fentence, according to his own underftanding of obedience. Therefore all attempts to explain away the fpirituality of the Sabbath, will be of no avail to thofe who make them.

B b b

Let me address this subject to two classes of people.

First, to those who see the necessity of family and civil subordination.

It is not uncharitable to suppose, there are some in this class, who feel little of their own spiritual needs, and do not wish a Sabbath for the purpose of piety. It is unhappy there should be any such. It is known they do not wish such a Sabbath as has been described; but from experience they have learned the need of family and civil order. On the support of these they are determined, though it be at the expense of some self-denial. Let all such know, that they cannot obtain their end without the christian Sabbath, or an institution so similar to it, that it ought not to be called by another name. A Decade of festivity cannot come into the place, and in society answer the purposes of the christian Sabbath. It may help to madden the people—to efface a sense of moral obligation—to enflame all the appetites for dissipation; and thus in the end destroy all order, government and social morality. The efficacy of a Sabbath, to preserve order in the family and in the state, arises from the impressions of morality and of our being in a responsible state, which are made on the minds of men. A Decade of sensual festivity and dissipated thoughts is a most potent instrument of hell and its apostles, and directly subverts the first principles of social compact and justice. The Sabbath derives its power, from bringing into the view of men, a holy God—a holy, just and benevolent law—a day of being judged and an eternity of rewards.

With this eternity of rewards, those whom I now address are not affected. Perhaps they do not believe it. But if God hath not enabled them to feel the force of higher motives, let them reverence the Sabbath of the Lord for the fake of prefent order.

If mafters of families ; let them fanctify the Sabbath in their houfes. If rulers of the ftate ; let them execute its laws, ordained by the wifdom of their fathers. Let all remember, that whether the fpirituality of religion, be agreeable or not, the beft order and happinefs of the world cannot be had without it. Alfo, let them propofe the ferious queftion to their own reafon and confcience ; whether, if the laws and inftitutions of the chriftian religion be actually neceffary for the good of fociety in this world, their neceffity for the blifs of another world may not be inferred.

Secondly, to chriftians who are fo in truth, as well as by profeffion.

Of you it is conceived that you delight in God—in his law—in his glory. You do not wifh a better heaven than it will be to ferve and glorify him. Be not defrauded of the benefit of his inftitutions by a fervile compliance with the cuftoms of the world. Remember your Sabbath to be a covenant feal and foretafte of your eternal reward. Remember that it is a means to know God, to glorify him and to do your duty. Remember, that you will find your graces in exercife, and your comforts made fenfible to you, in proportion as you obey the command of the Lord, to keep the Sabbath holy. Remember, thefe Sabbaths of the world are foon to ceafe, and one of eternal duration to commence. This is *the reft that remaineth for the people of God.* As you ferve him now his fovereign grace will reward you hereafter. As you now find delight in his day, in his ordinances, in your clofets; fo you will be delighted in the near approach to his glory. May unnumbered multitudes of guilty men draw near and enjoy this glory. AMEN.

END OF THE FIRST VOLUME.

www.ingramcontent.com/pod-product-compliance
Lightning Source LLC
Chambersburg PA
CBHW032010220426
43664CB00006B/202